LITURGY AND SPIRITUALITY

LITURGY AND SPIRITUALITY

by

GABRIEL M. BRASO, O.S.B,
MONK OF MONTSERRAT

translated by

LEONARD J. DOYLE

THE LITURGICAL PRESS

ST. JOHN'S ABBEY

COLLEGEVILLE, MINNESOTA

The original Spanish edition, *Liturgia y Espiritualidad* (Barcelona, 1956), is the first volume in the series *Biblioteca Vida Cristiana*. This English translation conforms to the revised and enlarged Italian edition, *Liturgia e Spiritualità* (Rome: Edizioni Liturgiche, 1958).

Nihil obstat: John Eidenschink, O.S.B., J.C.D., *Censor deputatus*. *Imprimatur*: ✝ Peter W. Bartholome, D.D., Bishop of St. Cloud. December 14, 1959.

FOREWORD

On a pilgrimage to Lourdes I was privileged to witness several miracles. The most impressive one was unquestionably the sudden cure of a blind man. It is impossible to describe the thankfulness and the enthusiasm of that happy man, who after so many years of darkness was imbibing for the first time the torrent of beauty, form and color which was pouring into his soul through eyes that had just been opened to the light. The faces of his relatives and friends, radiant with joy, the magnificent landscape of the Pyrenees illuminated by the brilliant June sunshine, all the little familiar objects that he had known previously only by touch—everything was a source of unaffected, almost childish admiration. He had discovered the light, and with it his life was becoming broader, richer, and yet, at the same time, simpler. What he found most amazing was the thought that this light was already in existence, and that he himself had lived all these years immersed in it without appreciating its reality.

More than once the memory of the blind man favored by Providence at Lourdes has come back to me at the end of a short course or a few days of retreat in which I sought to explain the principles of the spiritual life as practiced and taught by the Church in her liturgy. I had done no more than point out the rudiments of this magnificent supernatural life in which we are immersed and by which we are constantly nourished; but the participants in the course, whether laymen or ecclesiastics, had got the impression of having discovered a new world. And in reality such had been the case: they had discovered the liturgy as a source of life and as a norm of spirituality.

For the liturgy is just that: the Church's public worship and, at the same time, the basic food and the genuine rule of the spiritual life of the Christian. Yet there is no denying that, despite the widespread, energetic movement to promote a liturgical renewal, the liturgy remains for many people a closed book. The very ones who are concerned about it do not always appreciate its real value. Pope Pius XII says in the encyclical *Mediator Dei,* "There are places where the spirit, understanding or practice of the sacred liturgy is defective, or all but inexistent; elsewhere certain enthusiasts interlard their plans and hopes with principles which compromise this holiest of causes in theory or practice." In other words, ignorance of the liturgy is still quite common: to some it is simply unknown; others have only an inadequate, if not mistaken, conception of it.

And this is not to be wondered at, since a just appreciation of the liturgy in its twofold aspect of public worship and system of spiritual life encounters three great obstacles which make the liturgy something difficult or tend very readily to disfigure it. We refer to *individualism, superficiality* and *utilitarianism.*

For many centuries now, by reason of action or of reaction, the world has been living in an atmosphere of *individualism,* which has been suffocating the sense of community. As spontaneous fruit of liberal doctrines erected into a system by Protestantism; as Catholic reaction to bring man back to God, from whom he had been separated by the paganism of the Renaissance; as a natural defense against ancient and contemporary forms of socialism and statism which would absorb individuals and convert them into an impersonal mass—individualism has taken over in all fields of human activity: educational, religious, political, social.

Our mentality is saturated with this individualist view of life; and it is very hard to abstract from anything so deeply rooted within us, and let ourselves be penetrated with the concepts of church, community, mystical Body, which form the basis of the liturgy. The language of the liturgy will necessarily become difficult and incomprehensible. And even when we try to subordinate the individualist criterion to the communitarian mentality of the liturgy, we run the risk of falsifying the liturgical concepts, interpreting them arbitrarily, or thinking that we have reached the marrow when we have scarcely pierced the rind.

And here we arrive at the second obstacle: *superficiality.* Perhaps life has never been lived so superficially as it is in our day. This is natural: what has been gained in breadth has been lost in depth. The activity required by modern life leaves no time for reflection. Only the specialists attain any depth in their own specialties. There is too little thinking because there is too much talking. Because of so much writing and so much reading to be done, people have lost the habit of reflecting. The widespread and rapid dissemination of news has dulled the feeling for weight, and even the weightiest events are taken lightly by those who are not directly involved in them. Hence comes the need for sensationalism, and this in its turn is a new deterrent to reflection.

Nothing could be more contrary to the environment in which the spirit of the liturgy ought to develop. The liturgy is life, and supernatural life, which flows smoothly through the deepest channels of the spirit. The liturgy is eminently theological in its content, doctrinal in its structure, conceptual and symbolic in its expression. A right understanding of the liturgy presupposes seriousness, depth, intensity of life, perception of the transcendental value of even the simplest realities of this world.

For this reason too, people do not always have an accurate concept of what the liturgy is. They often confuse it with the complexus of rules which govern its celebration. This is rubricism, the most superficial view of the liturgy. Some, with more understanding, give the name of liturgy to the investigation of the history of worship and of its ideological and literary evolution. Thus they may stop at a mere archeologism, or they may finally arrive at the science of the liturgy. More profound and more exact is the concept of liturgy as the Church's public worship. Still this is not all. The marrow is reached only when the liturgy is understood and assimilated as source and norm of the spiritual life of the Christian.

There remains a third obstacle: *utilitarianism.* Properly speaking, it is no more than a concrete form of superficiality; but it presents special dangers. It is a fruit of the hustle and bustle in which we are living and which completely absorbs our activity. Confronted with the imperious demands of a great number of needs to which it is impossible to give sufficient attention, we seek the most practical and immediate solution. We do not attempt the best, we seize upon the most useful. In the spiritual life and in the apostolate, utilitarianism often smothers the best fruits of the liturgical spirit.

The liturgy is not so much interested in immediate, easily controllable results as in a normal life flowing along regularly and without disturbance. The liturgy requires a disinterested, generous spirit, capable of wide horizons which are not always compatible with the concrete, tangible interests of a religious pragmatism. The liturgy teaches us to forget ourselves in our zeal for the spread of God's kingdom, and leaves it up to Providence to take care of our spiritual growth and provide for our needs.

We are interested, therefore, in making known the true physiognomy of the liturgy, showing what is this "public worship which the entire mystical Body of Jesus Christ renders to the Father," pointing out the place and the function we are to have in it, and making clear the close connection that exists between the Church's liturgy, our status as Christians and the development of our spiritual life.

The priestly desire to help the Christian people discover once more the genuine spirit of the liturgy and find in it the purest and most abundant source of Christian life, is the motive that has given rise to this book.

In writing it, we have had in mind the priestly ministers of the divine worship to whom the Church has given as a rule of spiritual life the *imitamini quod tractatis* ("imitate what you are handling"); the seminarians who are orienting their life toward participation in the priesthood of Jesus

Christ; the many faithful Christians who are eager for learning, for spiritual orientation, for intimate union with the Lord.

We have sought to explain to them the rudiments of the liturgical life, that is, of the Christian life as the Church teaches and practices it when she celebrates her liturgy. We have begun by pointing out that the Church has established a chair of learning next to the altar. The worship which gives infinite glory to God is at the same time a school in which practical Christianity is taught.

In the school of the liturgy the Christian learns first of all that he is not an individual in a society but a member of a body; that for this reason there is an intimate compenetration, a vital unity, between the Church's activities of worship and his own spiritual life. What the Church accomplishes has its effect on him; and what he is and does, is communicated to the whole body of the Church. From this reality it follows that the pedagogical method used by the Church consists in unifying the action of Jesus Christ, that of the Church herself, and the private action of the Christian. Thus the maximum effect is obtained through the maximum of unity.

We have taken some time to describe the doctrinal foundations on which the liturgy rests. These give us an understanding of the place the liturgy occupies in the plan of the divine economy and, more concretely, in the priestly and redemptive work of Jesus Christ.

We have analyzed the elements that go to make up the structure of the liturgical action and its essential characteristics, to arrive in this way at a profound knowledge of the Church's public worship. These notions give us the key to understanding the reasons behind the organization of the liturgy in space, in time, in its inmost way of being, in its manifestations.

Then come the relations of the individual with the liturgy. In the first place we examine the contribution every Christian should make toward giving life to the liturgical rites and converting them into the true and sincere expression of the worship of the whole mystical Body; how he should pray if he wants to pray with the Church and in her name. Then we study the influence which the teaching authority of the liturgy should wield over the various aspects of private spiritual activity. This is a summary of the principal rules of Christian perfection derived directly from the teachings of the liturgy; it is the echo of the Church's public worship, which makes souls resound in unison with the canticle which the Spouse of Jesus Christ intones publicly to her Lord.

Finally, we have devoted a chapter to pastoral action, in order to illuminate it with the principles of the liturgy and direct it toward a strong parochial, ritual, communitarian and hierarchical life.

In the exposition we have striven for clarity and order, so as to bring the theological concepts within the grasp of all the readers, to bring out the organic unity of the Christian life centered in the priestly liturgy of Christ, and to facilitate the use of the book if anyone wants to employ it as a text for a course in liturgy.

The principal and almost exclusive sources upon which we have drawn are: the holy Scripture, the liturgical books, the theology of St. Thomas and the pontifical documents, particularly the encyclical *Mediator Dei*.

Let us allow ourselves still another word of direction for the correct reading and interpretation of the book. Our concern is simply to avoid the three reefs to which we have referred and which can upset everything that has reference to the liturgy. St. Benedict gives his monks a wise rule to make them realize all possible profit from their reading: let them read the books straight through from the beginning. In this book not all the chapters have the same character. Some are more doctrinal, while others contain practical applications rather than doctrine. To dwell on the latter and pass lightly over the former would be to succumb to the utilitarian urge. It is not easy to grasp the meaning and the compass of the practical norms without an intelligent understanding of the principles that have inspired them.

In illustration of the doctrine set forth, we have cited concrete facts, pointed out certain deviations, suggested orientations and possible solutions. All this has anecdotical value. Its purpose is to make the doctrine more accessible and to fix the attention, even if it be by way of examination of conscience, so as to move the reader to reflection and to help him assimilate the principles. To give too much importance to the anecdote could lead to a false or exaggerated interpretation of the text, and the proposed objective would not be attained. In such case, superficiality would impede the light and favor the scandal which usually results when the concrete facts of the liturgical movement are judged by those who have not assimilated its principles.

It has been our intention to make something positive: not to destroy but to build up. We want to make liturgical spirituality known, not to attack other forms of spirituality, be they ever so far removed from liturgical spirituality, and even contrary to it in certain points. If we have sometimes referred to these other forms, we have done so only to bring out more clearly, perhaps by way of contrast, some aspect of the spiritual life as formed in the school of the liturgy. Besides, there are many ways in the Church which lead to God. Pope Pius XII expressed this thought very graphically: "There are those who can eat solid food—bread—and those who have to subsist on milk."[1]

It is to be desired, however—and our work is directed to this end—that every day will see an increase in the number of those who can sit at the common table to eat the normal and substantial food which the Church in the liturgy prepares and offers to all her children.

Montserrat, September 3, 1956
Feast of St. Pius X

[1] Homily for the centennial of St. Benedict, in *A.A.S. (Acta Apostolicae Sedis)*, 1947, p. 456.

CONTENTS

Chapter

1   WHAT WE MEAN BY SPIRITUALITY 3

2   THE SPIRITUALITY OF THE CHURCH 11

3   HISTORY OF THE CHURCH'S SPIRITUALITY 30

    1. Formation and high point of liturgical spirituality 31

    2. Era of outward splendor and of lessening of solid
       interior piety 37

    3. Decadence of liturgical spirituality 41

    4. Rebirth of liturgical spirituality 50

4   THE LITURGY, THE CHURCH'S PUBLIC WORSHIP: DOCTRINAL
    FOUNDATIONS 56

    1. Christian worship 56

2. Jesus Christ in the plan of God 66

3. The priesthood of Jesus Christ 70

5 THE LITURGY, THE CHURCH'S PUBLIC WORSHIP: CHARACTERISTICS
OF LITURGICAL ACTION 77

1. The twofold finality of the liturgy 79

2. The priesthood of Jesus Christ made present and active 85

3. Communitarian character of the liturgy 96

4. Hierarchical character of the liturgy 106

5. Sacramentality of the liturgy 118

6. The liturgy, temporal center of the unity of the divine plan 123

7. Objectivity of expression in the liturgy 130

6 THE INDIVIDUAL CONTRIBUTION TO THE CHURCH'S PUBLIC WORSHIP 145

7 LITURGICAL SPIRITUALITY AND CHRISTIAN LIFE 160

1. Private spiritual activity as preparation for the liturgy 163

2. Private spiritual activity as vital assimilation of the liturgy 175

3. Devotions 189

8 LITURGY AND PASTORAL ACTION 205

1. Liturgy and catechesis 207

2. Liturgy, paraliturgy and participation of the faithful 218

3. Liturgy and parochial life 225

4. Roman character of our liturgy 244

LITURGY AND SPIRITUALITY

1 WHAT WE MEAN BY

SPIRITUALITY

The word "spirituality" has attained widespread use. Spirituality is treated of in specialized books and dictionaries. There have come to be "centers of spirituality" which celebrate congresses and "weeks" of spirituality. Speakers and writers treat of the spirituality of the laity, of married couples, of the working class. We may even find one or another article published on the spirituality of communism or of lamaist Buddhism.

As a consequence, the meaning of the term keeps becoming more ambiguous. For some it is equivalent to the life of Christian perfection, while others use it to designate the entirety of the activities of the human spirit. Some express by it a natural tendency to mysticism; for others it is synonymous with spiritual life. Others again indicate by the term "spirituality" the part of theology which some call ascetical and mystical. The followers of the existentialist philosophy or of the new theology use it to describe that indefinable "spiritual climate" in which our interior activity takes place.

For us, spirituality is *the particular way of conceiving and of realizing the ideal of the Christian life.*

Let us station ourselves, therefore, within the practice of the Christian life, which, though it is essentially one, can take on different modalities and show many aspects. In each individual, these modalities and aspects may vary according to his own state of life and his condition and according to

3

the circumstances in which his life goes forward; but they have their origin principally in the different ways of considering and appreciating the Christian life itself.

Any concrete program of life, if it is to be called Christian, must tend to a single ideal: union with God through Jesus Christ our Lord. For the term of perfection of the Christian's whole vital activity is one: God, the object of our beatitude. And the road which leads us to Him is also one: incorporation in Jesus Christ and the participation and imitation of His mystery in our life.

But the practical realization of this ideal must take the personal and subjective element into account. Every Christian, with grace acting upon him, must apply his own internal activity to the attainment of the supernatural ideal, ordering that activity toward the object of his perfection. Otherwise we could not speak of real life. Each one must have in view the object which will bestow that perfection, must let it make its mark on him, and must himself tread the path that leads to it.

And in this consists the diversity of kinds of sanctity. Herein is the reason for the various ways of conceiving and realizing the ideal of the Chrisitan life.

The most profound differences in spirituality are of an intellectual order. Everyone will seek to realize the concept of Christian life which he forms for himself. And since the first principle and the last end of the Christian life is God, the orientation of any spirituality will depend primarily on the idea of God which each person has formed for himself.

For God in His essential simplicity can be considered by our limited intellect from an infinite number of facets or aspects. Any one of them may stand out from the rest, shining with a more intense light and appearing especially attractive to the soul. This is a consequence of our imperfect way of knowing God. Only by analogy and by application of concepts drawn from creatures can we understand anything of the divine nature and the divine life. Thus we distinguish in God His essence and His attributes, and we consider each one of His perfections as distinct from the others, subordinating some to others, and establishing special relations between each one of them and ourselves. This is the principal source of the different shadings in theology and of the various attitudes of the soul with respect to God. Thus we can speak of a Pauline theology and a theology of St. John.[1]

---

[1] Let the doctrine of grace as seen and explained by the two Apostles serve as an example. St. Paul considers grace as the healing of a sick nature. He sees in it primarily the gratuitous justification of the sinner and the definitive restoration of the order which had been changed by sin; and this is brought about by the inclusion of all in Christ. He likes to emphasize the role of faith in the work of salvation, and he describes the splendors of the grace that is in us. From his theology of the mystical Body he derives the idea of our communion with Jesus Christ, Son of God (1 Cor. 1:9). This Christ, glorious after His Resurrection, is the Head from whom flows the vital and unifying principle of all the members (Eph. 1:22 f.; 4:15 f.; Col. 1:18).

St. John, on the other hand, sees grace rather as an elevation of created nature. He considers the grace of the Christian election as

The differences, sometimes profound, between the great theological systems have their ultimate root in the particular point of view from which they prefer to consider God. One, more metaphysical, insists on the ontological concepts of the divine existence; the other, more inclined to psychology, underlines the principles of relationship between God and man. According to some, of a rather intellectualist bent, God will formally satisfy our happiness by the vision of His own essence; while others, more on the affective side, locate our beatitude above all in the appeasement and the enjoyment of our will through union with God, supreme object of our love. This diversity of points of view is bound to have an influence on the particular manner of seeking God and of establishing personal relations with Him.

Something similar can be said of every one of the conclusions of speculative theology. Let us merely cite as an example the famous question of the infallibility of efficacious grace. What different directions the spiritual life takes, according to whether the Thomist doctrine or the Molinist thesis is accepted!

Aside from the method of posing and resolving the various theological questions, there are many other causes, psychological and moral in nature, which determine the differences in spirituality in as much as they influence effectively the choice of means for going to God.

We can point out first of all the intellectual ability and the whole temperament of each individual. Let us compare, for example, the spiritualities of saints as different in temperament as St. Jerome and St. Benedict, St. Francis of Assisi and St. Ignatius Loyola, St. Bruno and St. Francis de Sales.

The degree of culture also has a great deal of influence on the means that will be chosen for the Christian life. So do the kind of life, the person's own status or condition, his experiences, the preference for some one concrete means of sanctification, the circumstances of time and place, the particular vocation which inclines one toward a certain proximate, immediate end (education of youth, practice of the works of mercy, bringing the gospel to unbelievers, apostolate to the working classes, contemplative life, etc.); and we might also add the environment, and, in a particular way, the formation received.

All these elements contribute to the great variety of types of sanctity found in the Church and constituting so many spiritualities.

In a broad sense we might say that every soul has its own spirituality.

a sweet, tranquil possession of the soul by the glory of the divinity. He confounds, knowingly, in a single perspective of eternal life, the two phases, grace and glory. The principle of this life is Christ in His eternal pre-existence and in His Incarnation: the life which was already in existence "with the Father" *(apud Patrem)* has been made manifest and has been given to us; thus the faithful are united to Christ, united to the Father, united among themselves in the unity of the Life (1 John 1:1-3).

It is evident that the fact of emphasizing one of these viewpoints, even though they support each other and complete each other, can determine in practice two different lines of spirituality.

But, speaking more properly, since we are treating of methods of sanctity, and a method always supposes a common way of seeing and resolving certain problems, there will be as many spiritualities as there are practical solutions of the evangelical ideal, which have had a more or less collective character in the Church.

Prescinding from very personal and accidental shades of difference, it is obvious that there are certain categories of persons who, by reason of finding themselves in similar conditions of life, must find themselves in agreement also as they carry out the Christian ideal, setting out in the same direction and availing themselves of the same means. Such will be the persons who follow the same state of life, and hence have identical duties and live under similar conditions. Thus the method of tending toward the ideal of perfection must be very different for seculars and for ecclesiastics, for persons united in matrimony and for those who have made a vow of chastity. Every state of life, every social category, even some professions, will determine objectively the bases for establishing the proper spirituality of the persons who belong to it.

Sometimes the coincidence of finding the same solutions to the problem of spiritual perfection proceeds from a cause still more extrinsic: the fact of living under the same circumstances of time and of place may give a particular spiritual orientation to the individuals of that epoch. Then we have a *current of spirituality*. In the course of the centuries various currents of spirituality have been forming in the Church, originating almost always in great historical events or in the various circumstances that have characterized an epoch and have notably influenced the development of its spiritual life.

Thus, for example, there were the Crusades, which brought about contact of the West with the Holy Land; the spread of the mendicant orders; the Council of Trent and the reaction against the paganizing humanism of the Renaissance. These were facts which had resounding consequences in the moral life of the Christian people, sufficient to modify its mentality and its religious practices profoundly and to give them a characteristic shape.

It may also happen that a certain way of orienting and organizing the religious life becomes crystalized within the Church and builds up an organic structure, establishing norms and principles of spiritual orientation, creating a school of spirituality and at the same time acquiring extension and continuity. Then we have a *system of spirituality*. These organic and organized spiritualities are the ones in which we are most interested here. As a general rule, although the fact in itself is not necessary, these systems have been diffused and perpetuated through the religious orders in which they have become incarnate and which themselves sometimes owe their origin and their existence in the Church to these systems.

The founders of the various religious orders or congregations, men of God spurred on by zeal for God's glory and burning with love for their brethren, have translated their Christian ideal into reality in a concrete manner which corresponded to the necessities of their times and to the characteristics of their temperament and their formation, and which almost always originated in a reaction against the moral evils of their own age.

The disciples who gathered around these exceptional men inherited the teaching and the spirituality of the master, and they were very careful to preserve so great a spiritual legacy intact for transmission to posterity. Thus the spirit of the great saints has been perpetuated in the Church under the form of a spirituality which subsists and diffuses itself through the respective religious orders. The forms taken by this spirituality may be more or less faithful to its original purity; but, whether more faithful or less faithful, they favor its continuity, even though the individual or collective circumstances which gave rise to that spirituality are often substantially changed.

It can be said as a general rule that the forms of spirituality which have come down to us in this way have a unilateral, incomplete character: while they emphasize, perhaps too much, one of the aspects of the Christian life, and attribute too much importance to certain moral means of attaining perfection, they sometimes forget or detract from the value of others; so much the more if they are formed by way of reaction, which is always apt to become extremist. Since it is bound to be partial and particular in character, any spirituality is best adapted to those whose qualities and circumstances are most similar to those of the founder.

Considered in themselves, none of the spiritualities is necessary, and much less is any of the systems of spirituality necessary, for attaining Christian perfection. To succeed in becoming perfect, it is enough to observe the gospel according to the interpretation of the Church, which determines and adapts it sufficiently to the personal abilities and conditions of each individual. This is the essential thing, and suffices in itself. A system of spirituality has only the function of a tutor, supplementing the universal *magisterium* of the Church, to facilitate our understanding of the gospel ideal and lead us by the hand, as it were, to its effective realization. No tutor can arrogate to himself a monopoly over the Church's spiritual teaching.

We must distinguish in every spirituality, therefore, between that which is evangelical doctrine and that which is simply a means or a pedagogical device of that system. The former is essential and indispensable for arriving at a true Christian life; the other can be taken or left alone without compromising the attainment of this ideal.

Actually if we analyze the constituent elements of the different spiritualities, we shall find that they all have a common foundation, consisting of the basic principles of Christian doctrine and the practical rules of the gospel morality. It is this common and essential basis that gives them a title to legitimacy in the pale of the Church. The rest of their constituent elements are proper to each one, making it a specific, particular spirituality.

As to doctrinal orientation, every system of spirituality, if it is to fit the essential concept of Christian life, must be first of all *theocentric,* by reason of the ultimate end to which it is ordained. Next, it must be *christocentric,* since in the actual economy of redemption Jesus Christ is the necessary Mediator: according to the plan pre-established and ordained by God, no one can reach the Father except through Jesus Christ. Further, by the will of Jesus Christ, His work is continued and applied to individuals within the Church by means of the sacraments; hence every authentic spirituality will have to be *ecclesiastical* and *sacramental.* All these characteristics of a *doctrinal* nature, which correspond objectively to the essence of the religion established by Jesus Christ, are *essential* and must therefore be found in every spirituality, since it is precisely these notes which constitute the concept of Christian life.

As to the concrete, individual practice of the Christian life, every spirituality will have to make use of certain elements which are the *indispensable moral means* for attaining the ideal of Christian perfection. These means—often *subjective* in as much as they suppose an individual activity aimed at perfecting the individual himself—are derived in part from the generic concept of moral perfection, in part from the gospel teaching, and in part from the present condition of human nature.

First of all, every form of Christian perfection must be based on the *commandments*; they also are essential, and they are summed up in the precept of charity: You shall love the Lord your God with your whole heart, with your whole strength, with your whole mind; and your neighbor as yourself. Our individual powers will make their contribution through the practice of the *virtues,* and will be directed thereto in harmony with the spirit of the *evangelical counsels,* and also with their practice when the concern is with religious perfection. All these moral elements should inspire in the soul a twofold attitude of *penance* and *prayer*: penance to free us from the obstacles placed in the way of our sanctification, and prayer to unite us positively to God.

Besides these doctrinal and moral elements, common to all forms of Christian perfection, the individual spiritualities contain other characteristic elements. These are the *accidental* elements, that is, the concrete forms under which all these moral means of perfection can be put into practice and these doctrinal points can be exemplified. Such would be, for example, one or another exercise of mortification or of devotion, the practice of certain works of mercy, the use of specified methods of prayer, some concrete ways of expressing love for Christ or devotion for the Church.

In each spirituality this complexus of elements is combined in a different way. It is easy to see the variety of accidental forms which distinguish the various spiritualities; for each one has its methods, its practices, its favorite exercises. But even the doctrinal points themselves and the moral means, common to all spiritualities, are considered in each one of them under a special light, from a particular viewpoint, which brings out more prominently certain theological truths and certain aspects of perfection.

In order to specify the characteristics of a spirituality, therefore, we must evaluate and combine the various elements—common doctrinal and moral elements, and accidental elements—according to their value and their practical importance in that particular method of perfection. The resulting picture will be the characteristic physiognomy of that spirituality.

The differences among the various spiritualities do not depend on the elements employed, since these are the same in any system approved by the Church, but rather on the relative value attached to these elements and the way in which they are used to reach the ideal of Christian perfection.

The spirit of proselytism which is often noted in religious orders and congregations consists precisely in bringing about the spread of the religious concepts and the means of perfection which constitute their spirituality. Convinced of the goodness and efficacy of their spiritual orientation and of the means of sanctification which are proper to them, they strive to inculcate them in others. This is an impulse of zeal and of charity: to procure the spiritual good of others, according to the natural principle that "the good is diffusive of itself." On the other hand, there corresponds to the spread of its spirituality a growth of that order and of its spiritual influence in the Church, and this is a legitimate instinct of self-preservation and self-extension.

For the practical acceptance of a spirituality creates bonds of affinity with the order or congregation that embodies it, which affinity may develop into a real spiritual brotherhood. Such is the origin of many confraternities and congregations and especially of the third orders.

This moral kinship attains its maximum degree among the members of the same order, and finds its reason for being, precisely, in the practice of one and the same spirituality, which makes them children of the same father and confers on them the same spiritual temperament. Juridically, a religious belongs to his order from the moment he validly pronounces his vows. But this is not enough. In point of fact, he will be vitally incorporated into it only when he has accepted and assimilated the spirit proper to that order, its own particular spirituality. A religious who belonged canonically to an order and inwardly adhered to another spirituality would come to be like a guest and a stranger among his brethren.

Like every organized form of life, the systems of spirituality, with their efforts at conquest and their tendency to spread, invigorate and develop in the Church the most select nuclei of Christian life. But they also carry with them a danger: that of degenerating into a spirit of partisanship. It is easy to give too much importance to one's own methods, with disdain for the other systems and even with detriment to the essential unity of the Christian life. This position is so much the less justifiable, the more a spirituality is based on subjective or particularist points of view and the more prominent are the accidental elements in it.

If this pitfall is avoided, the organic systems of spirituality put the perfection of the Christian life within reach of all the faithful, according to each one's possibilities. They facilitate the acquisition of a spiritual personality in the Church, so that the Church increases its variety and its beauty. And they realize more concretely the various aspects of the holiness of Jesus Christ.

2 THE SPIRITUALITY

OF THE CHURCH

The Church as such has its spirituality, which is not just *a* spirituality, and not even the best among all, but simply *the* spirituality of the Church. Perhaps this idea seems to need no elaboration, but it is worth emphasizing, the more so if we take into account the fact that the Church is not *one* out of many tutors who can instruct us on the kingdom of God, but is simply *the* unique and universal teacher, instituted by Jesus Christ as depositary and interpreter of His doctrine, pillar and mainstay of Christian truth (1 Tim. 3:15).

Let us see how the Church exercises this teaching authority or *magisterium*. With reference to the determination of revealed doctrine, the Church's *magisterium* is unique and absolute. In herself she constitutes the proximate and immediate rule of Catholic faith, and she cannot share this right with anyone.

It is true that in the sphere of theological speculation there are various schools which the Church has accepted and whose doctrine she approves. But their role does not exceed that of private schools, mere auxiliaries to the official teaching authority of the Church. She uses them as subsidiary, specialized aids to bring about a deeper understanding of the revealed truths. She leaves to the scientific workings of these schools the task of analyzing theological doctrine and explaining it rationally, building it up into organic systems and preparing the elements for new statements of her *magisterium*.

But no school may usurp the right of establishing new doctrines in the Church's name, nor may it depart in its teachings from the truths and doctrinal principles established by the Church. Where doctrine is concerned, the Church exercises her *magisterium* authoritatively and by herself, whether in the determination of revealed truth or in anything pertaining to the norms of morality directed toward the attainment of the supernatural end.

On the other hand, when the concern is with translating doctrinal principles into practice and bringing the Christian ideal into concrete reality, the official exercise of her infallible *magisterium* is not enough for the Church. She feels the need of coming down from her chair to put herself into immediate contact with all the faithful and with each one, to become intimately acquainted with their needs and to lead them by the hand, as it were, to the actual realization of the supernatural ideal which she herself proposes to them.

To this end the Church has worked out a pedagogical method which she is pleased to apply herself. The purpose of this method is to point out to all men the supreme ideal of the Christian life, to bring it within the capacities of each one, and to render the means of attaining it easily available to all. The Church uses this method in her public relations with God, to show us in practice what must be the norm of our prayer life and of our daily Christian life in general.

In this particular, her pedagogical activity is essentially linked to her priesthood and her maternal action. For the Church's priesthood is concerned with the spiritual education of the Christians as a proper object; and this education has as its immediate end the perfecting of the supernatural life in each one of the faithful, and is ordained to the supreme and priestly end of the glorification of God through religious worship and through the worship which the Christian life exemplifies. Similarly, by reason of her maternity, the Church cannot limit herself to bringing forth children to God; she must also feed them and take care of their growth and their perfect development; her maternal mission cannot be called complete until she sees them changed into perfect men, "to the mature measure of the fulness of Christ" (Eph. 4:13).

We can reasonably assume, then, what must be the intrinsic perfection and the pedagogical effectiveness of a method worked out by the Church to meet the requirements of her priesthood, her teaching function and her maternal role.

Certainly the more a master succeeds in adapting himself to his disciple's capacities, to the point of working right inside him if that were possible, the greater will be his influence over the disciple. Now the Church, by reason of her maternity, can attain a compenetration and a power of adaptation greater than anyone else can attain, with those who are her disciples and also her children. Moreover, we must take into account her priestly zeal and even the special assistance of the Holy Spirit, who always inspires in her the means best adapted to attaining her end.

To be effective, her method must also be universal. All those whose sanctification has been entrusted to the Church must be able to find in her school the normal means for the perfect development of their supernatural life, without having to look for any means other than those she proposes to them.

This does not mean that each person may not seek new channels for his own personal devotion, provided they are approved by the Church. Nor does it mean that there cannot exist within the Church other subsidiary schools which, though using other means, can be of use to her in the spiritual education of such a variety of souls. We assert only that the means used commonly by the Church as such must suffice to satisfy completely any aspiration to sanctity, any ideal of Christian life, and that her pedagogical method must be objectively the most perfect, the easiest, the most effective and the most universal.

Still, we must keep in mind that the Church's *magisterium,* in as much as it is ordained to the practical realization of the Christian ideal, has restricted its own absolute authority according to the following rules, which in themselves bear witness to the wisdom and the prudence of her pedagogy:

1. In the application of her spirituality the Church does not always proceed authoritatively. She often acts by way of suggestion and persuasion, as befits a good tutor or a prudent educator.

2. She does not bar auxiliary teachers. On the contrary, she always admits them if they are in any way useful in the spiritual formation of the faithful. Such are the other spiritualities which have been forming in the Church. It must be noted that she admits them not only when they strive to render the Church's own pedagogical method more accessible and practical—just as the theological schools render her doctrine more accessible—but also when they aspire to use their own methods, different from those proposed by the Church as such, as long as those methods do not depart from the doctrinal and moral principles established by the Church's official *magisterium.*

3. The educational work of the Church, however universal and effective it may be, does not take the place of the individual's personal effort. Every educational work is a work of assimilation. It implies, therefore, a personal effort to receive and assimilate the elements which the educator proposes and whose acquisition he seeks to make easy by his pedagogical method. The interest of the educator, and in our case the interest of the Church, tends precisely to stimulate all the possibilities for personal actuation of the disciple, to increase them, to channel them and direct them toward their object; so much the more when it is considered that her spiritual *magisterium* has for its aim the development of the Christian's supernatural life, something which cannot be brought to fulfilment without the personal application of the

faculties to the Christian's own object. This constitutes, moreover, the basis of the individual contribution to the collective worship which only in this way can be a living worship "in spirit and in truth."

In the following chapters we shall attempt to set forth the content of the Church's spirituality and the applications of her method. Here we shall fix our attention only on the characteristic note that distinguishes it from all other systems: its tendency to unify the whole spiritual activity of the individual, conforming it to and incorporating it in the cultual action of the Church herself.

Let us examine this plan more closely and first of all establish its aim. Since the Church by her essential constitution is the extension of the mystery of Christ, she has received from the Lord a threefold function to be exercised in time, that her end may be achieved. The Church is to reproduce and actualize in time the mystery of Jesus Christ; she is to communicate the knowledge of that mystery to men; and she is to insert vitally into that mystery the life of every Christian.

In keeping with this threefold function, Jesus Christ has made her the depositary and the dispenser of a sacrifice, of a doctrine, of means of sanctification. The sanctifying power of the Church, which in itself has no limits, has its roots in this threefold deposit, supported by the impetratory force of her prayer.

All that is needed is to apply this power to each one of her members and bring about its assimilation on their part. This is precisely the pedagogical task of the spirituality of the Church. Perfect in her knowledge of the mysteries of God's kingdom and of the limited capacities of human psychology, she seeks first of all to bring the profound content of these mysteries within reach of all, even of the least cultured men and the simplest minds.

Guided by the Holy Spirit and by her delicate maternal instinct, she seeks the most suitable means for explaining the truths of a supernatural order in the simplest and most effective form. She breaks them up in order to communicate them a little at a time; she repeats them periodically according to a wisely contrived cycle; she facilitates the understanding of them by making use of symbols that excite the imagination and of external elements which can impress the senses.

No one knows as well as the Church does, how to make use with such dignity and effectiveness of external elements to reach the interior, of that which is concrete to express that which is abstract, of the sensible to communicate the divine, without altering or diminishing the mystery in any way. That is what she herself declares in the preface of Christmas: "through Him whom we recognize as God made visible we are carried away in love of things invisible" *(ut, dum visibiliter Deum cognoscimus, per hunc in invisibilium amorem rapiamur)*.

But the method would not be perfect if it did nothing more than adapt the mysteries to man's capacity. To complete his spiritual formation, it must raise man up and conform him to the objective reality of the mysteries. This accounts for the austerity of the Church's pedagogical system. It accounts also for its formative power. The adaptation of the individual to an objective reality is necessitated by the fact that the Church's method is meant for all men: to be completely within the reach of all, it must prescind from each one's individual characteristics.

But it is in the divine origin of the Church's *magisterium* and in its specific aim—to make people appreciate the realities of the supernatural order in their being itself and in all their purity—that we must seek the most profound reason why the spirituality of the Church is eminently objective.

It is objective first of all in the evaluation of doctrinal principles, which are given priority over the other elements involved in the subjective formation, in order to illuminate those elements and direct them into the way of salvation as God Himself has marked it out and chosen to reveal it to us. And even these doctrinal principles are related among themselves and subordinated one to another according to a criterion which corresponds perfectly to their ontological reality and to the place they really occupy in the supernatural economy. Hence the Church's spirituality is profoundly theological. And in consequence of this it is also eminently theocentric. Its doctrinal plan converges wholly on God, who must be reached through Jesus Christ in the Church.

Similarly, in the ordering of the practical means of the Christian life, the Church's spirituality subordinates that which is subjective to that which is objective, individual sensibility to theological reality, the accidental and concrete forms of personal devotion to the common means of perfection, and these to the objective means of sacramental sanctification.

Thus, if we were to establish a scale of values of the Church's spirituality and thereby draw up a program for applying the principles of that spirituality, we could say that the Christian must do penance and practice abstinence in order to acquire virtue and obtain the spirit of prayer; he must be virtuous and he must pray in order to receive the sacraments with greater purity and assimilate their fruits to greater effect; he must receive the sacraments in order to be configured to the mystery of Christ in the unity of the Church and to glorify God in Christ.

In thus adapting man to the objective reality of the supernatural economy, the rule of the Church's spirituality establishes him in unity, which is wonderfully resplendent in the divine plan as reflection of the substantial unity of God. The very complexity of human psychology becomes simplified, because man's faculties are hierarchically ordered and directed by more rationally suitable means toward the proper object, while this in turn is ordered to the attainment of the supreme common object. And the multiplicity which originated with subjective differences is overcome by disciplining the individual, by adapting him and uniting him to the other Christians in a community of thought, will and ideal.

This unification of forces is helped by everything that surrounds the life of the Christian. The creatures of which he makes use even in a purely natural order, the state of life in which he finds himself, his individual and social activities, are converted, with the blessing of the Church, into an extension of the kingdom of God, directed to an intensification of the Christian life. Jesus Christ by His most merciful coming has consecrated the whole world. The Church by her sacramental rites renews this consecration over every creature individually and communicates to it a power of supernatural irradiation. Thus everything is sanctified, everything is christianized, everything is directed toward the mystery of the Lord.

For the mystery of the Lord constitutes the key to the unity of the Church's spirituality. The motto of that spirituality might well be St. Paul's phrase, "to unify all things in Christ" (Eph. 1:10). The mystery of the Lord is at the same time the terminus and the center of the Church's spirituality, which tends to it and revolves around it.

Before all, the Church in her public worship renews the mystery of the Lord sacramentally, and thus represents it, that is, makes it present again amid the assembly of the faithful, emphasizing one of its aspects, to which it directs their attention.

Then, to make the mystery stand out more sharply and to bring its divine content within reach of the understanding of the faithful, she takes the sacred Scriptures of the Old and the New Testament suitable for illustrating it; in her explanation she makes use of theological science, of the writings of the Fathers and the doctors which can render it accessible to all intellects; and while disclosing the content of the mystery she fosters its reception and assimilation into each one's life. With all the means at her disposal, she seeks to impress the human senses and the human sensitivity with a view to a more fruitful perception of the mystery; and with the efficacy of her prayer she brings down from heaven the graces which will make possible the realization of the mystery in the life of the Christian.

Finally, as the greatest factor in this moral assimilation, she has the faithful participate sacramentally in the same mystery of the Lord.

It is up to the Christian to complete the action of the Church by conforming his mind and his life to it, that is, by looking to it for the nourishment and the norm of his spirituality.

Thus the whole spiritual activity of the Church and of the individual is unified; thus is assured the maximum sanctifying effect of her spirituality, which penetrates all the faculties of the Christian and his whole activity.

The special characteristic of the Church's spirituality, then, and the reason for its supreme efficacy lies in the unity which it establishes between the

Church's public worship, her sacramental action and the spiritual activity incumbent on each one of the faithful.

For this reason, the Church carries on the work of spiritual formation of her children principally when she gathers them to offer public worship. The faithful, assembled to offer God the supreme act of Christian worship, receive in return the gift of the Eucharist, which confers upon them a participation in the mystery of Christ, a greater understanding of that mystery and the strength to translate it into reality in their own life. On coming out of church, the Christian has only to assimilate and to exemplify in his deeds what he has heard in the liturgical assembly and what has been done in the sacraments.

This is why the Church's spirituality is called *liturgical spirituality:* it tends to reproduce in the private life of the Christians what the Church has done and has taught in offering God her public worship, her liturgy.

In a certain sense, every legitimate spirituality could be called liturgical, since it must always assign an essential place to the ritual action of the Church; just as every spirituality existing in the Church and approved by her can be truly called a spirituality of the Church.

Here, however, we call "spirituality of the Church" that particular way of conceiving and of realizing the ideal of the Christian life which is taught in practice by the Church herself without any additions or modifications drawn from private schools of spirituality.

In this sense, liturgical spirituality is that which seeks in its method and in its style of private sanctity (subjective piety, ascetical exercises, practice of the virtues, etc.) to imitate totally and exclusively the method and the style used by the Church in her official relations with God, that is, in her liturgy.

Many of the Church's prayers give evidence of this plan of her spirituality which unites the private activity of the Christian with the liturgical action according to the program set forth: the sacramental renewal of the mystery of Jesus Christ is to lead to the spiritual understanding of the mystery, which is then translated into the works of the Christian life. We shall cite only a few examples taken from the missal.

In the collect of the second Mass of Christmas the Church asks the Lord to grant "that as we are bathed in the new light of Your incarnate Word, that which shines in our mind by faith may be resplendent in our works."

The fruit which she desires to obtain from the communion on the feast of the Epiphany is that "our purified mind may grasp the mystery we celebrate in this solemn ceremony."

Here is the postcommunion of the third Sunday after Epiphany: "O Lord, You generously allow us to make use of these great mysteries. Deign, we pray You, to make us truly fit to reap their fruits."

In a similar way on Easter Tuesday, referring to her new children begotten in the waters of baptism during the Paschal Vigil, the Church delicately asks the Lord in her collect, "O God, who keep building up Your Church with new offspring, grant that Your servants may express in their lives the sacrament they have received through faith."

On Friday of the same week the collect expresses the need that the relation existing between the mystery of Christ and the Paschal sacrifice be verified also between the faith professed with the solemnity of the Paschal rites and the practical life of the new Christians.

On Low Sunday *(Dominica in Albis)*, when the white baptismal robes are taken away from the neophytes, the collect asks for them and for the whole Church that "now that the Paschal festivities are ended, by Your grace we may continue them in our life and in our deeds."

The same expression of the unity that should exist between sacrament, faith and works, is found in the secret of the fourth Sunday after Easter: "O God, through the sacred commerce You have established with us by means of this sacrifice, You have made us partakers of Your sovereign divinity. Grant, we pray You, that, as we know Your truth, we may lead a life worthy of it."

The splendid collect of Ascension day makes us raise our eyes to heaven, whither the Lord has risen, and then makes us pray that we too may dwell continually in heaven by the thoughts, affections and desires of our spirit.

Still more explicitly, a prayer of the Leonine sacramentary implored on this same feast of the Ascension the grace "to have our mind always directed toward the place into which the glorious Author of this solemnity has entered, that by a holy life we may arrive at the goal to which our faith is tending."

Very meaningful also is the postcommunion of Ember Saturday in September, which establishes an intimate relationship between the Eucharistic sacrifice and the heavenly glory, through the grace produced and the good works fostered in us by the sacrifice: "We pray You, Lord, that Your sacraments may effect in us what they contain, that we may arrive in reality at that which we are now celebrating in mystery."

We could cite many more prayers in which phrases such as these recur: *quod mysteriis agimus, piis affectibus celebremus; sacrosancta mysteria quae frequentamus actu subsequamur et sensu; sacramentis magnae pietatis aptemur; muneribus tuis possimus semper aptari.*

On this plan of unity the Church had already established her style of sanctity, her spirituality, from the very beginning. For many centuries this was the one organic method for directing the supernatural life of the Christians. Then, with the passage of time and in the face of the particular spiritual needs of the Christian people, other methods began to arise, other spiritualities. These the Church has accepted and approved and even recommended, whenever she has found in them a legitimate and expedient means for perfecting the Christian life, even if their procedures differ from the method practiced by the Church; for the form of sanctity is not essential to sanctify itself.

Despite this fact, the Church is aware that her own style is normally and objectively the most adequate and most effective for attaining holiness. For this reason she cannot renounce it: she offers it constantly to all. From time to time she makes her voice heard in favor of a better understanding of it and a more exact realization of its worth, and gives practical evidence of her desire by imposing some of its acts on everyone as a grave obligation in conscience.

Why, for example, are the prescriptions of canon 125—mental prayer, visits to the Blessed Sacrament, recitation of the rosary, examination of conscience —though considered effective means to priestly holiness, not required of the clergy with the same obligation as the recitation of a minor hour of the divine Office? This precept and the grave precepts of assistance at Mass on Sundays and holydays of obligation, of Lenten fast, etc., do not acquire their full meaning if they are considered only as duties of one's state or duties of religion or of Christian mortification. Their deepest meaning and their inmost reason for being must be sought in the high estimation the Church has of her own spirituality, to the point of requiring by a grave obligation the participation, at least external participation, in its most essential acts.

A greater understanding of this principle would do away with a good deal of casuistry, and the virtue of religion itself would thereby receive a more rational and more theological orientation.

The most recent popes have shown clearly what was their thinking on this point. Among the various writings of St. Pius X referring to the liturgy, we shall limit ourselves to quoting these sentences from his famous *Motu proprio* on sacred music: "We are filled with a burning desire to see the true Christian spirit flourish in every respect and be preserved by all the people. We therefore are of the opinion that before everything else it is necessary to provide for the sanctity and dignity of the temple where the faithful assemble for no other purpose than that of acquiring this spirit *from its primary and indispensable fount, that is, the active participation in the most sacred mysteries and in the public and solemn prayer of the Church.*"[1]

Pius XI also wrote a good deal on the liturgy. We should have to quote many paragraphs of his apostolic constitution *Divini cultus* of December 20, 1928, dedicated wholly to the sacred liturgy, on the occasion of the twenty-fifth anniversary of St. Pius X's *Motu proprio* just mentioned. We shall merely take a sentence from his encyclical *Quas primas* establishing the feast of Christ the King: "People are instructed in the truths of faith and brought to appreciate the inner joys of religion far more effectually by the annual

---

[1] *Acta S. Sedis*, 1903, p. 331; translation in *All Things in Christ*, ed. by Vincent A. Yzermans (Westminster, Md.: Newman Press, 1954), p. 200.

celebration of our sacred mysteries than by any official pronouncements of the teaching of the Church."[2]

The same Pius XI, in an audience granted on December 12, 1935, to Dom Bernard Capelle, abbot of Mont-César, said that the Church permits certain prayers and devotions "because she has pity on poor, weak men. 'So be it,' she says. 'Since you cannot pray in any other way, pray like that, provided you are really praying!' But when anyone wants to know how *she* understands prayer, that is another thing: the answer will be found in the liturgy. You must imitate the holy Church, and not prohibit that which she is content to accept by way of prayer. But you must seek to raise up the faithful, little by little, and teach them to pray as she does. The liturgy is a great thing. It is the most important organ of the Church's ordinary *magisterium* . . . . The liturgy is not the school of this or that party, but the school of the Church!"[3]

Among all the pontifical documents emanating from the Holy See to set forth its thinking on liturgical worship and the spirituality which flows from it, none can be compared to the encyclical *Mediator Dei* issued by Pope Pius XII on November 20, 1947.[4] Extracting from it the paragraphs referring most directly to the spirituality of the Church, we find the following principles and norms established:[5]

1. Proper dispositions of the soul and private spiritual activity are neces-

---

[2] *A.A.S.,* 1925, p. 603; translation in *Social Wellsprings,* Vol. 2, ed. by Joseph Husslein, S. J. (Milwaukee: Bruce, 1942), p. 39.

[3] *Les Questions Liturgiques et Paroissiales,* 21 (1936), 4. Cardinal Pacelli, referring to the report of this audience, later wrote to Abbot Capelle that the mind of the supreme Pontiff had been rightly interpreted and that he had conformed fully to the Pope's desires. Cf. Bernard Capelle, *Le Saint-Siège et le mouvement liturgique* (Louvain, 1937), p. 3.

[4] The official text in Latin is found in the *A.A.S.,* 1947, pp. 521-600. The quotations in English are taken from the Vatican Library translation as published by the National Catholic Welfare Conference, 1312 Massachusetts Avenue N.W., Washington 5, D. C.

[5] The encyclical speaks of *objective piety* and *subjective piety.* For the right understanding of the doctrine there set forth, it must be noted that these two expressions do not always have the same value in a pontifical document. *Objective piety* may signify: 1) the Church's public worship; 2) liturgical spirituality, or private spiritual activity based on the spirit of the liturgy; 3) the excess of this tendency carried to the point of disdain for any act of piety that is not intimately related to public worship. In opposition to these three meanings of the expression *objective piety,* the other expression *subjective piety* may designate: 1) private spiritual activity; 2) the forms of private piety not inspired by the liturgy and not related to it; 3) the exaltation of personal activity in the way of spirituality to the point of belittling the importance of sacramental action. In the encyclical, *subjective piety* is equivalent simply to *private piety,* and it designates every personal spiritual activity, without which the *objective* efficacy of the Redemption and of the sacraments cannot be applied to us individually. *Subjective piety* is taken in the first meaning, therefore. To it is opposed *objective piety* in its third meaning of *reprehensible excess,* in as much as it represents new theories which belittle every kind of personal piety and teach "that all other religious exercises not directly connected with the sacred liturgy and performed outside public worship, should be omitted" (n. 29). There is not a strict parallelism, therefore, in the use of the two terms. Still the thinking of the Pope is made very clear by the whole context and by the repetition of the same concepts under different forms which illuminate and complement each other.

sary in order that the intrinsic power of the sacraments and of the sacrifice of the altar may obtain the proper effect.[6]

2. In the spiritual life there can be no repugnance or discrepancy between the public action of the Church and the private activity of the faithful. On the contrary, both are animated by the same spirit and tend to the same end.[7]

3. Beyond a doubt, liturgical prayer, being the Church's public prayer, is more excellent than private prayer.[8]

4. The holy sacrifice of the Mass must be for all Christians the center and the principal source of the life of piety.[9]

5. The sacred liturgy is an overflowing source of the life of piety.[10]

6. The piety which is derived from the sacred liturgy possesses the greatest efficacy for the spiritual life of all Christians and of each one individually.[11]

[6] See *Mediator Dei*, nn. 31-35, 54-57, and many other passages.

[7] "In the spiritual life, consequently, there can be no opposition between the action of God, who pours forth His grace into men's hearts so that the work of the Redemption may always abide, and the tireless collaboration of man, who must not render vain the gift of God. No more can the efficacy of the external administration of the sacraments, which comes from the rite itself *(ex opere operato)*, be opposed to the meritorious action of their ministers or recipients, which we call the agent's action *(opus operantis)*. Similarly, no conflict exists between public prayer and prayers in private, between morality and contemplation, between the ascetical life and devotion to the liturgy" (n. 36).

[8] "Unquestionably liturgical prayer, being the public supplication of the illustrious Spouse of Jesus Christ, is superior in excellence to private prayers" (n. 37).

[9] "The Mass is the chief act of divine worship; it should also be the source and center of Christian piety" (n. 201).

[10] "All the elements of the liturgy, then, would have us reproduce in our hearts through the mystery of the cross the likeness of the divine Redeemer according to the words of the Apostle of the Gentiles: 'With Christ I am nailed to the cross. I live, now not I, but Christ lives in me'" (n. 102). "By these suitable ways and methods in which the liturgy at stated times proposes the life of Jesus Christ for our meditation, the Church gives us examples to imitate, points out treasures of sanctity for us to make our own; since it is fitting that the mind believes what the lips sing, and

that what the mind believes should be practiced in public and private life" (n. 153). "But at that time especially when the faithful take part in the liturgical service with such piety and recollection that it can truly be said of them, 'whose faith and devotion is known to You,' it is then, when with the high Priest and through Him they offer themselves as a spiritual sacrifice, that each one's faith ought to become more ready to work through charity, his piety more real and fervent, and each should consecrate himself to the furthering of the divine glory, desiring to become as like as possible to Christ in His most grievous sufferings" (n. 99). The Church through the sacred liturgy demonstrates "the wisdom of the teaching method she employs to arouse and nourish constantly the 'Christian instinct'" (n. 50). "The worship she offers to God is a continuous profession of Catholic faith and a continuous exercise of hope and charity" (n. 47). See also n. 161, etc.

[11] "The liturgical year . . . is rather Christ Himself who is ever living in His Church . . . with the design of bringing men to know His mysteries and in a way live by them. These mysteries are ever present and active . . . in the way that Catholic doctrine teaches us. According to the doctors of the Church, they are shining examples of Christian perfection, as well as sources of divine grace, due to the merits and prayer of Christ; they still influence us because each mystery brings its own special grace for our salvation. Moreover, our holy Mother the Church, while proposing for our contemplation the mysteries of our Redeemer, asks in her prayers for those gifts which would give her children the greatest possible share in the spirit of these mysteries through the

7. The whole private activity of the faithful should tend to the sacred liturgy, serving as a means for getting a better grasp of the liturgy and for obtaining more abundant and effective fruits.[12]

8. Besides the piety which feeds on the liturgy, there are many other exercises of devotion in the Church, approved and recommended by the popes, but without any intimate or direct relation to the sacred liturgy.[13]

9. The Pope gives three reasons for explaining and recommending the many practices of private piety not related to the liturgy:

a) They are good in themselves and capable of leading souls to God.[14]

b) Not all Christians are sufficiently prepared to understand the liturgical rites and formulas correctly and thus to nourish their life of piety with them.[15]

c) The Holy Spirit can make use of means that are quite varied for bringing about holiness in souls, and can lead souls to God by very different ways.[16]

merits of Christ. By means of His inspiration and help and through the cooperation of our wills we can receive from Him living vitality as branches do from the tree and members from the head; thus slowly and laboriously we can transform ourselves 'unto the measure of the age of the fulness of Christ' " (n. 165).

[12] "Such action on the part of individual Christians, then, along with the ascetic effort prompting them to purify their hearts, actually stimulates in the faithful those energies which enable them to participate in the august sacrifice of the altar with better dispositions. They now can receive the sacraments with more abundant fruit, and come from the celebration of the sacred rites more eager, more firmly resolved to pray and deny themselves like Christians . . ." (n. 35). "As we have previously stated, such spiritual exercises are most useful and even necessary to instil into souls solid virtue, and to strengthen them in sanctity so as to be able to derive from the sacred liturgy more efficacious and abundant benefits" (n. 178). "Since these multiple forms of piety develop a deeper spiritual life in the faithful, they prepare them to take part in sacred public functions with greater fruit, and they lessen the danger of liturgical prayers becoming an empty ritualism" (n. 175).

[13] "It is Our wish also that the faithful, as well, should take part in these practices . . . . From these multiple forms of piety, the inspiration and action of the Holy Spirit cannot be absent. Their purpose is, in various ways, to attract and direct our souls to God, purifying them from their sins, encouraging them to practice virtue and finally stimulating them to advance along the path of sincere piety by accustoming them to meditate on the eternal

truths and disposing them better to contemplate the mysteries of the divine and human nature of Christ" (nn. 174-175).

[14] "But when devotional exercises, and pious practices in general, not strictly connected with the sacred liturgy, confine themselves to merely human acts, with the express purpose of directing these latter to the Father in heaven, of rousing people to repentance and holy fear of God, of weaning them from seductions of the world and its vice, and leading them back to the difficult path of perfection, then certainly such practices are not only highly praiseworthy but absolutely indispensable; because they expose the dangers threatening the spiritual life; they promote the acquisition of virtue; and because they increase the fervor and generosity with which we are bound to dedicate all that we are and all that we have to the service of Jesus Christ" (n. 32). See also the preceding note.

[15] "Nor are all capable of understanding correctly the liturgical rites and formulas. So varied and diverse are men's talents and characters that it is impossible for all to be moved and attracted to the same extent by community prayers, hymns, and liturgical services. Moreover, the needs and inclinations of all are not the same, nor are they always constant in the same individual" (n. 108).

[16] "It is perfectly clear to all that in the Church on earth, no less than in the Church in heaven, there are many mansions; and that asceticism cannot be the monopoly of anyone. It is the same Spirit who breathes where He will; and who with differing gifts and in different ways enlightens and guides souls to sanctity. Let their freedom and the super-

10. Nevertheless, pastors should foster a deeper knowledge of the liturgy among the faithful, that they may be able to nourish their spiritual life more substantially with it, since the liturgy is the normal and most potent source of life for souls.[17]

11. As for the other practices of piety, the spirit of the sacred liturgy must exercise a beneficent influence on them. More than that: the touchstone by which to judge the legitimacy of the particular exercises of devotion will be the greater or lesser efficacy with which they bring it about that the sacred liturgy will be better understood and more esteemed, and will wield a greater influence over the life of the Christians.[18]

To treat of a more recent document where the doctrine to which we are referring is found in a very clear and explicit way, we cannot fail to mention the decree *Maxima Redemptionis nostrae mysteria* of November 16, 1955, promulgating the new liturgical *Ordo* of Holy Week. Its introductory part contains the following paragraph: "The liturgical rites of Holy Week not only have a special dignity, but have also a special sacramental power and efficacy in nourishing the Christian life, and cannot be adequately replaced by those pious exercises of devotion usually called extraliturgical, which take place during the sacred triduum in the hours after noon."[19] This text refers

natural action of the Holy Spirit be so sacrosanct that no one presume to disturb or stifle them for any reason whatsoever" (n. 179).

[17] "We earnestly exhort you, venerable brethren, that after errors and falsehoods have been removed, and anything that is contrary to truth or moderation has been condemned, you promote a deeper knowledge among the people of the sacred liturgy so that they more readily and easily follow the sacred rites and take part in them with true Christian dispositions" (n. 186). "Here then is a better and more suitable way to raise the heart to God. Thenceforth the priesthood of Jesus Christ is a living and continuous reality through all the ages to the end of time, since the liturgy is nothing more nor less than the exercise of this priestly function" (n. 22). We should have to quote in their entirety nn. 187-209, in which the Pope promotes and inculcates the participation of the faithful in the sacred liturgy. In the epilogue of the encyclical he specifies the purpose which has moved him to address the bishops of the Catholic Church in such a solemn way: "that your children, who are also Ours, may more fully understand and appreciate the most precious treasures which are contained in the sacred liturgy"; and the last desire the supreme Pontiff expresses is "that during our earthly exile we may with one mind and one heart participate in the

sacred liturgy which is, as it were, a preparation and a token of that heavenly liturgy...."

[18] "If the private and interior devotion of individuals were to neglect the august sacrifice of the altar and the sacraments, and to withdraw them from the stream of vital energy that flows from Head to members, it would indeed be sterile, and deserve to be condemned" (n. 32). "Any inspiration to follow and practice extraordinary exercises of piety must most certainly come from the Father of Lights, from whom every good and perfect gift descends; and of course the criterion of this will be the effectiveness of these exercises in making the divine cult loved and spread daily ever more widely, and in making the faithful approach the sacraments with more longing desire, and in obtaining for all things holy due respect and honor. If, on the contrary, they are an ·obstacle to the principles and norms of divine worship, or if they oppose or hinder them, one must surely conclude that they are not in keeping with prudence and enlightened zeal" (n. 181).

[19] "Sacrosanctae hebdomadae liturgici ritus, non solum singulari dignitate, sed et peculiari sacramentali vi et efficacia pollent ad christianam vitam alendam, nec aequam obtinere possunt compensationem per pia illa devotionum exercitia, quae extraliturgica appellari solent, quaeque sacro triduo horis postmeri-

explicitly to the liturgical rites of Holy Week; but it is easy to infer the general doctrine implicitly contained in it.

The inference is justified by a parallel text found in the instruction of the Sacred Congregation of Rites for the correct application of the aforesaid decree. The instruction recommends to shepherds of souls that they instruct the faithful "on the supreme value of the sacred liturgy, which always, but especially on these days, far excels by its nature all the other customs and kinds of devotion, even the best."[20]

We could cite many more pontifical documents.[21]

From all of them we can draw the conclusion expressed by Monsignor Montini in a letter of the Secretariate of State (June 30, 1953) to the Liturgical Week of Oropa: "Nothing is more urgent in this hour, so grave and yet so rich in hopes, than to call the people of God, the great family of Jesus Christ, back to the substantial food of liturgical piety, revived by the breath of the Holy Spirit, who is the soul of the Church and of each one of her children." Thus "the faithful will resume contact with the values of the Christian life so often forgotten. In this way they will more easily come to know once more in a conscious way what is the substance of religion and piety for the Christian, namely the justice of the gospel, by which we are all to live, changed into new creatures, after the model of Jesus Christ."[22]

Despite the eloquence of her teachings, the Church shows herself condescending as far as the spirituality of the laity is concerned. On the other hand, she shows great concern and insistence when she addresses those who belong to her by a twofold title and who for that reason are repeatedly called *ecclesiastics*.

For it is not enough to have a canonical title indicating that one belongs to the Church juridically; to be truly *ecclesiastic* in the full sense of the word, one must be united spiritually to the Church through the acceptance and the assimilation of her spirituality. So much the more must this be said of the ecclesiastics who form part of the hierarchy and who by reason of their state and their ministry are called upon to spread the life and the spirit of the Church. Their life would turn out to be a contradiction if they themselves, who are to renew the mystery of Christ sacramentally in the Church and communicate it to the faithful, did not realize it at the same time in their lives, just as the Church herself teaches and lives it.

It is very significant that with the conferral of the first tonsure the new cleric is appointed to a church, which is at the same time a temple and a

---

dianis absolvuntur" (*Ordo Hebdomadae Sanctae Instauratus*, decree, near beginning).

[20] "Edoceantur porro fideles de summo valore sacrae liturgiae, quae semper, et his praesertim diebus, ceteras devotionis species et consuetudines, quamvis optimas, natura sua longe praecellit" (*ibid.*, instruction, IV, 23).

[21] See: *Documenta pontificia ad instaurationem liturgicam spectantia, 1903-1953* (Rome: Edizioni Liturgiche, 1953); and *Les Enseignements Pontificaux: La Liturgie* (Solesmes, 1954).

[22] See *Rivista Liturgica*, 1953, p. 85.

congregation of the faithful. It is the environment in which, from now on, he will have to sanctify himself by serving the Church.

To the subdeacon is entrusted a particular mission, to pray in the name of the Church, and for this he is given a breviary, that is, the book of ecclesiastical prayer. In it is contained the prayer of the Spouse of Christ, the deepest thoughts and the most refined emotions awakened in her by the presence of the Lord and the contemplation of His mystery. In it, with words inspired for the most part by God Himself, the Church sings to Him and praises Him, rejoices in His infinite sanctity and His indescribable perfections, admires Him in His works, glorifies Him for His Redemption and for His communications to creatures. And in the name of all, she thanks Him for His goodness and shows Him, confidently and humbly, the needs and the miseries of all. In return, and still in the same prayer, the Lord instructs the Church by imparting new light on His mysteries and infuses into her a more fervent love for Himself and for men.

All this the Church carries out through the ministry of the new subdeacon, on whom the daily duty of fulfilling this mission is incumbent henceforth. The Church's thoughts, affections, words will become realities through the person of her minister. It would be very deplorable, therefore, if, while the Church in the act of her greatest intimacy with her Spouse associates herself with the sacred minister to the point of identifying herself with him in the outward performance of her prayer, the minister on his part did not identify himself with the Church in the spirit which informs and gives life to that same prayer. After the Church has entrusted to her minister the task of giving reality to her relations with the Lord, and has given him at the same time the opportunity of making his own the prayer which she dictates to him, it would be something incomprehensible if he fulfilled that office only outwardly, as a canonical duty of his state in life, and then, being unsatisfied, had recourse to other formulas and other thoughts for *his* prayer, in the margin of the Church's prayer.

In the rite of ordination, the lector receives from the bishop a book, the lectionary; the subdeacon receives the book of the epistles; the deacon is assigned the book of the gospels; that they may enlighten the Church of God with the divine word, the epistles and the gospels respectively. There is no doubt that the reader himself should be the first to profit from that which he reads for the benefit of the faithful. It would be a sad thing if, after having administered to others on the Church's behalf the spiritual food which she has selected as most suitable and nourishing, he himself would then feel the need of looking for his own food in other writings, unless he uses them to penetrate more deeply into the Church's doctrine and assimilate it better.

Similarly, the priest's own book is the missal. The Church puts it into his hands, entrusting him with the mission of presiding over the public prayer and offering the sacrifice of the ecclesiastical community. By means of the missal she suggests to him the content and the formulas of everyone's prayer. If there is anyone who can and should assimilate this prayer and make it his own, it must be the priest himself, beyond any doubt.

It is only to be expected, then, that in conferring holy orders the Church should insist that the newly ordained make it the spiritual ideal of their lives to conform their own personal conduct to the public ministry conferred on them through their ordination. This is the program of sanctification traced for them by the Church; the program and the method: to realize in their own lives what they do in the name of the Church. This is so much the more true because the Church in her rites and her liturgical formulas is not interested in studying archeology and preserving souvenirs of antiquity, but is preoccupied with communicating the Christian life in the most substantial way, which is always a way that is present.

According to this plan, the porters are told, "See to it that, just as you open and shut the visible church with material keys, in the same way you close to the devil and open to God, by your words and examples, the invisible house of God, that is, the hearts of the faithful."

The bishop exhorts the lectors, "What you read with your lips, you must believe in your hearts and practice in your works . . . so that you give the example of a heavenly life to all those by whom you are heard and seen." And he prays for them "that what they read, they carry out in their works." And then, more explicitly: "Instructed and trained by constant application to reading, may they say what is to be done, and themselves carry out in deed what they say, that in both these ways they may serve the holy Church by the example of their holiness." It must be noted that these readings are precisely those which are read in the celebration of the liturgical rites; in them, therefore, the spiritual life of the lector is to be founded and nourished, so that his life will eventually be conformed to them and become a living proclamation of what is written in the liturgical books.

In the exhortation which precedes the ordination of exorcists we read, "See to it, therefore, that, just as you cast out devils from the bodies of others, so you remove from your own minds and bodies all uncleanness and iniquity." In other words, the sacramental rite is held up to the exorcists as the model of their own holiness.

The same kind of exhortation is given to the acolytes, under the imagery of light, which is proper to this order: "You cannot be pleasing to God if, while carrying the light for Him in your hands, you serve the works of darkness . . . . Walk as children of light . . . . Be fervent in all justice, goodness and truth, that you may enlighten yourselves and others and the Church of God. For then you will worthily offer wine and water for the sacrifice of God when you have offered yourselves in sacrifice to God by a chaste life and good works."

The bishop prays for the acolytes "that as they carry the visible light in their hands, they may also send forth a spiritual light by their conduct . . . . Inflame, O Lord, their minds and hearts with the love of Your grace, so that, enlightened by the splendor of Your countenance, they may faithfully serve You in Your holy Church."

In the ordination of subdeacons the bishop admonishes them, "See to it, therefore, that, while performing these visible services properly and with careful attention, you perform also the spiritual services symbolized by them." And after having explained the spiritual significance of the altar, the altar cloths and the corporals, the bishop adds, "Be such, therefore, as to assist worthily at the divine sacrifice and to serve the Church of God, which is the body of Christ . . . . Consider what ministry is entrusted to you; therefore I exhort you so to conduct yourselves as to be pleasing to God."

The admonition to the deacons is permeated with this concept of the unity between the liturgical ministry and the personal works of holiness. The deacons, who are separated from the rest to approach the altar, are to shine forth by their sanctity, being clean and undefiled, pure and chaste, as is becoming to ministers of Christ and dispensers of the mysteries of God. Toward the end of the exhortation they are told to "take care to teach the gospel by living deeds to those to whom you are proclaiming it."

But the best clue to the Church's way of thinking, expressed in a more concise and exact way, lies in the admonition which precedes the ordination to the priesthood. "Seek to become well acquainted with what you are doing," the ordinands are told; *imitate what you are handling;* so that in celebrating the mystery of the Lord's death you seek to mortify your members by fleeing all vice and concupiscence. Let your teaching be a spiritual medicine for the people of God; let the sweet odor of your lives be a delight to the Church of Christ; so that by your preaching and example you build up the house, that is, the family of God." And again in the prayer which follows the solemn preface of ordination to the priesthood the same program of Christian and priestly life is indicated: "May they believe what they read, teach what they believe, and practice what they teach."

In short, the Church in all these texts not only urges on her ministers the necessity of being holy because they are to administer holy things, but moreover determines for them the form, the style of their sanctity. She advises them to use as means of sanctification the sacred rites themselves which they are to perform in the name of the Church, taking care to learn their deepest meaning, assimilating their content in a vital way and putting them into practice in their deeds.

It is clear enough, then, that the Church wants all the faithful, and particularly the ecclesiastics, to receive as their own the spirituality which she offers them and which consists primarily in a plan of vital unity between public worship and piety, between the Church's official action and the spiritual activity of individuals.

The most profound reason for this desire of the Church is found in the fact that this is the plan of sanctification established by God, according to the explanation of St. Thomas. We shall develop St. Thomas's explanation later. Here it will suffice to indicate some points of his doctrine on the sacraments.

Jesus Christ has in fact established man's supernatural life and religious perfection on the sacraments as a foundation. Hence by analyzing the structure of the sacramental economy we shall see what is the divine plan of our sanctification in the Church. And the first thing to do is to determine the final cause, which will specify and give form to this whole sanctifying organism.

According to St. Thomas[23] the sacraments have the positive and ultimate purpose of "disposing and perfecting the soul with a view to the worship of God according to the rite of the Christian religion." To this end they confer grace on us, and some of them configure us to Jesus Christ the Priest by means of the sacramental character. By virtue of the character, we are consecrated definitively and specifically to rendering God a suitable worship by taking part in the public worship offered Him by the Church, with the power of administering or receiving the sacraments. The character even endows all the virtuous acts of the Christian life with the value of worship.

This destination to the divine worship is something of supreme value for St. Thomas in the sacramental economy, since the sanctification of man and the sacramental grace which causes it have the purpose of making such a consecration possible. Actually the Church's public worship, to be a worship "in spirit and in truth," must be interior and personal too: the outward rites of Christian worship can be acceptable to God only when they correspond to an interior attitude, that is, when the members of the Church are holy with the holiness of the Head, when those who render this worship—the sacred ministers and the faithful, in the role which belongs to each of them—are spiritually united to Jesus Christ, supreme Priest and principal offerer.

Thus the character which consecrates us to the divine worship calls for a further perfection, the sacramental grace which sanctifies us to make us worthy of that worship. The supreme purpose to which the two effects of the sacrament, grace and the character, are ordained is the divine worship: that we may be able to offer it to God, the character is conferred on us; that we may be able to offer it worthily, grace is given us.

This order of values tells us what should be the norm of our actuation of the sacramental grace through the practice of the Christian life, and gives us the characteristic purpose of the Church's spirituality. We do not render God an exterior and interior worship to sanctify ourselves; but we sanctify ourselves and the sacraments sanctify us, that we may be able to unite ourselves to the public worship of the Church. And to unite ourselves to the worship

[23] St. Thomas, *Summa theol.*, III, qq. 62 and 63.

with which the Church honors God does not mean only to take part in the external acts of worship which she exercises or practices, but also, and principally, to impart to those acts of worship the internal perfection of a sanctity and a spiritual activity which will inform the external rites.

Essentially, it suffices for this purpose that the members be vitally united by grace to the Head and by the baptismal character to the high Priest Jesus Christ. Thus every Christian in the state of grace, provided he performs good actions, participates by that fact alone in the divine worship according to the rite of the Christian life, and lends it the interior value of his holiness, even though he be unaware of this.

But his consecration will be fully actuated and the participation in the Church's worship will reach its perfection only when, besides this essential contribution of his sanctity, the whole interior activity of the soul, in unison with that of Jesus Christ and of the Church, lends to the liturgical rites the spirit and the inward feeling which they express outwardly.

But the Christian will not succeed in having this spiritual attitude at the time of liturgical prayer, and in fact the prayer will always turn out to be somewhat unreal for him, if his soul is not trained in the school of public worship and if in fact his actions are not habitually informed by the spirit of the liturgy.

It is precisely to this end that the spirituality of the Church tends, and this constitutes her particular style of sanctity.

3   HISTORY OF THE

CHURCH'S SPIRITUALITY

The ideal of the Church's spiritual pedagogy has not always been embodied in concrete realities. Like every manifestation of the activity of the human spirit, the common spirituality of the Christians has been subjected to the fluctuations of the various facts and circumstances which have contributed to forming its history.

We can distinguish four great periods in the history of the Church's spirituality:

1. Formation and high point of liturgical spirituality because of the unity established from the beginning between public worship and private piety. This period attained its perfection during the pontificate of St. Gregory the Great.

2. Era of splendor and exuberance in the external forms of the common piety of the Church and the faithful, while the true sense of worship and of piety is being lost. The twelfth and thirteenth centuries mark the high point of this exteriority.

3. There follows an age of decadence for the liturgy and for private piety, and the division between the two parties is established. While the liturgy turns toward formalism, individual piety seeks new ways in the margin of the liturgy. This epoch culminates with the Renaissance, and extends to the end of the last century.

4. Rebirth of liturgical spirituality with the return to unity between the Church's public worship and the private spiritual activity of the faithful, both being purified of the defects that had brought about the separation. This new era of rebirth of liturgical spirituality opens at the beginning of the twentieth century.

We shall confine ourselves to the principal facts that characterize each of these periods.

1. Formation and High Point of Liturgical Spirituality

The plan of sanctification based on the unity which the Church expresses so insistently in her liturgy is no mere idealism; its value and its efficacy have been proved by many centuries of wonderful experience. Actually this unity shaped the whole spiritual life of Christian antiquity and produced excellent fruits of holiness.

A mere look at the documents that have come down to us from those centuries will suffice to show what a vital unity existed between the public worship and the practical life of those first generations of Christians. What is more: with reference to those times, it would be absurd to imagine a private spiritual activity separated from the activity that constituted the public worship of the Church. The sense of unity in Christ through the Church was profoundly rooted in those Christians, and their spirit could be nourished only on the solid and abundant food which the Church distributed to them in common.

It was in the liturgical assembly that the catechumens received their initiation; the readings that were recited there supplied them with the doctrinal instruction on which they were to base their faith and build up their supernatural life; the liturgical rites completed the preparation for baptism and conferred on them, in the sacraments of the Christian initiation, the divine sonship, the fulness of the Christian life, the sacramental communion with Jesus Christ and the communion of love with the Church.

All the fruits of sanctity of the primitive Church, in times of persecution and later in peaceful times, ripened in the warmth of the liturgy. The ideal of purity which inspired the virgins and the continent; the fervor of love for Christ which imparted strength and joy to the martyrs and found concrete expression in the enthusiastic "I am a Christian!" so often pronounced before the judges; the delicacy of brotherly love which made the early communities "a single heart and a single soul"; the burning desire for intimate union with God which populated the deserts of Egypt and Asia Minor with hermits and monks—all had been inspired and had taken shape in contact with the rites of the liturgy.

The Acts of the Martyrs offer a magnificent testimony of the intense ecclesiastical spirit which animated the life of those perfect Christians. Those artless narratives show us plainly what was their spirituality. At the supreme moment of their existence, their expressions reflect vividly what they felt and lived most intensely, and they are a relic much more precious for us than their mortal remains, since they put us into contact with the inmost sentiments of their souls. The words that came spontaneously from their lips were often the same expressions they were accustomed to using in the liturgical gatherings. The gestures with which they took leave of their brethren while they awaited the palm of martyrdom were the same ritual gestures they were accustomed to repeating in the synaxes.

Deo gratias is the exclamation with which they usually welcomed the sentence of the judges, the same exclamation with which they welcomed the reading of the sacred Scriptures in the liturgical assemblies. This is true of St. Cyprian and most of the African martyrs.

The *Amen* which had so often ratified and sealed the Church's public prayers, and which they were used to pronouncing as a profession of faith when receiving the Eucharist, now sealed the offering of their life, introducing them to the bloody participation of the Lord's Passion.

This is declared explicity by the Acts of St. Afra, the famous martyr of Augsburg. Alluding to her former life of sin, she said before the judge, "As I am unworthy to offer a sacrifice to God, I want to sacrifice myself for the glory of His name, that the body by which I have sinned may be purified in the torments." And while she was being led to the scaffold she offered the Lord the following prayer, which savors strongly of the liturgy: "I give You thanks, Lord Jesus Christ, that You have seen fit to accept me as a victim for the glory of Your name, You who were immolated as a single Victim on the cross for the salvation of the whole world, the just One in place of the unjust, the good One in place of the evil, the blessed One for the cursed, the sweet One for the bitter, the One untouched by sin for the sake of all sinners. To You I offer my sacrifice, who with the Father and the Holy Spirit live and reign for ever and ever. Amen."[1]

We could cite the prayers of martyrs such as Severus of Adrianopolis, Euplius of Catania, Theodotus, Phileas of Thmuis, Paul of Gaza and many others. In their content and in their very expression those prayers are reminiscent of the liturgical formulas which the martyrs had so often heard or recited and which had nourished their spiritual life. The diversity of origin of these martyrs bears witness to a practice universal in extent.

Let us recall only the magnificent prayer of St. Polycarp, celebrated bishop of Smyrna, martyred in 155. When he was led to the place of torment, raising his eyes to heaven he said, "God of the angels, God of the archangels, our resurrection, forgiver of sins, ruler of all the elements and of every dwelling-place, protector of the whole race of the just, who live in Your sight: I, Your servant, bless You for having held me worthy to receive my share and crown

---

[1] *Passio S. Afrae*, nn. 1 and 2: *Monumenta Germaniae Historica*, Scriptorum Rerum Merovingicarum, III, pp. 61 and 63.

of martyrdom, the beginning of the chalice, through Jesus Christ in the unity of the Holy Spirit, that when the sacrifice of this day is complete I may receive the promises of Your truth. Therefore I bless You in all things, and I glory in Jesus Christ, almighty and eternal high Priest, through whom be glory to You, together with Himself and the Holy Spirit, now and forever, world without end. Amen."[2]

Of particular interest are the prayers of the martyrs who, forgetful of themselves, offered up to the Lord in their supreme moment a prayer for the whole Church, reminiscent of the *oratio fidelium* of their synaxes, which is found already in St. Paul and is not lacking in any of the ancient liturgies; in fact, a souvenir of it has come down to us in the *orationes solemnes* of Good Friday.

The martyr Paul of Gaza was condemned to be beheaded. When he arrived at the place of execution he asked the executioner for a few moments in which to recollect himself and pray. The Acts tell us that first he prayed for the whole Christian people, then he made a commemoration of the Jews and the Samaritans, and offered supplication for the pagans and for the curious and excited multitude that surrounded him. Finally he interceded for the judge who had condemned him, for the emperors who had instigated the persecution and for the executioner who was to behead him.[3]

Of St. Polycarp we are told also that after a long prayer of two hours by which he desired to prepare himself for martyrdom, he raised his voice and commemorated the whole Church, the well known and the unknown, the good and the bad, and all the Catholics, wherever they were scattered, who remained united to the one Church.[4]

Beautifully expressed also is the reply of St. Fructuosus, bishop of Tarragona, to a Christian who asked for a particular remembrance of himself as the saint was being led to the stake: "I must keep in mind the holy Catholic Church, spread out from the East to the West."[5]

But it is not only in their prayers that the martyrs echo the liturgical prayers. Even many of their spontaneous expressions reveal how deeply the words of the Church's public prayer had penetrated into their lives.

The Acts of the martyrdom of St. Saturninus of Carthage tell us that among the faithful arrested with Bishop Saturninus was the lector Emeritus, in whose house the sacred liturgy had been celebrated. Here is the dialogue between the proconsul of Carthage and the lector Emeritus:

[2] Martyrdom of St. Polycarp, XII; *Actas de los Mártires*, p. 275.—As the basis of our citations from the Acts of the Martyrs we take the edition of the Biblioteca de Autores Cristianos, *Actas de los Mártires*, prepared by Daniel Ruiz Bueno (Madrid, 1951). It gives the Latin text and a Spanish translation, and we consider it sufficiently critical. (The American agent for the Biblioteca de Autores Cristianos is the Academy Library Guild, Fresno, Calif.)

[3] Eusebius, On the Martyrs of Palestine, VIII; *Actas de los Mártires*, p. 921.

[4] Martyrdom of St. Polycarp, VIII; *Actas de los Mártires*, p. 270.

[5] Martyrdom of St. Fructuosus, Bishop of Tarragona, and of Eulogius and Augurius, Deacons, III; *Actas de los Mártires*, p. 791.

"Is it true that you hold the celebration in your house contrary to the emperor's edict?"

"Yes, we have celebrated the liturgy of the Lord."

"And why have you let so many people enter?"

"Because they are my brethren and I cannot put them out."

"You were obliged to put them out."

"No, I could not do it, because we cannot live without celebrating the liturgy of the Lord."[6]

Let us recall the expressions of the martyr St. Ignatius: "You could not do me a greater service than to let me be immolated to God while the altar is still prepared." "I am God's wheat, and I shall be ground by the teeth of wild beasts that I may be found pure bread of Christ."[7]

The lector Ampelius, one of the martyrs of Albitina, declared to the proconsul the treasures he possessed, namely: the communion with the brethren, the celebration of the *dominicum*, the sacred Scriptures and in his heart the praise of Jesus Christ.[8]

Very interesting under this same aspect are the Acts of the bishop of Tarragona, Fructuosus: "Along the way many, moved by brotherly love, offered the martyrs a mixture prepared for drinking. But the bishop refused it, saying, 'It is not yet the hour to break the fast.' For it was the fourth hour of the day. On Wednesday they had already solemnly celebrated the fast in prison. And now on Friday, the holy bishop was hurrying on, looking forward with joy and assurance to breaking the fast with the martyrs and the prophets in the paradise which the Lord has prepared for those who love Him."[9]

The martyrs are often described in the narratives of their sufferings as praying with their arms extended in the form of a cross. This was the attitude that used to accompany liturgical prayer. That is why they assumed it again when the hour of their own sacrifice arrived, remembering what they had been accustomed to doing in the liturgical gatherings: *solitae consuetudinis memores,* say the Acts of St. Fructuosus and of his deacons Augurius and Eulogius, referring to their attitude in their last prayer amid the flames at the stake.[10]

The historian Eusebius, describing the martyrs of Tyre, mentions a youth whose hands were not tied as were those of his companions, and who, extending his arms in the form of a cross, prayed serenely and intrepidly, waiting motionless for the bear or the leopard that was to devour him.[11]

---

[6] Martyrdom of SS. Saturninus, Dativus and Many Other Martyrs in Africa, X; *Actas de los Mártires*, pp. 983-984.

[7] St. Ignatius of Antioch, *Letter to the Romans*, II, 2, and IV, 2 (PG 5, 688 and 689).

[8] Martyrdom of SS. Saturninus, Dativus and Many Other Martyrs in Africa, XII; *Actas de*
los Mártires, p. 987.

[9] Martyrdom of St. Fructuosus, III; *Actas de los Mártires*, p. 791.

[10] Martyrdom of St. Fructuosus, IV; *Actas de los Mártires*, p. 792.

[11] The Martyrs under Diocletian, according to the Account of Eusebius of Caesarea, VII; *Actas de los Mártires*, p. 877.

At various times the Lord granted His martyrs the grace of uniting their sacrifice with the Eucharistic sacrifice: they shed their blood during the celebration of the holy mysteries, thus fulfilling even physically the supreme desire of union with Jesus Christ and with the Church. And in the Eucharist they always found the strength to overcome pain and death.

On the day of her death St. Melania was able to assist at the celebration of the Mass. It was a Sunday. The noble Roman matron, lying in the little cell of her monastery at Jerusalem, was expiring in terrible agonies. In the adjoining house the priest Gerontius was offering the holy sacrifice, so grief-stricken, as he himself tells us, that he could not pronounce the prayers distinctly and was reciting them in silence. Then the dying woman cried out, "Pronounce the prayers in a louder voice, please, that I may hear them and be strengthened by their power!"[12]

During the persecution of Gallus, St. Cyprian wrote to Pope Cornelius, advising him to admit to holy communion those who had apostatized and now wanted to return to the Church; and he gave this reason: "because the Eucharist serves precisely to strengthen those who receive it . . . . Fervor and courage wane if the reception of the Eucharist does not sustain and enkindle them."[13] It should be kept in mind that in those ages the Eucharist was conceived only as a sacramental participation in the mystery of the Lord and in the unity of the Church.

Convinced as the martyrs were that the sacrifice of their life would be a continuation of the sacrifice of the Lord in the members of His Church, before taking leave of their brethren they tightened the bonds of love with them through the kiss of peace, just as they had done during the celebration of the holy mysteries. And that sign of brotherly love and of ecclesiastical unity prepared them for the act of supreme love and the final union with Christ.

In the *passio* of SS. Perpetua and Felicitas we read that when Perpetua found herself in the *iugulatorium,* she summoned her brother and another Christian and said to them, "Remain steadfast in the faith, love one another, do not be scandalized at our sufferings." Then, joining the other martyrs, she went out bravely with them into the amphitheater. There they solemnly gave one another the kiss of peace and, silent and motionless, awaited the stroke of the sword.[14]

The *passio* of the African martyrs Lucius, Montanus and companions tells us that while these martyrs were taking leave of their Christian brethren with the kiss of peace, the *sacramentum legitimae pacis,* the martyr Fabian imposed silence and said to them, "We give you peace, beloved brethren, and our peace will abide with you if you remain at peace with the Church and

---

[12] M. Card. Rampolla del Tindaro, *Santa Melania Giuniore Senatrice Romana* (Rome: Vatican Press, 1905), pp. 38-39.

[13] St. Cyprian, *Epistola* 57, 2 and 4 (CSEL III, II, pp. 652 and 654).

[14] Martyrdom of SS. Perpetua and Felicitas and of Their Companions, XX; *Actas de los Mártires,* p. 438.

preserve the unity of love. And do not think that my words are of little value, since our Lord Jesus Christ just before His Passion also spoke in this way: 'This is My commandment, that you love one another as I have loved you.' "[15]

In the Passion of the soldier martyrs Marcian and Nicander it is related that Marcian's wife, who was a pagan, sought to prevent her husband's martyrdom, and therefore he had sent her away. But when the time for receiving the mortal blow arrived, he summoned her to him, embraced her and said, "Now, in God's name, depart. You could not look upon me while I celebrate my martyrdom, because your soul is still in the devil's power." Then he said goodbye to his little son, kissing him and saying, "Lord, God all-powerful, take care of this child." Finally the two martyrs Marcian and Nicander exchanged the kiss of peace and knelt before the executioner.[16]

In many other incidental details the Acts reveal how the martyrs and the editors of their *passiones* were saturated with a liturgical spirituality which showed itself spontaneously everywhere.

On various occasions the Lord sought to comfort and fortify His martyrs supernaturally before the great trial, with some intimate and extraordinary manifestations which gave them a foretaste of the reward that awaited them in heaven.

It is curious to observe that, as a pledge of eternal life and a symbol of what the Eucharist was for them, there appears to them a young man of extraordinary nobility in the act of offering a vessel of milk which, with the sweetness of its taste, cures them of the ailments contracted in the prison, fills their hearts with heavenly consolation, fortifies them for the struggle and assures them of victory. It is an allusion to that milk which they had been given to taste as a sensible expression of their new life in Christ after they had been begotten to supernatural life with the reception of the Paschal sacraments. The Passions of SS. Montanus, Lucius and companions and of SS. Perpetua and Felicitas are very interesting in this respect.

Still more frequent is the representation of heaven as a banquet in the midst of a delightful garden. It is a heavenly idealization of the brotherly *agape* which they had so often tasted on the occasion of their liturgical gatherings. The same idea was repeatedly expressed in the pictures in the catacombs, thus creating an atmosphere of peace and hope among the sepulchers of the departed.

Many more references could be given. We could go down into the Roman cemeteries and examine the paintings of primitive Christian art, or read the ingenuous epitaphs that have been preserved for us in such great numbers. We could page through the writings of the Fathers, especially their catecheses and homilies, and analyze the ecclesiastical legislation in the decrees of the councils.

[15] Martyrdom of SS. Montanus, Lucius and Companions, XXIII; *Actas de los Mártires*, p. 822.

[16] *Passio SS. Nicandri et Marciani MM.*, n. 9; *Acta Sanctorum Iunii IV* (Paris and Rome: Victor Palmé, 1867), p. 221.

All this accumulation of precious relics of Christian antiquity would strengthen our conviction that the spiritual life of these centuries of ardent faith proceeded from the liturgy, was nourished on the liturgy and reproduced in each one of the faithful that which the Church was celebrating for all: the mystery of Christ.

2. Era of Outward Splendor and of Lessening of Solid Interior Piety

This method of conceiving and practicing the ideal of Christian perfection lasted in all its purity and ardor during the centuries that constituted the ancient era of the Church. But the Middle Ages too, despite the general upheaval of ideas and customs they brought with them, formed and preserved their own efforts at spiritual perfection, bringing into the life of individuals the influence and the exemplarity of the liturgical rites.

It is true that the invasions of the barbarians, which completed the political destruction of the already weakened and divided Roman empire, threatened also to drag down with it civilization, culture and even the Christian life itself. But, even if it was only by an instinct of self-preservation, the more gravely the general level of the faithful's morality and piety was threatened, the more they felt the need of basing themselves solidly on the foundations that sustained their spiritual life.

Actually it was the liturgy and the traditional ecclesiastical sense, taking refuge in the monasteries, that maintained the strong vitality of the Church, converted the barbarian tribes, saved European civilization and infused the Christian spirit into the new institutions and the new society which was rising from the ruins of the empire.

In this era the liturgy underwent a profound modification in its outward forms. Being the only source of spirituality for those new generations, it had to adapt itself to the character of youthful life, which is always inclined to exuberance, to grandiose displays, to exteriority.

These new generations had a taste for solemn forms under which to partake of the immense riches of spiritual life which the Church offered them. Thus they gradually increased the splendor of worship, the number of feasts, the duration of the Office. The ceremonies were multiplied, and the liturgical action was overloaded with new rites.

Some liturgical solemnities acquired a new plastic and lyrical form, to the point of becoming *liturgical dramas* in the tenth and eleventh centuries, and later becoming the miracle and mystery plays produced in the church which exerted so much influence on the social life of the sixteenth century.

The Middle Ages are also the time of the construction of the great abbey and cathedral churches, in which the plastic arts sculpture on the stone and picture in the frescoes of the walls and in the many-colored windows all that the liturgy is doing with its words, rites and feasts.

But in this very splendor of the liturgical life which was linked to the piety of the Christian people, we find a cause of eventual decadence. The outward exuberance of the liturgy was smothering its spirit.

If public worship ought to be the norm and the food of the spiritual life of individuals, this is in order that it may bring the mystery of Christ within reach of men's minds and wills. The outward forms which immediately affect the senses and the emotions contribute to the association of all men and even of all nature in the Church's worship. But in their function of educating and regulating individual piety, they must be only a means to facilitate the understanding and the assimilation of the mysteries of worship.

But as we advance into the medieval centuries these outward forms take on the character of an end in themselves, and hence the knowledge of the liturgy becomes more superficial. A great appreciation of its outward manifestations is felt; but its content, the reality of the mystery of Christ in the liturgy and in the Christian life, is already far from the minds of the faithful. Little by little the theological basis is being forgotten, while the love of everything that arouses the feelings is increasing. What is sought is not so much the participation in the sacramental life and the understanding of the mysteries, but the material apparatus of worship and the kind of devotion that affects the senses.

This process was very slow and was at work for several centuries. If the age of St. Gregory the Great represents the high point in the formal and ideological development of the liturgy and of its spirituality, the twelfth and thirteenth centuries reach the high point of an outward development, exuberant and disproportioned. Suddenly there begins a rapid decline which leads to the disaster of the age of the Renaissance.

Following in a sort of parallel fashion the curve of the outward development of the liturgy, the solid spirituality of the first Christians was being modified under the influence of a twofold tendency, which impelled the spirits of the faithful in new directions unknown to the preceding centuries. On the one hand there was the urge to concretize and materialize piety and worship; on the other hand, a marked and growing sensible devotion toward the humanity of Christ and toward the Virgin Mary. The two currents increased progressively under the influence of the general tendency to exteriority, and at the same time they influenced that tendency.

The first of these two currents, that is, the desire to seek what is concrete and palpable in piety, is proper to the human spirit, especially when the intensity of a profound spiritual life is decreasing. In the era with which we are concerned, we find the most important manifestation of this tendency in the development of the cult of the martyrs. We shall pause for a while to examine so important a factor in the modification of medieval piety.

From the very beginning the Christians had the devotion of possessing some object sanctified by the heroes of the faith. Thus, according to the account given in the Acts, the faithful of Carthage hastened to soak some cloths in the blood of their Bishop Cyprian; the soldier Pudens exulted in the possession of a ring bathed in the blood of the martyr Saturus, one of the companions in suffering of SS. Perpetua and Felicitas. With ever greater interest and concern, the faithful sought to gain possession, when it was possible, of some particle of the martyrs' bodies mangled by the teeth of the wild beasts or of their bones burned to a powder at the stake. Let us recall, among many similar cases, what happened after the martyrdom of SS. Fructuosus, Augurius and Eulogius.

But when their remains received burial, this was considered inviolable in virtue of the Roman law, at least in the West. When the Christians visited the tombs of the martyrs, the purpose was to make spiritual contact with those heroes of the faith in the places sanctified by the presence of their bodies. As a material souvenir of their pilgrimage they carried away a little earth taken from around the tomb, or some drops of oil from the lamps burning there, or some pieces of cloth—the *brandea*—with which they had touched the place of burial.

In the East, however, there is mention of the transferral of relics as early as the fourth century. The relics were highly prized and sought after, and their presence in any place or any city was always looked upon as a pledge of heaven's protection. When the bodies of the martyrs were exhumed, they were divided so that their relics could be distributed and thus their presence and protection could be extended.

This desire came to be felt in the West also, but for many centuries it met with the obstacle of "Roman custom." Thus, at the time of St. Gregory the Great many important persons asked him for relics of the Roman martyrs.

The empress Constantina, wife of Emperor Mauricius, asked the Pope to send her the head of St. Paul or some part of his body as a relic for the new basilica just constructed in the Apostle's honor at Constantinople; but she received only some *brandea* which had touched his tomb.

St. Gregory did the same thing with the bishops of Rieti and of Milan, who were asking respectively for the relics of the martyrs Hermas, Hyacinth and Maximus and the relics of SS. Paul, John and Pancratius.

The same pope received a priest named John who had been commissioned by Queen Theodelinde to ask him for various relics of Roman martyrs. The priest John had to be content to carry to the sovereign of Monza some bottles containing a little oil gathered from the lamps that were burning in the shrines he visited during his stay in Rome.

St. Gregory gives us the reason for this procedure in the letter addressed to the empress Constantina on the occasion of the request she made of him: "Her most serene Highness must be informed that it is not the custom of the Romans when they give relics of saints to presume to touch any part of the body; they merely put a *brandeum* into a pyx and place it near the

sacred bodies of the saints . . . . In Roman territory or anywhere in the
West it would be an intolerable and sacrilegious thing for anyone to want
to touch the bodies of the saints."[17]

The current finally became so headlong that the Roman *consuetudo* could
not resist it much longer. Bishops and abbots especially vied with one another
in enriching their respective churches with numerous and celebrated relics.
No means were spared to obtain them: assaults on churches and monasteries,
armed robberies. The literature on the thefts of relics is very abundant in
the eighth and ninth centuries.

At the beginning of the ninth century there took place at Rome something
which greatly facilitated the acquisition of relics. To avoid the profanation
of the Roman cemeteries on the occasion of the barbarian invasions, Pope
Paschal I ordered the transferral of the martyrs' relics into the churches of the
city. The tombs of martyrs and non-martyrs were opened, and at once we
find an association organized for the sale of relics. Its most notable member
was the deacon Deusdona, whose adventures throughout France and Germany, as he distributed relics everywhere, have become famous. The bodies
of certain martyrs seem to have multiplied under his hands.

About two centuries later, the contact of the West with the Holy Land on
the occasion of the Crusades revived the desire for relics. If it was the bodies
of martyrs that were desired before, now it was personal souvenirs of our
Lord and of the Blessed Virgin that were eagerly sought; and the treasuries
of the great abbeys and cathedral churches were enriched with the most
extravagant and unlikely relics brought from the East.

And here there is a confluence of this current which delights in seeing
and touching, and the other current we have pointed out, the sensible devotion to the humanity of Jesus. In various writings of the eighth and ninth
centuries there is already noted a deeply rooted inclination toward an affective
and tender piety, which keeps increasing in the following centuries and exerts
a powerful influence, until it comes to predominate, later, in the liturgy and
in popular piety.

All that is needed for an evaluation of this influence is a look at the
artistic expressions of liturgical vitality in the decorative and plastic arts.
In the centuries of the late Middle Ages Jesus Christ had almost always been
represented as the Dominus, the Lord of majesty; later, in the centuries of
the great theologians, He was represented as Master or Teacher, and if He
sometimes carried the cross, it was usually a triumphal cross adorned with
precious stones. On the other hand, when we come to the fifteenth century,
the favorite themes of writers and artists are the tender scenes of Jesus'
childhood and of His Passion, a realistic and tragic Passion; the *Dominus* has
been transformed into the "Man of sorrows," naked, bloody, crowned with

---

[17] *Monumenta Germaniae Historica: Gregorii   1, book 4, ep. 30, ed. Paul Ewald (Berlin:
I Papae Registrum Epistolarum*, vol. 1, part   Weidmann, 1891), pp. 264-265.

thorns, surrounded by the instruments of the Passion, or stretched out lifeless on the knees of His sorrowing Mother.

These two tendencies of medieval piety differ greatly from the ecclesiastical spirituality of the first centuries; but, like that spirituality, they are united to the liturgy of the Church. Until well into the fourteenth century the liturgy and popular piety live the same life, and there is no antagonism between them. They both develop by following new paths and creating new forms, but they still compenetrate each other and form a unity.

Yet they carry within themselves a principle of separation. The atmosphere in which they live is highly favorable to the development of the virus which is suffocating their common vitality, to the point of creating between them the total separation which will be completed in the period of the Renaissance. Subsequently, it will be hard to turn around and re-establish the unity that has been destroyed, despite the efforts of liturgical spirituality at restoration.

3. Decadence of Liturgical Spirituality

We can assign various causes for the separation between public worship and the spiritual life of individuals.

In the first place there is the complicity of the liturgy itself in the deformation of popular piety. As Dom Guéranger says, "instead of being the rule of faith for the people, the liturgy turned itself into an instrument at the service of popular passions." Following the tendencies then in vogue, it abandoned its dogmatic depth and its objective sobriety.

To get some idea of the level to which the liturgy descended at that time, we need only page through any missal or breviary of that era. In almost all of them we find, among the innumerable feasts of saints which were being introduced, formulas of popular and sentimental character, which can often be classified as superstitious and vulgar, and which sometimes even become crudities.

Most characteristic, however, are the hymns of the breviary, the sequences and proses of the missal and the tropes which invade the texts of the Mass and the Office. The religious ignorance which was already infiltrating everywhere did not permit people to see the profound meaning of the traditional liturgical texts, and they had to depend on new formulas which would express their pious feelings according to the new vogue.

Sequences are found for all tastes and in almost all Masses, not only on the feasts of saints but also in the Masses of the common, in Sunday Masses, in votive Masses. Almost all the missals of the fifteenth century contain a hundred sequences, which, as may be supposed, echo all the apocryphal stories and legendary occurrences.[18] It is hardly necessary to mention the fact that

---

[18] See, for example, the following fragment which the missal of Langres, of the year 1491,

the Masses with which every church celebrated the feast of its principal relics also had their proses or sequences.[19]

The tropes came to be commentaries of popular appeal on all the texts of the Mass and the Office. The people appreciated them because they understood them and because the tropes made worship more dramatic. Very soon all the texts were crammed with tropes: the fixed parts of the Mass and the changeable parts, the *Pater noster,* the versicles, the antiphons, even the *Benedicamus Domino* at the conclusion of the Offices.[20] The most famous

assigns to the feast of St. John the Evangelist, in which an attempt is made to reconcile the Apostle's death with the Lord's statement, "That disciple does not die."

Tibi seni	"Appearing to you in your old age,
Christus apparens	Christ invites you,
invitat, dicens ita:	saying,
Veni, care,	'Come, beloved,
et epulare	and feast
cum sancta fratrum turma.	with the holy throng of brethren.'
Audiens haec Ioannes	Hearing this,
vivus intrat sepulcra.	John enters the tomb alive.
Et requirentes corpus	And those who seek his body
nil vident nisi manna.	see nothing but manna."

[19] The following will serve as an example. It is a fragment of a prose which the church of Taranto sang during the Mass to the *tear of Jesus Christ* which they claimed to be preserving. It is not to be called a model of historical reliability!

A Christo quae nata	"Coming from Christ,
Angelo collecta,	Gathered by an angel,
Magdalenae data,	Given to Magdalene,
Maximino vecta,	Brought to Maximin,
Imperatori graecorum,	Emperor of the Greeks,
Inde praesentata	Then presented
Gaufrido, Vindocinorum	To Godfrey, and transferred
Ad locum translata.	To Vendôme."

And it continues in this style to its conclusion with the invocation:

O benigna, o benigna, o benigna,
quae semper inviolata permansisti!

[20] We shall cite only some examples taken from the Office of Peter of Corbeil. The *Gloria* for the Mass of the Circumcision begins thus:

Gloria in excelsis Deo, cuius reboat in omni gloria mundo.
Et in terra pax, Pax perennis,
Hominibus bonae voluntatis, Qui Deum timent in veritate.
Laudamus te, Te decet laus.
Benedicimus te, De die in diem.
Adoramus te, Cum prece, voto, hymnis adsumus ecce Tibi.
Glorificamus te, Qui in caelis gloriosus es.
Gratias agimus Tibi, De beneficiis tuis. Etc.

The epistle for the Mass of the Holy Innocents begins in this way:

Lectio libri Apocalipsis Iohannis apostoli, Qui testimonium perhibet de his. *In diebus illis,* Ecce ego Iohannes *Vidi supra montem Sion Agnum stantem,* Qui tollit peccata mundi, *Et cum eo centum quadraginta quatuor millia,* Quos trucidavit frendens insania, herodianae fraudis ob nulla crimina, *Habentes nomen eius,* Haec est enim Innocentum gloriosa concio, *Et nomen Patris eius,* In sancti Spiritus clementia, *Scriptum in frontibus suis,* De quo scriptum est: erit nomen meum ibi, dicit Dominus. Etc. — Better known are the tropes that have given names to many pieces in our Kyriale, such as the Kyrie *Fons bonitatis, Orbis factor,* etc.

example of an Office completely fitted with tropes is that of Peter of Corbeil,[21] known improperly as *Office of the insane* or *of the ass,* which took the greater part of the day to recite.

Something similar was occurring in the monasteries with the multiplication of Offices and of choir prayers. To every canonical hour were added the *psalmi familiares* according to the intention of relatives, friends or benefactors. The *psalmi familiares* were followed by the penitential psalms. When the recitation or chant of the Office of the day was completed, the Office of the dead was recited or sung, then that of All Saints, and there was still time to add the Office of our Lady.

In other churches there was the custom also of reciting by way of devotion the Office of the Cross or that of the Incarnation or of the Trinity or of the Holy Spirit. Some parts of the Office were chanted in fixed places outside of the choir. Thus the commemorations of the saints were made before the respective altar, if there was one in that church; the chants of the *Benedictus* at Lauds, the *Magnificat* at Vespers, the *Te Deum* at Matins were assigned each to a special chapel, to which the community went in procession while singing the antiphon of the saint to whom that chapel was dedicated.

Obviously the divine Office could no longer be the expression and the food of the spiritual life of those monks who spent almost all their time in these endless choral Offices. Thus prayer ended by becoming a burdensome task, while the true monastic labor and the typical *lectio divina* of the monk were disappearing, and the observance and the regular discipline were being relaxed as a natural consequence of so many hours of nervous tension passed in choir.

While the liturgy was becoming formalistic and devoid of spirit, a series of calamities of a religious nature was bringing about the religious crisis of the Christian people: the decay of the feudal system with all its consequences, the continual wars and disturbances, the struggle of the states against the Church, and later the great schism of the West. A number of heretical sects, which were then multiplying rapidly in a ground well fertilized, were propagating their doctrines among the people, while the monasteries and the parochial life were falling into a deplorable decadence. Cathari, Waldenses, Albigenses formed so many sects, all basically opposed to the sacraments, and exercising so much the more influence over the people as the people were becoming more ignorant and abandoned by their shepherds, and were taking refuge in devotional practices without doctrinal foundation.

The souls that were most elect and desirous of spiritual perfection reacted strongly against this vice of their age. To the exteriority of worship, to the abounding and empty formalism of certain liturgical formulas, and to the

---

[21] *Office de Pierre de Corbeil. Texte et Chant d'après le Manuscrit de Sens (XIII siècle). Introd. et notes par* H. Villetard (Paris, 1907).

sterile polemics of the decadent scholastics, they opposed a spiritual activity wholly interior and personal, freed as far as possible of the traditional outward means of sanctification and completely dedicated to the perfection of the individual, to fostering affective devotion and to seeking union with God in the practice of the interior life.

These new tendencies, begun by the mystical authors of the end of the twelfth century but greatly intensified in the two following centuries until they took organic form at the beginning of the fifteenth century, bore excellent fruits of sanctity which succeeded in checking the decay of the monastic and ecclesiastical life and the general moral weakening of the Christian people.

Toward the end of the fourteenth century a community of clerics known as the "Brothers of the common life," which very soon constituted the congregation of the Canons Regular of Windesheim, in Holland, gave order, a name, and diffusion to this new spiritual current, which had arisen in the Benedictine and Cistercian monasteries, had been strengthened with the foundation of the mendicant orders, and was to exert a powerful and dominant influence down to our own times. The spiritual doctrine they spread is known by the name of *devotio moderna,* and advocates perfection as an ideal of life eminently interior, based on self-analysis and individual piety, and independent of exterior means of sanctification.

The transition from the traditional liturgical spirituality to the new forms of modern piety did not take place suddenly, and for many centuries they can be found mixed together and living more or less like brothers, although in reality the new spirituality was definitely predominant, while only the outward appearances of liturgical piety remained.

In the monasteries, as a general rule, the ancient liturgical spirituality resists more tenaciously, although perhaps it is not always by conviction, but rather by tradition and inertia. With the new *devotio* predominating almost exclusively in all the schools of spirituality which are being formed in this time, great figures representative of the traditional *mystique* are still found in the monasteries. But not even these are immune from the new spiritual orientation. St. Mechtilde (d. 1298), for example, and St. Gertrude (d. 1302) still have a profound sense of the liturgy: their extraordinary communications with the Lord take place on the occasion of liturgical acts and solemnities of worship; the basis of their prayers is always formed by the texts of the Office and the Mass; and the divine revelations they receive have for their object, as a rule, the liturgical rites and the observances of the conventual life. Yet together with this profound liturgical sense there are found in their writings clear indications of the new forms of spirituality.

On the other hand, typical of the documents of this period of transition which are now completely under the inspiration of the *devotio moderna* but which still preserve an appearance of liturgical character, are the "Books of Hours," beautifully handwritten and illustrated by miniatures in the fourteenth and fifteenth centuries, and printed in the sixteenth century. Their content is made up of a collection of devotions which take their formulas and their elements from the liturgy or are inspired by the liturgy; but the criterion of the choice, the immediate purpose and the very distribution of the texts has no relation to the liturgy. According to Dom Festugière[22] "the Books of Hours are derived from the liturgy, but they put souls outside of the current of the liturgy."

Actually the *devotio moderna* opened a chasm between the individual ideal of Christian perfection and the liturgical life of the Church. Its characteristic note is *individualism,* and for that reason it finds itself diametrically opposed to liturgical spirituality, which is essentially ecclesiastical and communitarian. The various spiritualities, each with its particular character, will arise from the *devotio moderna* in the course of time; but at the basis of all will be found a predominating individualism as a common inheritance.

The individual has come to be the principal center of interest of spiritual activity. The Christian is considered primarily as an individual who has to save and sanctify himself. Self-knowledge and self-analysis are put at the basis of perfection. The personal dispositions and circumstances of each subject determine what will be the best means for him to obtain perfection. The highest importance is attributed to individual activity in reforming one's life, on the basis of ascetical exercises, austerity and acts of private piety. Liturgical acts and participation in public worship are replaced by devotions of private character. The sacraments, the rites of the Church and even the Church itself are appreciated in so far as they offer themselves as means of purification and of individual sanctification. The very relations with God always have a personal character, with predominance of affective elements and with a tendency to an attitude of intimate friendship and even of familiarity.

Individualism characterized all the aspects of the age of the Renaissance. As a force dissolvent of and hostile to the Church and the Christian life, it was manifested in the paganizing humanism, and later in the great heresy of Protestantism, essentially opposed to the sacraments. The Church also took advantage of this current of individualism as a force of reaction, principally by means of the *devotio moderna,* which she adapted to the needs of the moment, intensifying it in some of its manifestations, and embodied in a series of institutes and religious congregations that arose in the sixteenth and seventeenth centuries, animated by the best apostolic spirit. These congregations labored untiringly to revive the Christian life in the Church; and the fruits of their zeal were not long in appearing, but always along the lines

[22] Dom M. Festugière, *La Liturgie catholique, Essai de synthèse* (Maredsous, 1913), chapter 7, section 2, note 1.

of the *devotio moderna* and influenced inevitably by the general atmosphere of individualism in which they drew their breath.

Following the preachers of penance and continuing their work were the founders, zealous for a holy reform. To bring souls back to the right road and to the practice of Christian perfection, they used the means that came naturally to them, the means which they themselves practiced and which could best move their contemporaries: there came to be more and more ascetical practices, exercises of devotion, public preachings and private meditations on sin, the Last Things and the Passion of Jesus Christ; exercises of charity and the works of mercy were fostered and organized; confraternities and pious associations of the faithful flourished.

But the abyss that separated the faithful and the liturgy remained permanently open. The faithful did not stop assisting at Mass, receiving the sacraments and even using the sacramentals. Rather, with the renewal of the spiritual life these things were increasingly frequented. They were considered and esteemed as abundant sources of grace. But as rites of the Church's public worship and guides to individual piety they had little or no influence on the minds, the wills, even the sentiments of the faithful. Between those rites and private piety there no longer existed an intimate, vital bond which would make them vibrate in unison. We are not surprised, therefore, to find at this time the first religious order which renounces officially, in its constitutions, the choral recitation of the divine Office.[23]

[23] With this statement we do not intend to judge an institution, but an epoch.

We certainly do not mean that St. Ignatius renounced the choral Office because he did not understand or appreciate sufficiently the spiritual value of the Church's public prayer. It is known that the saint experienced great consolation in assisting at or taking part in liturgical celebrations and the chant of the divine Office. At Manresa "he sings the high Mass, Vespers and Compline every day" (*Monumenta Ignatiana, Fontes Narrativi de Sancto Ignatio*, I, 390). When he was a priest, he daily prepared with the missal the texts of the following day's Mass (*ibid.*, p. 644) and strove to penetrate the meaning of the prayers and the spiritual understanding of the texts (*Monumenta Ignatiana, Constitutiones*, II, p. 442, n. 15; II, p. 93, n. 60). It has been rightly said that the holy Mass occupies the center of St. Ignatius' spirituality (Dr. Ángel Suquia, *La santa misa en la espiritualidad de san Ignacio de Loyola*, Madrid, 1950).

On the other hand, the fact of the suppression of the choir in the Society of Jesus is a very significant sign of that era in which the social value of liturgical prayer was being lost: while the devotion of Christians was being emancipated from the teaching authority of the liturgy, the essential elements of public worship were held in great esteem by pious souls, because they found in those elements the most effective means of fostering their private piety. Typical in this respect is the composition by a Benedictine abbot, Garcias de Cisneros, of a "Directory of the Canonical Hours" in which, availing himself of the structure of the divine Office, he strives to keep the soul united to God through pious considerations and sentiments which have nothing to do with the meaning of the canonical hours or with the formal content of liturgical prayer. Similar in spirit was the prescription in the Constitutions of the Society of Jesus: ". . . Vespers alone could be said. Likewise ordinarily on Sundays and feast days, without organ or plain chant, but in a devout, quiet, simple tone: *and this with the aim of moving the people, and in so far as it was judged that they would be moved, to greater frequentation of confessions, sermons and readings and not in any other way . . .*" (*Monumenta Ignatiana, Constitutiones*, II, 549).

It is interesting to note the reasons given by the Jesuits for opposing the decree of Paris issued against them, which accused them

The doctrinal struggle against the Lutherans and the Calvinists, who were teaching the essential corruption of human nature by original sin and denying freedom of choice before the irresistible action of grace, contributed no little to a re-evaluation of the possibilities of personal activity in the work of one's own sanctification, and prompted a systematization of the new theories for explaining the efficacy of grace and its relation with human freedom. With these theories the doctrinal foundation for piety of the individualistic type was established.

There is no doubt that the *devotio moderna* from its very beginning breathed new life into the Church. On it depended many conversions, many reforms of monasteries, and many foundations of new institutes; and by it the Christian spirit was strengthened and enkindled.

But it also completed and consolidated the separation between the liturgy and the spiritual life, between the Church's prayer and that of the Christian. Henceforward the Church's acts of worship will no longer be the universal, substantial and indispensable food of private piety; this piety will find nourishment in other dishes, more easily digestible but not so solid and nutritious, which will be more to its taste and will keep it from feeling the need of recourse to the teachings of the Church's liturgy.

Thus the unity of ecclesiastical prayer and even of the Christian life remains broken. Liturgy and piety will be two distinct realities, each following its own course, independent of one another, perhaps misunderstanding each other or looking on each other as strangers. If certain acts of worship are still prescribed, they will be considered as an obligation in conscience by virtue of a precept of the Church, or as a complement of the general duty of religion, or, at most, as an efficacious means of sanctification. But even during assistance at these acts of worship, the soul will seek union with God by recourse to her own devotions, foreign to the sense of what the Church is meanwhile saying and doing in her rites. The sacred minister himself, once his ministry has been performed, will feel the need of procuring some spiritual food for his own soul.

Obviously such a separation cannot constitute permanently the normal state, still less the ideal, of the Church's spiritual life. The restoration of the original unity, however, could become possible only if each of the two

among other things of the novelty of suppressing the choir. The principal reasons they allege to justify this decision are of a pastoral nature. But to these is added also: "Members of other orders, serious men, outstanding in piety and learning, taught by their own experience, are high in their praise of the Society's dispensing with choir, that the disadvantages of vain glory may be avoided and that better things may be sought . . . in the pursuit of mental prayer and in progress in the spiritual virtues to which our society is

dedicated and to which it will be better spurred on by not having the choir" (*Monumenta Ignatiana*, Epistolae et Instructiones, XII, 618-619).

We may well say with Father de Guibert (Joseph de Guibert, S.J., *La spiritualité de la Compagnie de Jésus. Esquisse historique,* Rome, 1953, p. 557) that "in the matter of common exercises of prayer, public ceremonies, the Jesuits adapted themselves largely to the customs and tastes of their contemporaries."

elements, liturgy and spiritual activity of the individual, contributed a little to overcoming the obstacles and to seeking in the other the complement necessary for re-establishing the shattered vital unity.

As far as the liturgy was concerned, the thing to be done first of all was to purify it of all the extraneous elements which were disfiguring its authentic shape. Then it had to be reinvigorated and its forms brought up to date, with the aim of making it more apt to attract new generations to the understanding of the mystery of Christ and to participation in it.

Individual piety, on its part, had to renounce its sentimentalism and its deeply rooted individualism, in order to raise itself toward the liturgical spirit with a greater depth of life and a more solid doctrinal foundation.

Only the Church is competent to adapt the liturgy. And in reality she has never neglected this mission: at various times she has tried, with more or less effect, to reform the liturgy by bringing it back to its original purity. As early as the end of the eleventh century, Gregory VII had sought to re-establish the ancient Roman rite, giving it back its original prestige and splendor after having purified it of extraneous elements. But the work which Hildebrand in his papacy carried to a conclusion with great energy did not last long. Localized in Rome, it suffered the effects of the absence of the papal court, and very soon only the church of the Lateran remained faithful to the Pope's reform.

In the face of the great movement of liturgical restoration promoted by the sons of St. Francis of Assisi, Gregory IX entrusted to Haymo, fourth general of the Franciscans, a revision of the breviary of the Curia. This revision was promulgated by Nicholas III, though not imposed on the whole Church.

Let us pass over the intended reform entrusted by Leo X to the humanist Zachary Ferreri, approved by Clement VII,[24] because this work, which set out to celebrate the liturgical feasts with classical odes, loaded with pagan terminology, should be called a deformation rather than a reform.

On the other hand, the Spanish Franciscan Cardinal Francisco de Quiñones undertook with the best of intentions the reform of the breviary approved by Paul III. But instead of making a revision Quiñones composed a new breviary, prescinding from the Church's tradition and from the whole of

---

[24] Compare the two versions of one stanza of the hymn for Matins during Lent, according to the primitive text ascribed to St. Gregory the Great as probable author, and according to the version of Ferreri:

Primitive text:	Text of Ferreri:
Utamur ergo parcius	*Bacchus abscedat, Venus ingemiscat,*
Verbis, cibis et potibus,	*Nec iocis ultra locus est, nec escis,*
Somno, iocis, et arctius	*Nec maritali thalamo, nec ulli*
Perstemus in custodia.	*Ebrietati.*

In these hymns of the humanistic reform, the Blessed Virgin is often called such names as *felix dea, dearum maxima, nympha candidissima,* and the Most Holy Trinity is called *Triforme numen Olympi.*

liturgical antiquity. Because of its brevity the new breviary won many users; but with the passage of time its lack of discretion and the novelties introduced under the influence of particularistic tendencies earned general opposition to it.

Another reform, with a criterion of respect for traditional forms, was attempted by Cardinal Caraffa. Raised to the papacy with the name of Paul IV, he continued the work he had started, but died without having promulgated it. Yet his effort was not in vain, and his work was consigned by Pius IV to the commission of the Council of Trent, that it might serve as a basis for the definitive liturgical reform.

The Council of Trent, in fact, concerned itself deeply with the desired reform of the liturgy, to purify it of the many elements foreign to it and unworthy of it. Various dogmatic documents and many disciplinary arrangements have a direct relation to the liturgical reform. To be seen especially are the acts of Sessions IV, VII, XXII and XXIII. Basic to the matter under our consideration are the decisions of the council with regard to the tradition of the Church, the holy sacrifice of the Mass, the sacraments and the rites of the Catholic Church.

In the disciplinary part, it is established that liturgical prayer must always be considered as public prayer of the Church; private Masses "must be deemed truly communal," and the reason is that the celebrant offers them in the name of the whole mystical Body of Christ, and that the people also take part in them at least spiritually. In fact the council manifests its desire that "at every Mass the faithful in attendance take part in the sacrifice not only by a spiritual desire but also by the sacramental reception of the Eucharist." It recommends to deacons and subdeacons that they communicate when they serve as ministers of the altar.

The holy council commands all shepherds of souls, and especially the bishops, to explain to the faithful, together with the gospel, the texts that are recited during the celebration of the Mass on Sundays and other festive days, "that the sheep may not suffer from hunger." It prescribes moreover that the catechisms published from that time on, devote a special section to the teaching and the explanation of the liturgy. It treats also in a special way of the cult of relics and the veneration of the images of saints.

As for the reform of the liturgical books, in the third decree of its last session the council decrees that all the work done up to that time for the reform of the breviary and the missal be turned over to the Pope, that he may decide about it according to his own judgment and by virtue of his authority. This conciliar decree found its fulfilment in the bulls *Quod a nobis* and *Quo primum tempore* of Pius V (July 9, 1568, and July 14, 1570), with which the new breviary and the new missal, reformed according to the decree and the mind of the Council of Trent, were finally promulgated.

In 1588 Pope Sixtus V founded the Congregation of Rites, with the special mission of watching over the purity of the legitimate rites of the Church and preventing spurious infiltrations.

Still other popes took a hand in the liturgical reform. Clement VIII, for example, corrected various legends of the saints in the breviary, modified the degree of solemnity of many feasts, and made the revision of the text of the Vulgate.

More important, but more unfortunate, was the effort of Urban VIII with regard to the hymns of the breviary. Wishing to give them a classical elegance, he had them revised and corrected according to the laws of prosody; and hands were laid on the venerable texts of Prudentius, Venantius Fortunatus, St. Ambrose. In all, 952 passages were corrected. If they gained anything in metrical finesse, they lost it in meaning and in the patristic flavor of their texts. The corrections of Urban VIII are still kept in the Roman breviary.

4. Rebirth of Liturgical Spirituality

In the course of the last two centuries many popes have tried to preserve and increase the purity of the liturgy and make it more intelligible and more attractive to the minds of the faithful. Outstanding among these supreme pontiffs for their zeal and their labors on behalf of the restoration of the liturgy have been Popes Benedict XIV, Pius X and Pius XII.

The achievements of the great Pope of the encyclical *Mediator Dei* on the liturgy are the restoration of the Easter Vigil and the renewal of the entire Holy Week, the new version of the Psalter, the new decrees on the Eucharistic fast and on the celebration of evening Masses, the introduction of the vernacular into some parts of the ritual and of the Mass of the catechumens, a principle of reform of the rubrics of the breviary and of the missal. The work of reform of the calendar, the breviary and the missal is still going on.

In this way the liturgy, while remaining perennial and unchangeable in its principles and its inmost structure, will once more be contemporary, intelligible, capable of communicating to all men the understanding of the mystery of Christ and the realization of the ideal of Christian perfection.

This reforming activity on the part of the Church has always been accompanied by her zeal for reviving the knowledge and love of the liturgy among Christians. Her attempts to bring the faithful nearer to this goal, inspired and fostered by the popes, have found their most faithful echo in the Benedictine monasteries, in which liturgical worship very soon recovered its purity and vitality. It is to the monastic churches that the Christian people have turned to discover the meaning and the dignity of the liturgy, together with the spiritual riches contained in it. From the monastic *scriptoria* has issued that abundance of scientific and pastoral literature which has contributed so powerfully to the present reflowering of liturgical spirituality. It may well be said that the liturgical movement has been inaugurated and propagated in the various countries in the measure in which the Benedictine monasteries rose from their state of decadence and found their authentic spirit and their true mission in the Church.

Dom Prosper Guéranger, who restored the monastic life in France, was also the one who initiated the liturgical revival in his country and in all of Europe and brought it to a high level of achievement, so that he is rightly considered the father and the soul of the present movement of liturgical rebirth. In the monastery of Solesmes, restored by him in 1833 and headed by him as its first abbot, Guéranger formed a powerful center of liturgical culture and spirituality. This center gave to the movement the great men and the great scientific and popularizing works which formed, and still form under many aspects, the basis of specialized studies on the liturgy.

The diffusion of Guéranger's writings and of those of his disciples awakened the passion for liturgical studies in various European countries. At the same time, sad events put the monks of Solesmes into contact with other monasteries beyond the boundaries of France. These contacts led to the revival of interest in the knowledge of the liturgy and in the spirituality which is nourished on it. New centers arose, especially in the abbeys, where the studies could be better organized, where the liturgy could be practiced with greater purity and where its spirituality found a favorable environment in the simplicity and seriousness of the monastic life.

Around the monasteries, and often in contact with them, important figures in the liturgical movement arose among the diocesan clergy and even among the laity; and these were joined by noted members of other religious orders.

Thus it may well be said that the present movement of liturgical restoration, in its various aspects, must always be related more or less directly to the names of Guéranger and Solesmes.

Other centers of the liturgical movement have exercised great influence with their scientific studies and their works of popularization. In France there is the abbey of Ligugé, founded from Solesmes. In Belgium are the abbeys of Maredsous, Saint-André at Lophem-lez-Bruges, and Mont-César, which have been joined by those of Afflighem and Steenbrugge. In Germany the primacy goes to the monastery of Maria Laach for its special importance; others are Beuron, St. Joseph of Westphalia, Grüssau, etc. Notable in Austria is the monastery of canons regular of St. Augustine of Klosterneuburg. In Holland there is the abbey of Oosterhout, an important center for the spread of the liturgical life.

In Italy, various monks of the monasteries of Parma, Finalpia, Praglia and others have published works on the liturgy; but particular importance attaches to the abbey of St. Paul outside the walls of Rome, for having given to the Church the famous Cardinal Schuster, archbishop of Milan, who contributed so much to the reflowering of the liturgy as historical science and as spiritual life. In Spain the liturgical movement was begun and is still

promoted especially by the monasteries of Silos and of Montserrat, which
have been followed by the abbey of Samos and other monastic centers. Similarly, the Benedictine monasteries in the United States, in Argentina, in
Brazil, in Chile, have been in the vanguard of the liturgical movement in
the American republics.

Perhaps the pre-eminent place occupied by the Benedictine monasteries in
the liturgical renewal has led some people to believe that liturgical spirituality
is the exclusive or particular heritage of the Benedictines and that their proper
end is that of dedication to liturgical worship. This is not so.

We have already indicated sufficiently that liturgical spirituality is nothing
but the common spirituality of the Church. If the life in the monasteries is
lived according to the spirit of the liturgy, this is precisely because the Benedictines have no spirituality of their own: their spirituality is simply that
which the Church teaches and practices, without any additions peculiar to
themselves. The dignity and splendor of worship in the abbeys is merely a
consequence of this spirit, lived with the intensity which a perfect Christian
life demands.

As for the liturgical movement, though begun in the monasteries, it now
has a universal character: the Church has made it her own. Noted prelates
are its most ardent promoters and propagators; and there are many priests,
religious and even lay people who are working ardently, by themselves or
in well organized groups, to intensify and spread the liturgical restoration.
Pius XII declared that "the chief driving force of the liturgical movement,
both in doctrine and in practical application, has come from the hierarchy."[25]

The liturgical movement was preceded by a preliminary stage in which
romanticism predominated. The lyrical and poetical value of the Church's
rites and ceremonies was brought out. Authors delighted in going back to
the first centuries of Christianity to get a picture of the life of the first
Christians and to put themselves in contact with their tombs and catacombs,
not so much in order to draw upon those sources for a scientific knowledge
of the traditional doctrine and the religious principles that inspired those
centuries of ardent faith, but rather out of a sentimental attraction for past
times and ancient things.

A reminder of this romantic phase is the naïve position of those who make
the liturgical spirit consist in a mere archeologism or in an attachment to a
certain form of ornamentation, to a style of the furnishings or the houses of
worship, and who speak of liturgical chasubles, liturgical designs or liturgical
chalices solely by reason of form or style.

Despite its obvious shortcomings, romanticism as applied to the liturgy
contributed no little to reviving interest in real, positive values which had
been almost completely forgotten.

---

[25] "Allocution," *The Assisi Papers,* proceed-
ings of the First International Congress of
Pastoral Liturgy, Sept. 18-22, 1956 (Collegeville, Minn.: Liturgical Press, 1957), p. 223.

A concept of the liturgical movement that is too limited and deficient is that which reduces the liturgy to a mere ceremonial.

Being an action of a public and social character, the liturgy must have its laws to order and regulate it. This complexus of ecclesiastical decisions which go to make up the ceremonial must be well known and observed if the celebration of the rites and the practice of the ceremonies is to be worthy and orderly and is to express the meaning which the Church wishes to give it. But this will always be something merely external to the liturgy.

Still, there are many who have confused, and still do confuse, the liturgy with ceremonial jurisprudence, in spite of the clear definitions by Pius XII in the encyclical *Mediator Dei*.[26] There are still ecclesiastics who have not got beyond this idea. For them, a liturgist is nothing but a good master of ceremonies or a connoisseur of rubrics, who knows how to resolve in accordance with the rubrics the cases that may be proposed, and who has a ready ability for preparing and directing a pontifical function.

Many books which are presented as "manuals of liturgy" are nothing but ceremonial codes, perhaps with the addition of some historical notes, and they contribute no little to this false and minimizing concept of the liturgy. And in the majority of seminaries the course in liturgy is simply a lesson in rubrics, with some reference to their history.

A result of the first spontaneous flowering of the liturgical movement was the revival of interest in historical and doctrinal studies on Christian worship and its various manifestations. Christian antiquity and the various liturgies, Eastern and Western, were studied scientifically; the origin of the different liturgical rites and texts was investigated; the principles of historical criticism were applied to the documents that were used as sources for these labors; scholars probed in the field of philosophical and theological studies to determine the nature of the liturgy and of worship, its position in the domain of theological science, its relation with the mystery of Jesus Christ. The fruits of this scientific aspect of the liturgical movement are very abundant and positive, and efforts are being made on all sides to increase them.

But the liturgy, although it may indeed be the object of scientific investigations, is not in itself a science: it is public worship and supernatural life. To this object must tend all the scientific and pastoral activities of those who want to reanimate the liturgical life, the spirituality of the Church.

The circumstances of our times seem most propitious for raising the faithful to a piety solidly founded on the understanding of the mystery of Christ and of our own insertion into it through the unity of the Church. To the individualism of other times has succeeded a sense of community and a need of union or federation in all fields of human activity. In the economic, social

---

[26] "It is an error consequently and a mistake to think of the sacred liturgy as merely the outward or visible part of divine worship or as an ornamental ceremonial. No less errone- ous is the notion that it consists solely in a list of laws and prescriptions according to which the ecclesiastical hierarchy orders the sacred rites to be performed" (n. 25).

and political orders, everything tends to the formation of great collectivities. This tendency undoubtedly has its effect in disposing people towards getting out of religious individualism and subjectivism and beginning to understand and to live practically the notion of Church, of Christian community, of public worship.

The sentimentalism so proper to uneducated souls has diminished in our times, in which the general level of culture and civilization has been raised so much; and, the more the religious instruction of the faithful and the knowledge of theological truths has grown, the more the need has been felt of founding and nurturing the spiritual life on something more solid than many of the devotions that have no doctrinal basis. This accounts for the popularity of missals for the laity; the enthusiasm with which the laity take part in the rites and chants of the Church, the more so when the Church brings these rites back to their primitive purity and makes them vitally accessible, as she did with the new order of Holy Week; it accounts also for the extraordinary interest demonstrated when people discover the boundless spiritual riches accruing to their souls from intelligent contact with the sacred liturgy.

Here is how Pius XII sums up this movement of restoration of the liturgical spirit and its fruits in the encyclical *Mediator Dei*:[27]

"You are of course familiar with the fact, venerable brethren, that a remarkably widespread revival of scholarly interest in the sacred liturgy took place towards the end of the last century and has continued through the early years of this one. The movement owed its rise to commendable private initiative and more particularly to the zealous and persistent labor of several monasteries within the distinguished Order of St. Benedict. Thus there developed in this field among many European nations and in lands beyond the seas as well, a rivalry as welcome as it was productive of results. Indeed, the salutary fruits of this rivalry among the scholars were plain for all to see, both in the sphere of the sacred sciences, where the liturgical rites of the Western and Eastern Church were made the object of extensive research and profound study, and in the spiritual life of considerable numbers of individual Christians.

"The majestic ceremonies of the sacrifice of the altar became better known, understood and appreciated. With more widespread and more frequent reception of the sacraments, with the beauty of liturgical prayers more fully savored, the worship of the Eucharist came to be regarded for what it really is: the fountainhead of genuine Christian devotion. Bolder relief was given likewise to the fact that all the faithful make up a single and very compact body with Christ for its Head, and that the Christian community is in duty bound to participate in the liturgical rites according to their station."

More recently, in the discourse on pastoral liturgy pronounced at Rome on September 22, 1956, at the conclusion of the International Congress of Pastoral

[27] Nn. 4-5.

Liturgy held at Assisi, the Pope renewed the expression of his thoughts in these words: "The liturgical movement is shown forth as a sign of the providential dispositions of God for the present time, of the movement of the Holy Ghost in the Church, to draw men more closely to the mysteries of the faith and the riches of grace which flow from the active participation of the faithful in the liturgical life."[28]

So profound a renewal of the Church's spirituality could not be achieved without the occurrence of obstacles and difficulties by way of excess in action or reaction. We have already indicated that the process of getting the liturgy and the Christian people together could not be accomplished unless each gave up some impediment and made a corresponding effort to reach the other.

As far as the faithful are concerned, it was up to their shepherds to initiate them, stimulate them and lead them to the more luxuriant pastures of the liturgy. But some of them, whether by reason of the formation previously received, or because of a certain degree of ignorance or timidity, or through lack of interest or a partisan spirit, have abstained from this liturgical renewal, if they have not gone so far as to oppose it. Others, more daring, have rather gone to excess by an imprudent zeal to get the people and the liturgy together, or have presumed to bring the liturgy to the people on their own authority, whereas this is the exclusive competence of the Church.

"Indeed," wrote Pope Pius XII, "though We are sorely grieved to note, on the one hand, that there are places where the spirit, understanding or practice of the sacred liturgy is defective, or all but inexistent, We observe with considerable anxiety and some misgiving, that elsewhere certain enthusiasts, over eager in their search for novelty, are straying beyond the path of sound doctrine and prudence."[29]

To obviate these difficulties and mark out the true and proper path of the liturgical renewal, Pius XII composed his magnificent encyclical *Mediator Dei*. The encyclical is an answer to the present concern for a purer and more intense liturgical life. It indicates the channels to be followed by this movement of restoration and opens out wide horizons for further progress of a spirituality based on the liturgy, offering, from now on, that absolute security which can be found only in the teaching authority of the Church.

[28] "Allocution," *The Assisi Papers*, p. 224.   [29] *Mediator Dei*, n. 8.

4 THE LITURGY,

THE CHURCH'S PUBLIC WORSHIP:

DOCTRINAL FOUNDATIONS

Since liturgical spirituality is based on the Church's public worship, the first thing to be done is to specify in what the liturgy consists.

For St. Thomas, liturgy is the same as "divine worship according to the rite of the Christian religion."[1] Pius XII with theological precision defined it thus: "The sacred liturgy is consequently the public worship which our Redeemer as Head of the Church renders to the Father as well as the worship which the community of the faithful renders to its Founder, and through Him to the heavenly Father." And then, more briefly: "the worship rendered by the mystical Body of Christ in the entirety of its Head and members."[2]

These definitions demand a brief exposition of the concepts included in them.

1. Christian Worship

Worship and religion

Worship or veneration, in Latin *cultus,* is the honor which, together with an acknowledgment of dependence, is given to a higher being because of his excellence.

[1] St. Thomas, *Summa theol.,* III, 63, 1.   [2] *Mediator Dei,* n. 20.

The generic notion of *cultus* presupposes, therefore, in the one to whom the *cultus* is directed, an excellence which makes him worthy of honor and at the same time places him in a state of superiority with respect to others. The honor is offered him through the recognition and the acknowledgment of his excellence; while to the concept of superiority there corresponds a recognition of dependence and the consequent submission on the part of those who are inferior to him. This twofold offering of honor and of submission constitutes precisely the act of *cultus*.

If these generic concepts are applied to our relations with God, the divine worship will consist in the honor with which man proclaims God's infinite excellence and the submission with which he recognizes in practice the supreme dominion of God.

Worship, thus conceived, constitutes the proper object of the virtue of religion. All the acts by which man bears witness to the divine excellence and to his own subjection to God as his supreme Lord are cultual or worshipful acts and are derived in some way from the virtue of religion.

They proceed immediately from the virtue of religion if by their very nature they are ordained to proclaiming the excellence of God and the consequent submission of man. Such, for example, are prayer, adoration, sacrifice, genuflections, etc.

But the acts of the other virtues can also be worshipful acts. Although by their proper nature they are not referred directly to the honor of God but to the perfecting of man, still they can receive from the virtue of religion an orientation of purpose which directs them to procuring God's honor or to disposing man for the divine worship. This holds of such acts as abstinence and almsgiving. All virtuous acts can be worshipful acts, if only they be ordained to bearing witness in some way to the infinite excellence of God.

The divine excellence, and the corresponding dependence and submission of man, are based in the first place on the relation of first principle and of supreme dominion which God has with respect to all creatures. All that man is or possesses, he has received from God, who has in Himself His own reason for being and His own complete fulness. Before the supreme and necessary Being on whom he depends absolutely for his being and existence, man must acknowledge the infinite excellence of God, first principle and supreme Lord of all creation, and must bow down before Him in an act of honor and of submission. Such is the primary act of worship.

To the necessary dependence founded in the very nature of the divine Being and the created being, must be added another dependence, which results from the free action of God in as much as He is first principle of every good that is not required by an essential reason. Under this aspect God is our supreme Benefactor. From His bounty we have received gratuitously all the goods that we enjoy. Hence we should answer Him by the worship of gratitude.

But there is still another fact that binds us to God in a relation of dependence. God is not only our essential and free first principle; He is also our last end. It is to Him that we are going, and it is only in Him that the innermost tendencies of our being will find complete satisfaction. It is only right that we recognize Him and submit to Him as our last end.

Now this twofold ordination of man towards God, that is, his submission to the first cause and his tendency to the ultimate end, is united in those acts which have the character of worship. As proceeding from the virtue of religion or commanded by it, they tend to honor God and revere Him as first principle and supreme Lord. As virtuous acts, that is, perfective of our powers, they bring us closer to our last end.

Twofold finality of the acts of worship

From this it follows that every act of worship has a twofold finality, which confers on it, by the same token, a twofold efficacy. By its very nature in the first place the act of worship, considered as such, has a latreutic finality, the term of which is the glorification of God. In as much as it proceeds from a virtue—which always has as its reason for being the perfecting of some one of our faculties—it acquires a soteriological finality which works for the sanctification of man. Thus the same acts by which man honors God and submits to His supreme dominion, bring about purity in man and give him that firmness which is necessary that the mind may apply itself to God as ultimate end and first principle; a purity and a stability which, according to the teaching of St. Thomas,[3] constitute sanctity, which for that very reason is identified essentially with the virtue of religion.

In this way the acts of worship realize that "sacred commerce" to which the secret of the fourth Sunday after Easter refers, and through which, according to the expression of St. Thomas,[4] we offer something to God and receive a divine exchange.

Among the various acts of worship, some, such as sacrifice, adoration, vows, have a predominantly latreutic character, by reason of their intrinsic finality or by the positive will of God; others, like the sacraments and the acts of virtue commanded by the virtue of religion, display rather a soteriological aspect. But in all the acts there is fulfilled what the Church affirms with regard to the sacrifice of the Mass: "which You have granted us so to present for the honor of Your name that they may also serve for the healing of our ills" (quae sic ad honorem nominis tui deferenda tribuisti, ut eadem remedia fieri nostra praestares).[5]

The ultimate reason for the intimate connection between the latreutic finality and the sanctifying effect of the acts of worship is the following. All the honor and reverence we render to God is not addressed to Him objective-

---

[3] St. Thomas, Summa theol., II-II, 81, 8.   [5] Secret of the tenth Sunday after Pentecost.
[4] Summa theol., II-II, 81, 3 ad 2.

ly by reason of Himself, since our homage cannot add anything to the infinite glory He possesses in His own Being, nor can our prayers make Him better aware of our needs or predispose Him more in our favor. The more we seek the divine glory subjectively by our acts of worship, the more perfect they will be; the motive that must stimulate us and the end we must seek in the acts of religion is the glorification of God; as to the effect, however, that is solely to our own advantage, so that by its tribute of reverence and honor our spirit honors God and submits to Him as it should, and thus finds its own perfection; for every being is perfected by putting itself under the influence of a more perfect being.

This is the traditional doctrine of the Fathers of the Church, which St. Thomas takes up and determines with precision in various passages of his writings[6] and which might be summed up thus:

Glory is clear knowledge together with praise of the excellence of another: *clara notitia cum laude*.[7] Honor is the acknowledgment of this same excellence.[8] Honor and glory, then, are acts by which our intellect recognizes an excellence existing in another being and finds it worthy of praise. Our will, on its part, accepts this superiority as a good to which it is well to tend, and, rejoicing in that good which another possesses, proclaims it and bears witness to it before others.

By these acts, this good of another redounds in a certain way on our faculties and communicates to them something of its own perfection; for our intellect is enlightened by the truth recognized, and the tendency of our will toward that superior good is already a certain union and conformity with it. Thus, while the proclamation of another's excellence does not add anything objectively to that excellence, it does rather perfect the powers of the one who recognizes that excellence, accepts it and proclaims it.

Our supernatural finality, then, consists precisely in the clear knowledge of the infinite perfection of the divine being: the highest perfection of our being and our supreme happiness are found in the contemplation of God and in the love and the joy which follow upon that perfect knowledge and redound from it onto our will.[9] In paradise, therefore, the "clear knowledge together with praise" will attain its maximum perfective and beatifying reality.

But this plan of the divine will cannot succeed if man does not accept it, that is, if he does not direct himself freely to the recognition of the divine excellence and to the consequent submission to God. In other words, man cannot attain perfection and beatitude if he does not freely take a religious, worshipful attitude before God. To make this possible and to facilitate it

[6] St. Thomas, *Summa theol.*, II-II, 81, 7; 132, 1 ad 1; *in Matth.*, VI, 32; *Catena Aurea, in Matth.*, VI, 32; etc.—"It is to our advantage, not His, that we know God" (St. Augustine, *Tract. in Ioan.*, 58, 3; PL 35, 1793).

[7] St. Thomas, *Summa theol.*, II-II, 132, 1 and ad 1; I-II, 2, 3; II-II, 103, 1 ad 3.

[8] St. Thomas, *Contra Gent.*, III, 28; *Summa theol.*, II-II, 103, 1 and 2.

[9] St. Thomas, *De Malo*, 9, 1 ad 4.

for us, God Himself has given us the means conducive to it.[10] Among them, the law and the commandments spell out for us how we are to recognize the divine sovereignty in practice, subjecting our will to it. Moreover, He has shown us what are the acts of worship which will serve most perfectly for expressing our recognition and attestation of the divine excellence.

God desires and demands, therefore, the fulfilment of the law and the offering of acts of worship to Him, because He loves man, who in these acts finds His right ordering to God, and because through these same acts the divine plan of making us sharers in His glory is fulfilled.

Under this aspect it can be said that, for the realization of His plan, God needs men and needs those acts by which men direct themselves freely toward Him, such as the acts of worship.[11] This interpretation must be attached also to the expression that the world was created for God's glory; that is, it was created as a manifestation of His excellence and as a means for helping the rational creature to obtain beatitude.[12] We must understand in the same way the anthropomorphism that sin is an offense against God: God cannot be offended by us except in so far as we work against our own good, which is willed by God, when we sin.[13]

God demands worship, therefore, because man in justice must recognize and proclaim the divine excellence, and because by this worshipful attitude man's intellect and will are placed in contact with God and thus find their supreme perfection, while God's loving design in the creation of the universe is fulfilled.[14]

Interior worship and exterior worship

From this it is easy to deduce that worship is essentially a spiritual activity. Only through acts of the intellect and the will can man tend to God, most pure Spirit, and be united to Him. The Father wants to be adored in spirit and in truth (John 4:23-24). This is the essential worship, the only one acceptable to God and the one which must be found in any form of true worship whatsoever. It is the principal worship, in as much as we distinguish these interior acts of religion from the exterior acts which manifest or accompany them. For our interior dedication to God can be manifested by exterior acts, which reflect in a material way the religious attitude of the spirit; then we shall have exterior worship.

The very fact of our being made up of a twofold nature, bodily and spiritual, demands that our body also have its part in the worship which the soul renders to God, and that in its own way it express its total dependence on the Creator. The participation of the body in the divine worship is meaningful and legitimate only in so far as it is related to the interior

---

[10] St. Thomas, *De Veritate*, 23, 2.
[11] St. Thomas, *Summa theol.*, II-II, 81, 7; 91, 1 and ad 3.
[12] Conc. Vat., sess. III, c. 5. — St. Thomas, *Summa theol.*, I, 44, 4.

[13] St. Thomas, *Contra Gent.*, III, 122; *Summa theol.*, I-II, 47, 1 ad 1.
[14] St. Thomas, *Summa theol.*, II-II, 30, 4 ad 1; I-II, 102, 4 ad 3; *in Ier.*, cap. 7; *in Is.*, cap. 1.

worship of the spirit; whether as a means of awakening it and fostering it, since man needs the sensible to arrive at the spiritual; or as an effect and expression of the intensity of the interior life, which overflows into our sensibility and our body.

Even before any positive institution of worship, writes St. Thomas, certain men, moved by a sort of divine instinct, had known how to find the external rites which by suitably expressing their interior worship would honor God and would be a prefiguration of the mysteries of Christ.[15]

In distinguishing between interior worship and exterior worship, it must be noted that these two forms of worship are not being compared as excluding each other, or as two logical species of one common genus, which in this case would be worship. In speaking of interior worship as opposed to exterior worship, we mean to express a wholly spiritual actuation of the virtue of religion, an application of the mind and the will to God without sensible expression of the religious activity of the spirit. On the other hand, although exterior worship supposes by definition an intervention of the body, it does not in any way exclude interior worship; rather, it is ordained to interior worship and proceeds from it, as has been said, and receives from it its whole moral entity: its being a human act and its being a worshipful act.

A pretended act of worship which was purely external would be a body without soul, a cadaver. In no way could it be acceptable and pleasing to God, as He Himself has declared in various passages of sacred Scripture: "This people honors Me with their lips, but their heart is far from Me; in vain do they worship Me" (Is. 29:13; Matt. 15:8-9). "I am full, I desire not holocausts of rams and fat of fatlings and blood of calves and lambs and buck-goats . . . . And when you stretch forth your hands, I will turn away My eyes from you; and when you multiply prayer, I will not hear" (Is. 1:11 ff.). "He that offers praise as a sacrifice glorifies Me; and to him that goes the right way I will show the salvation of God" (Ps. 49:23).

By contrast, exterior worship informed by a spirit of interior dedication to God, permits the whole man to prostrate himself before the divinity and to exercise his function of priest of the universe. By the mere fact of existing, every creature proclaims in its own way the excellence of God, who has given it being. But its cultual value can be increased beyond measure if it is used by man as matter for sacrifice and as a means of arousing or expressing a religious attitude of his spirit. Then the material universe attains its greatest dignity by being integrated with the nobler destiny of man. Then the unity of God's plan in the work of creation shines most brightly.

Every creature has its purpose, in which it finds its own perfection. But all are related and subordinated hierarchically so as to form a universal unity which, placed in the hands of man as king of creation, can be offered

---

[15] St. Thomas, *Summa theol.*, I-II, 103, 1.

with himself to God as the supreme act of worship of the whole universe. And in the unity of a finality related to worship, all the creatures are ennobled beyond their natural dignity.[16]

Private worship and public worship

Worship in itself has an individual character; that is, it realizes or exemplifies the relation of religious dependence between the individual and God. The individual is the proper subject capable of recognizing by himself the divine excellence and his corresponding dependence as a creature with respect to the supreme Being. For this reason we cannot speak of true worship where this act of intellect and of will is not found.

It is not only the individual, however, but also society as such, which depends on God; and in its organic structure society has special bonds of dependence which transcend the cultual value of individual acts of religion. The individual offers God a *private worship,* whether the concern is with purely interior worship or with interior worship accompanied by its outward and sensible expression; whether the subject of this worship is a single man or whether the concern is with a collectivity of men accidentally united to celebrate the same worshipful act together.

To society as such there corresponds a *public worship.* It is not enough that a person or a collectivity of persons render their religious homage to God; society will not satisfy its duty of worship unless it addresses itself to God as a moral entity, a social unity, not a mere aggregate of individuals. For public worship includes a formal element which specifies it and distinguishes it from the other species of worship and gives it its social character, by reason of which the acts of religion have as their subject not an aggregate of individuals but the organic unity of the social body.

In public worship, then, we find two elements: one which places it in the genus of worship; the other which specifies it, turning it into public worship.

The generic element that is required for any act to have the nature of worship is, as we have explained, the recognition of the divine excellence on the part of the intellect and the acceptance of the corresponding submission on the part of the intellect and of the will. From this we can deduce that public worship, being worship, will have to be offered by individuals, since only they have intellect and will.

The specific and formal element will be that which, added to this individual worship, will give it its nature of public worship. This is the official deputation by which the society or moral body authorizes one or more individuals, as its ministers or priests, to exercise officially and legitimately the acts of worship which belong to the society as such. By this delegation of

---

[16] "Lord, God all-powerful, who confer even on inanimate creatures the honor of being destined for Your worship" (from the bless- ing of the molten metal for a bell; *Rituale Romanum,* Ed. prima post typicam 1954, Tit. IX, n. 4).

powers, the worshipful acts which they perform as an individual physical entity, under determined conditions established by the same society, will have the value of acts of public worship. Obviously, by reason of their representative and social value, these acts will have to take on an outward form, perceptible to the senses.

Among all the outward acts of public worship, that is, of the worship which society as such renders to God, the most excellent and the most perfect is the offering of sacrifice. For that very reason, sacrifice requires, more than any other act of public worship, the intervention of a minister, a priest, invested with a special faculty of representing the people before God.

Sacrifice is the most solemn recognition of God's supreme dominion and of His absolute power to create and to destroy. To manifest outwardly his acceptance of the divine right over life and death, man offers God the goods that are most dear to him, and destroys them in God's presence, or deprives himself of them or of their use by dedicating them to the divinity. Hence sacrifice, whether it has a private and individual character or whether it is offered in the name of a society, requires a religious attitude of the spirit more perfect, if possible, and more absolute than that which can and must be found in any other act of worship. The material and sensible offering in which the act of sacrifice consists is only a symbol and an outward expression of a total dedication of the soul, or, better, of society, to God. This accounts for the excellence of sacrifice over any other act of worship.

Holy Scripture and the Fathers apply to sacrifice in a special way the general doctrine on the finality of worship as we have explained it.

According to St. Irenaeus, God desires sacrifice because the good of the offerer himself is thereby obtained,[17] in as much as the offering of sacrifice allows him to be spiritually fruitful and to show his gratitude,[18] for which reason "the one who offers is glorified in the very thing which he offers, if his gift is acceptable to God."[19]

St. Augustine develops at length the point that whatever we can offer God in sacrifice "is to man's advantage, not God's." For no one will say that he helps the fountain by drinking from it, or the light by seeing.[20] And after having gone through the various sacrifices demanded by God, he draws this conclusion: "that which is called sacrifice by all" (the external rite) "is only a sign of the true sacrifice" (the interior dedication to God). From this he infers the following definition: "True sacrifice is every work performed with the aim of adhering to God in a holy union, that is, every work aimed at obtaining that good which is capable of making us truly blessed."[21] St.

---

[17] St. Irenaeus, *Adv. haereses*, IV, 17; PG 7, 1019 ff.

[18] St. Irenaeus, *ibid.*; PG 7, 1023, 1029.

[19] St. Irenaeus, *ibid.*, 18; PG 7, 1024.

[20] St. Augustine, *De Civitate Dei*, X, 5; PL 41, 281-282.

[21] *Verum sacrificium est omne opus, quod agitur, ut sancta societate inhaereamus Deo, relatum scilicet ad illum finem boni, quo veraciter beati esse possimus* (St. Augustine, *De Civitate Dei*, X, 6; PL 41, 283).

Thomas makes these ideas his own, with almost the very words of St. Augustine.[22]

Christian worship

The concepts proposed thus far refer to the general notion of worship and can be applied to a purely natural religion, based on the simple relation of dependence with respect to God which is inherent in the creature by the mere fact of existing. In that religion every man would be the priest of his own sacrifice, as the father would be the priest of his family and the chief would be the priest of his tribe or people. Such, for example, are the sacrifices described in the first chapters of Genesis.

But God has in fact established a plan superior to the requirements of nature: He has chosen to be the object of beatitude in the most perfect way possible, raising us to a supernatural order in which we become sharers in His nature, destined to the vision of His very essence and destined to be introduced into the enjoyment of His own happiness. Obviously this divine plan must have required a new and more elevated form of worship, since it is principally through worship, as we have indicated, that man attains his ultimate end.

Actually God has established a positive religion, not proportioned to the natural possibilities of creatures but worthy of Himself and adequate to His infinite excellence. Since man was to be admitted to participation in the divine life, his relations with God, his worship, had to transcend the human order also and partake of the glory which God has in Himself.

For there is a glory that is necessary to the perfection of the divine being: it is the "clear knowledge together with praise" by which God knows His own excellence and rejoices infinitely in that knowledge. This essential and most perfect glory God expresses in an eternal and substantial Word: His Word, His Son, *the brightness of His glory* and the image of His substance" (Heb. 1:3).

Here, then, is God's plan: the Word will unite with a human nature, and the human family will thereby be introduced into the divine family. As He will be Son of God and Son of man also, all men will share divine sonship in Him. At the same time, having the Son of God in their midst, they will possess Him who is the splendor and the manifestation of the Father's glory. He Himself, being appointed high Priest of mankind, will be able to present Himself to the Father as mankind's tribute of glory; and men, united in a vital way with Jesus Christ in the unity of one mystical Body, will be able to unite their worshipful acts to the sacrifice of Jesus Christ. Thus they will cooperate with Him in the formation of a single worship, the worship of the Christian religion.

Thus the essential glory of God brings His splendors down to creatures.

---

[22] St. Thomas, *Summa theol.*, III, 22, 2.

This is the mission of the Word, *splendor gloriae,* who enlightens the minds of men with a new light to communicate to them the "clear knowledge," basis of the new Christian worship. Hence the liturgy of Advent sees the coming of the Lord as a light: "in that day there will be a great light." And Christmas day is a feast of light: "for today a great light has come down upon the earth." Jesus Christ is He, "the mystery of whose light we have known on earth," who was begotten by the Father "before the day-star." He is the true light who enlightens every man that comes into this world (John 1:9); through Him, as the preface of the Nativity sings, a new ray of the splendor of God has illuminated the interior of our mind.

If the mission of the Word is the "clear knowledge," foundation of Christian worship, the praise which is to follow upon it is nothing but the sacrifice of Jesus Christ. The Word, whose generation in the bosom of the Trinity is the adequate expression of the divine glory, will introduce all men and all creation with them into that glorification through the immolation of His humanity in time. Still, men will not add anything to the glory which God has in Himself; but their acts of worship will enter with Jesus Christ into the eternal act of the infinite divine glorification.

Christian worship will have a new capacity for sanctifying, so that the sacrifice of Jesus Christ will not be an isolated and transitory act, but will be perpetuated across space and time, and will always actualize the real presence of the Lord and the force of His priestly action, which will thus be able to reach all men. In this way the external acts of religion, the rites of the Christian religion, will not only arouse and foster interior devotion psychologically, but also contain and communicate grace and holiness.

Christian worship constitutes the center of the divine economy. In it is manifested and fulfilled the unity of the divine plan and its finality as far as worship is concerned. In Jesus Christ, high Priest of Christian worship, are revealed to us the unsearchable ways of the Lord (Rom. 11:33) and the mystery of His will, which He intended to realize in the fulness of time and which was hidden from eternity in God (Eph. 1:9; 3:9).

According to the doctrine of St. Paul, God has created all things that the manifold wisdom of God may be made known by the Church to the principalities and the powers in the heavens according to the eternal purpose which He has accomplished in Jesus Christ. For in Him God has willed to unite all things, those of the heavens and those of the earth, predestining us to be adoptive sons through Jesus Christ, that all those who hope in Christ may become praise of His glory (Eph. 1-3).

In order to sketch the doctrinal foundations of Christian worship, therefore, we must first examine the place which Jesus Christ occupies in the plan of the divine economy in relation to His supreme priesthood.

2. Jesus Christ in the Plan of God

Jesus Christ, center of creation

The writings of the New Testament reveal Jesus Christ to us as center of God's plan. He is "the first and the last" (Apoc. 1:17; 2:8), "the Alpha and the Omega, the beginning and the end" (Apoc. 1:8; 21:6; 22:13) of all things. St. Paul tells us that He is "the firstborn of every creature. For in Him were created all things in the heavens and on the earth . . . . All things have been created through and unto Him, and He is before all creatures, and in Him all things hold together . . . . He is the beginning, the firstborn from the dead, that in all things He may have the first place" (Col. 1:15-18). In Him God has chosen to unite all the things of heaven and of earth (Eph. 1:9-10). He is the center to whom all creation tends, even material creation, which groans and travails in pain until it reposes in Him (Rom. 8:22).

Adam, despite his greatness as head of the human race, is only a figure of Christ, *forma futuri* (Rom. 5:14). And if God has permitted the fall of Adam and has subjected us to a law, and after this, sin and iniquity have abounded on earth, everything has been arranged to make the victory of Jesus Christ more splendid (Gal. 3:22-24; Rom. 5:20; 10:4; 11:32).

For this reason St. Paul can conclude that all creatures will attain their highest end and God will be glorified in creatures when all has been subjected to Jesus Christ: "when all things are made subject to Him, then the Son Himself will also be made subject to Him who subjected all things to Him, that God may be all in all" (1 Cor. 15:28).

Jesus Christ, Redeemer and Sanctifier

With the same clarity with which it has shown us the christocentric character of the divine economy, the sacred Scripture shows us its finality, manifested in the twofold mission of Jesus Christ: to redeem men and to form with them a priestly people. This is declared by the principal texts of the New Testament which refer to His mission.

The mission of Jesus Christ is essentially one of redemption. In the sacred Scripture the mission that God wishes to entrust to a man is usually manifested in the name that God Himself confers on him. "You shall call His name Jesus," said the angel to Mary (Luke 1:31); and later, in reaffirming the command to Joseph, he gives him the reason: "for He shall save His people from their sins" (Matt. 1:21). Zachary sees Him prophetically as Redeemer of His people: "the Orient from on high will visit us, to shine on those who sit in darkness and in the shadow of death" (Luke 1:78-79). The angels of Christmas announce His birth to us under the same title: "Today there is born to you a Savior" (Luke 2:11). Thirty years later Christ will show us God's great love: "I have come to call sinners, not the just" (Matt. 9:13; Mark 2:17; Luke 5:32). "I came that they may have life, and have it more abundantly" (John 10:10). "The Son of Man came to seek and to save what was lost" (Luke 19:10).

It is not strange, then, that St. Peter in bearing witness to Christ before the Sanhedrin should call Him "Prince and Savior, exalted by God to grant repentance to Israel and forgiveness of sins" (Acts 5:31), and that he should write in his first letter, "You were redeemed . . . with the precious blood of Christ . . . . Foreknown, indeed, before the foundation of the world, He has been manifested in the last times for your sakes" (1 Pet. 1:18-20).

The two great theologians of the New Testament, St. John and St. Paul, also give us the same reason for Christ's coming: the Redemption.

St. John writes, "You know that He appeared to take our sins away" (1 John 3:5) and "that He might destroy the works of the devil" (1 John 3:8). The Father "has sent His only-begotten Son into the world that we may live through Him" (1 John 4:9), "that those who believe in Him may not perish, but may have life everlasting . . . and that the world may be saved through Him" (John 3:16-17).

St. Paul repeats the same concepts: "Jesus Christ came into the world to save sinners" (1 Tim. 1:15), "so that in Him we might become the justice of God" (2 Cor. 5:21), "that He might redeem those who were under the Law" (Gal. 4:5), "that through death He might destroy him who had the empire of death, that is, the devil; and might deliver them, who throughout their life were kept in servitude" (Heb. 2:14-15).

The redemptive efficacy of Jesus Christ is not limited to destroying sin and reconciling us with God, as if Christ were only a supplement, a mere compensation for the damage Adam had caused. Christ's action not only repairs all the damage done by sin and re-establishes the original order of our relations with God, but merits for us moreover the unexpected grace of becoming sharers in the divine nature and being raised to the dignity of adopted sons of God. "He sent His Son . . . to redeem those who were under the Law, that we might receive the adoption of sons," writes St. Paul (Gal. 4:4-5). And St. John, after having revealed to us the mystery of the Incarnation of the Word, adds, "To as many as received Him He gave the power of becoming sons of God" (John 1:12).

Thus Christ is not only our Redeemer, He is also our Brother; so that the whole work of our sanctification according to God's plan is to consist in making us "conformed to the image of His Son, that He should be the firstborn among many brethren" (Rom. 8:29).

Jesus Christ, Head of mankind

This brings into prominence a new aspect of Christ's relation with mankind. By the union of the Word with our nature, Jesus Christ becomes not only the most perfect member of the human family, but also its Head, replacing Adam's headship with a much higher reality.

Adam is head of the human race in so far as he is the vital principle from whom we all proceed by way of generation. His influence is so effective that all men, through him, form a single family, the great family of mankind. And our union with him is so intimate that in the very instant that we begin to be human beings, we share in Adam's sin.

In opposition to this solidarity of all men in Adam's sin, God has made Jesus Christ the universal principle of supernatural life, which proceeds from Him and is communicated to us through Him, not by way of natural generation, as life was communicated by Adam, but through the personal action of Christ, who makes the superabundant fulness of grace of His soul flow out over all those whom He has redeemed.

The fulness of sanctifying grace which enriches the soul of Christ as necessary and immediate consequence of His personal grace of union with the Word, makes Him the Saint *par excellence*. By the will of God, all supernatural grace, all communication of divine life to men will be realized only as a participation in the fulness of the sanctity of Jesus Christ.

By reason of the relation between Christ's sanctifying grace and ours, the supernatural destiny of mankind is linked to the grace of Jesus Christ and dependent on it. Thus, according to the actual divine economy, no supernatural grace can be granted us if it does not proceed *from Jesus Christ* as a participation in the fulness of grace which He possesses; if it does not come to us *through Jesus Christ* as fruit of His merits and by the intercession of His humanity, which, as instrument united to the Word, applies God's sanctifying action to us; and if it is not directed *to Jesus Christ* in as much as every supernatural vocation and every personal grace finds its reason for being and its specification in the particular relation with Christ to which God has predestined us.

The mystical Body of Christ

The same supernatural reality that sanctifies the soul of Jesus Christ and endows it with the inherent power of acting supernaturally, constitutes Him, therefore, as principle of all supernatural life and of every supernatural act for all men. Hence in the supernatural order there is established between Christ and us a vital unity so profound that it can be compared only with that which exists among the various members of a living body, and can even be said to surpass that unity in a certain sense by its very quality of constituting a supernatural organism. Using the Pauline and patristic expression, we have called this organism the *mystical Body of Christ;* and St. Augustine, with the expressive force of his language, gives it the name of the *entire Christ,* the *whole Christ.*

It is a *Body* because it possesses a variety of living members which, endowed with proper functions and suitably organized, find themselves united and coordinated with one another to form a single undivided being, with a finality specific to the organism and supreme for all and each of its members.

This Body is given the qualifying adjective of *mystical* to specify it and distinguish it from other bodies, both physical and moral. For in any physical body the various parts that go to make it up lack independence and personality, subsisting only as parts in the whole. By contrast, in a moral body the various members exist independently of one another, with no other principle of unity than a common tendency towards the same end, to attain which they all work together. In the mystical Body, however, every member keeps his own personality, but is endowed, on the other hand, with an internal principle, real and active, which has an effective influence on the whole Body and on every one of its parts.

Finally, it receives its denomination and differentiation *of Christ* from the fact that He is its Founder, Savior and Sustainer, and also from the fact that He is the noblest and most excellent part of this mystical Body.

Jesus Christ is in fact the *Head* of the mystical Body (Col. 1:18) by reason of His excellence, which places Him in the higher part of the Body, and because He possesses the fulness of grace, overflowing in its superabundance from Him and spreading through the other members, to which it communicates life and movement, whose actions it governs and influences in a vital way.[23]

The vital unity that Jesus Christ communicates to His mystical Body is so profound that the various members which go to make it up cannot attain their perfection unless by their inclusion in the Body they find themselves in organic connection with the other members; so that all have need of one another and complement one another in their respective operations. The members can do nothing without the salutary influence of the Head;[24] nor would there be any profit in the spiritual activity of a member who, centered on himself, would want to prescind from the other members or from the Body to which he is united;[25] nor would the Body be able to attain the fulness of perfection if the Head did not concern Himself with us, His members.[26]

St. Augustine, who has such beautiful, profound passages on the unity between Christ and His Church, considers our compenetration with Jesus Christ so intimate that our weaknesses can be predicated of Him and His properties can be attributed to us: "in that Man, Christ, the Church also is taken up by the Word."[27] "We are sons, we are the Son: for we many are such that we are one in Him."[28] And in many other places he affirms that the Church is none other than Christ, who evangelizes Himself,[29] preaches Himself to Himself,[30] goes toward Himself through Himself and loves Himself.[31] This is the mystery of charity in the mystery of unity.

[23] St. Thomas, *Summa theol.*, III, 8, 1.
[24] John 15:5; Col. 2:19; Eph. 4:15-16.
[25] Rom. 12:5; 1 Cor. 12:25-27; Eph. 4:25.
[26] Eph. 4:11-13.
[27] St. Augustine, *Enarr. in Ps.* 3, 9; PL 36, 77.

[28] *Enarr. in Ps.* 122, 5; PL 37, 1634.
[29] *Enarr. in Ps.* 74, 4; PL 36, 949.
[30] *Sermo* 305, 4; PL 38, 1399.
[31] *In Io.*, 69, 2; PL 35, 1816; *ibid.*, 70, 1; PL 35, 1818.

Jesus Christ and the supernatural economy

All that we have explained gives us an understanding of the place Christ occupies in the plan of the supernatural economy. Jesus Christ came to *recapitulate*[32] in Himself all mankind, which is incorporated in Him and introduced by Him to participation in the divine life and the divine glorification. Jesus Christ is the Head of the new line of children of God, not by physical generation but by spiritual transmission of grace. St. Paul expresses this in the first letter to the Corinthians: "The first man, Adam, became a living soul; the last Adam became a life-giving spirit . . . . The first man was of the earth, earthy; the second man is from heaven, heavenly. As was the earthy man, so also are the earthy; and as is the heavenly man, such also are the heavenly. Therefore, even as we have borne the likeness of the earthy, let us bear also the likeness of the heavenly" (1 Cor. 15:45-49).

From this point of view it is seen clearly that, in the organic unity of the divine plan, the state of original justice was only a transitory period, an initial and precarious phase. The true regime of grace began with sin. The state of fallen mankind was foreseen and permitted as a remedial experience which would impress upon us our frailty and weakness, to orient us once and for all to the Redemption of Christ and to participation in the divine life through our insertion into Jesus Christ. That is why the Church sings, "O surely necessary sin of Adam! . . . O happy fault, which merited such a Redeemer, so great as this!"

3. The Priesthood of Jesus Christ

Jesus Christ, Priest

We have seen the vocation of Jesus Christ in relation to mankind and in relation to the whole created universe. We can now examine Christ's ultimate end in relation to God after He has united all creatures in Himself. And with this we shall arrive at the supreme purpose which God had in establishing the plan of creation, of redemption and of the elevation of men and angels to the supernatural order through participation in the divine life in Jesus Christ.

Having created all things "for the adornment of His majesty" and oriented all things to Himself according to a relation of finality in worship, God has willed to receive this worship unified and sublimated in Jesus Christ: "Through Him and with Him and in Him there is to You, God the Father all-powerful, in the unity of the Holy Spirit, all honor and glory."

Jesus Christ was predestined to be the Priest of God's glory: His priesthood

---

[32] In our modern languages there is no word that can translate exactly the thought St. Paul expresses with the word ἀνακεφαλαιώσασθαι of the Greek text, which properly signifies "to unite under a single head." Jesus Christ is the Head who by drawing all things to Himself will establish them once more in the organic unity they had when they issued from the hands of God, a unity diminished by sin.

is the center, the supreme idea and the principle of unity of the actual divine economy. Christ was foreseen and willed by God as supreme Priest and Pontiff. Because He is Priest, He is also Redeemer; and because Christ's priesthood was to be supreme, the Father made Him Head of mankind and center of creation.

We see, then, in what the priesthood of Jesus Christ consists.

In the well known description of the priest in the epistle to the Hebrews (Heb. 5:1-4), four essential elements are indicated: the disposition and the human figure of the priest; his divine vocation; his deputation to the worship of God; his primary function, sacrifice.

We have indicated sufficiently Christ's role as representative. We need only examine the other three elements of the priesthood in Him.

His priestly vocation

Holy Scripture makes known to us the act of the election of Jesus Christ to the high priesthood. We find this election mentioned in Psalms 2 and 109, the words of which are concretely applied to Christ by the epistle to the Hebrews (Heb. 5:5-6). According to the testimony of the epistle, the priestly vocation of Jesus Christ is linked to the very generation of the Word in eternity: "So also Christ did not glorify Himself with the high priesthood, but was glorified by Him who said to Him, 'You are My Son, this day I have begotten You.'" The eternal predestination of the humanity of Jesus Christ to the divine sonship makes this humanity the closest possible tie between God and creation, and determines the mission which Christ is to realize in time and in eternity. This is His priestly vocation, sealed with a divine oath: "The Lord has sworn, and He will not repent: 'You are a priest forever, according to the order of Melchisedech.'"

Priestly consecration of Jesus Christ

When the fulness of time has come, this design of God is brought to its fulfilment. The grace of the hypostatic union with the Word, which fulfils in time the eternal vocation of the humanity of Jesus Christ to the divine sonship, brings about also His priestly consecration and His deputation to the worship of God.

Christ's priestly grace is not a new energy grafted onto the powers of His soul, or a mere accidental character which imprints a new modality on the actuation of His intellect and His will; it is the grace constitutive of His being as incarnate Word. It is a substantial grace, the grace of union, by which the person of the Word elevates Christ's humanity, making it subsist with His own divine being and consecrating it substantially for the worship of God.

The fulness of the divinity which penetrates and takes possession of the human nature of Jesus is, according to the biblical figure, the *oleum exsultationis,* "the oil of gladness," which makes Him the *"Christ" par excellence,* the Anointed of the Father, to be Pontiff of men; a Pontiff whose acts will be wholly worshipful and infinitely pleasing to the Father, as proceeding from the person of His Son, but will still remain human, that He may have compassion on the ignorant and the wayward, as we are told in the letter to the Hebrews: "Therefore because children have blood and flesh in common, so He in like manner has shared in these; that through death He might destroy him who had the empire of death, that is, the devil . . . . Wherefore it was right that He should in all things be made like His brethren, that He might become a merciful and faithful high Priest in matters pertaining to God to expiate the sins of the people" (Heb. 2:14-17).

This is the reason for the Incarnation of the Word, then, with all its consequences; in particular, the fact of an Incarnation in a mortal, weak nature, and the fact of a painful and sorrowful Redemption.

The sacrifice of Jesus Christ

The same letter to the Hebrews reveals to us the inmost disposition of Christ's soul at the moment of His entrance into the world and of His priestly consecration, applying to Him David's prophetic words: "Sacrifice and oblation You did not wish, but You have fitted together a body for Me. You took no pleasure in burnt offerings and sin offerings. Then I said, 'Here I am; I have come to do Your will, O God,' as it is written in the roll of the book" (Heb. 10:5-7; cf. Ps. 39:7-9).

The first act of Jesus Christ, therefore, was a priestly act of offering His life as a sacrifice acceptable to the Father. In Christ's priestly oblation the symbolism and the substitutive value, which are found in every sacrifice, had to be turned into reality. This oblation will be perfect and infinitely pleasing to God, not only by reason of the dignity of the offering priest, but also by reason of the dignity of the Victim and the perfection of the act of sacrifice, which will realize fully its meaning. God willed the real immolation of the creature who was most perfect, most pure, closest to the divinity. Jesus Christ had to be the Victim of His own sacrifice.

The Lord's whole life was oriented toward the cross. By reason of the inmost disposition of His soul, all His acts had the value of worship. But the Father's will was not satisfied with this moral offering, and demanded the real, physical, bloody immolation of the Son. The same eternal decree which constituted Christ the Priest of the universal worship of God, pre-destined Him to be the adequate Victim of that same worship.

Thus St. Peter speaks of Jesus Christ as the "Lamb without blemish and without spot, foreknown before the foundation of the world, and manifested in the last times for your sakes" (1 Pet. 1:19-20); and St. John sees Him as a Lamb slain (Apoc. 5:6).

The sacrifice of the cross is therefore the center of the divine plan. The whole religious activity of mankind converges on it and derives from it.

God has founded upon it the work of our redemption and sanctification, so that the supernatural action of grace in man becomes a moral reproduction of the sacrifice of Christ.

Such is the teaching of St. Thomas[33] when he says that, for the full attainment of his true supernatural end, man must traverse three stages: die to sin, live again to the new life of grace, and be admitted to the perfect and definitive union with God in glory. Now this process coincides with the three aspects found in the Lord's total act of sacrifice. Jesus Christ died, rose and ascended to the right hand of the Father; this is the threefold mystery that goes to make up the one sacrifice of Christ, which for the same reason is a paschal sacrifice.

Christ died. His death placed Him in the status of Victim, not by the material action of the executioners, blameworthy in the eyes of God, but by a free act of His will, which brought the physical fact of the crucifixion under the action of His priesthood and conferred on it the cultual value of sacrifice. "He was offered because it was His own will" (Is. 53:7). "No one takes My life from Me, but I lay it down of Myself," we read in St. John's gospel (John 10:18).

This is the most human aspect of sacrifice, and constitutes its essential act, so that sacrifice in the proper sense supposes the immolation of a victim in acknowledgment of God's supreme dominion. The redemptive effect of His bloody death is our death to sin: "He was delivered up for our sins" (Rom. 4:25). "He is a propitiation for our sins, not for ours only but also for those of the whole world" (1 John 2:2).

Christ rose. The immolation of the victim withdraws it from profane use. But beyond that it must be positively consecrated to God. This is the positive aspect of sacrifice, which Jesus Christ realizes by communicating to Himself a new life, everlasting and glorious, which shows Him and proves Him to be God's possession and property. "For though He was crucified through weakness, yet He lives through the power of God" (2 Cor. 13:4). "The death that He died, He died to sin once for all, but the life that He lives, He lives unto God" (Rom. 6:10). To this consecratory aspect of Christ's sacrifice St. Paul relates the grace of our life in God: "We were buried in death with Him by means of baptism, in order that, just as Christ was raised from the dead by the glorious power of the Father, so we also may conduct ourselves by a new principle of life" (Rom. 6:4).

The third phase, which gives the final perfection to sacrifice, is its real acceptance by God and the final introduction of the victim into the presence of the divinity. The sacred Scripture often throws this aspect into relief: "And they offered a holocaust on the altar. And the Lord breathed the sweet odor of it." In the Old Law this introduction had a symbolic character, corresponding to the substitutional value of the immolation of the victim.

---

[33] St. Thomas, *Summa theol.*, III, 22, 2.

But in the sacrifice of Jesus Christ, whose immolation was real, His introduction to the presence of God had to be equally real. The Lord's ascension
into heaven and His sitting at the right hand of the Father give a perfect
complement to His priestly action. "The main point in what we are saying,"
reads the letter to the Hebrews, "is that we have such a high Priest, who
has taken His seat at the right hand of the throne of Majesty in the heavens"
(Heb. 8:1). The introduction of the blood of animals into the "Holy of
Holies" was the figure of it (Heb. 9:7-12).

This perfective aspect of Christ's sacrifice merits for us the fulfilment of
the process of our sanctification, so that, according to St. Paul, we die to
sin with Jesus Christ, to rise with Him to a new life and be introduced with
Him into the presence of God. "When we were dead by reason of our sins,
He brought us to life together with Christ . . . . Together with Christ Jesus
and in Him, He raised us up and enthroned us in the heavenly realm"
(Eph. 2:5-6). The hope of all the redeemed is based on the Lord's Ascension
and rests on it in the end (Heb. 4:14; 10:19-22).

For St. Paul, the Lord's death, Resurrection and Ascension go to make up
the one paschal sacrifice of "Christ Jesus who died, yes, and who rose again,
who is at the right hand of God and who intercedes for us" (Rom. 8:34).
For this reason the Roman Church in the solemn moments of the offering
and the consecration of the Eucharistic sacrifice makes express mention of
the three-fold aspect of the Lord's sacrifice: *quam tibi offerimus ob memoriam
passionis, resurrectionis, et ascensionis Iesu Christi Domini nostri.—Unde
et memores, . . . eiusdem Christi Filii tui Domini nostri tam beatae passionis,
nec non et ab inferis resurrectionis, sed et in caelos gloriosae ascensionis . . . .*

Christ's priesthood perpetuated in the Church

It was God's will that the sacrifice of Jesus Christ should be ever renewed
and made present again until the consummation of the world. Adapting
Himself once more to the human way of being, He was pleased that all
men, in whatsoever time and place, should be able to be present at the
unbloody renewal of the sacrifice of the cross, which had reached all by its
power. Thus the essential priestly action of sacrifice would not die out in
the Church, the Lord's Passion would be perpetuated, and the fruits derived
from it would be more effectively applied to us.

According to the expression of St. Thomas,[34] Jesus Christ "by His Passion,
offering Himself as an oblation and victim to God, inaugurated the rite, that
is, the worship, of the Christian religion," so that "the whole rite of the
Christian religion is derived from the priesthood of Christ,"[35] who did not
limit Himself to offering a sacrifice that would have a power transcending
space and time and fruits capable of reaching all men, but with that sacrifice
chose to inaugurate a new worship, having His sacrifice as its center; chose

---

[34] St. Thomas, *Summa theol.*, III, 62, 5.   [35] *Summa theol.*, III, 63, 3.

to institute a new positive religion, a social religion, organized and founded on participation in His priesthood. Such are the Christian religion and worship, through which all the members of the mystical Body share, in different ways, the grace of the priestly consecration which is found in its fulness in the Head.

St. Thomas writes,[36] in fact, that whatever exists or is realized in the Head must be verified in some way also in His members, who are incorporated with Him. Since Christ, our Head, is Son of God, we share in the divine sonship; since Christ died and rose and ascended into heaven, we die and rise with Him and are called to share in His glory.

In a similar way, if Christ, by virtue of the hypostatic union, was consecrated Priest and Pontiff, we Christians, by virtue of union with our Head, receive a participation in His priesthood. "Draw near to Him," writes St. Peter, "a living stone, rejected indeed by men but chosen and honored by God. You also, as living stones, are being built into a spiritual edifice, so as to be a holy priesthood" (1 Pet. 2:4-5). "He has made us to be a kingdom, and priests to God His Father!" exclaims St. John (Apoc. 1:6).

We can state, therefore, that, just as the vocation of Christ's humanity to the divine sonship is identified with His priestly vocation, so we also by our vocation to Christianity are destined to a configuration with the priesthood of Christ, so as to be able to offer to God with Him the worship of the Christian religion and the Christian life.

Christ's Passion merited for us, besides the grace of the divine sonship, a new way of being assimilated with Him, that is, a perfection which disposes us to participate in the divine worship according to the rite inaugurated by Jesus Christ.[37]

In virtue of this first configuration with the priesthood of Jesus Christ, received with the grace of baptism, every Christian, when he acts as such, actualizes his participation in our Lord's priesthood and is able to perform an act of true Christian worship, if he refers it to God in union with Christ.

But there are certain acts of Christian worship which are celebrated by the Head Himself, making use of one of His ministers, in the name of the whole Body; or, better, they are celebrated by the whole Body in as much as it forms an organic, living unity, vivified by the Head. These acts constitute Christ's priestly action, perpetuated in the Church; they are the essential acts of Christian public worship. In that worship Jesus Christ is the one true priest, just as He was the one true priest of His bloody sacrifice.

But now, inseparably united to Christ and to His priesthood is the Church, which, together with Him and in as much as she forms with Him a single priestly entity, offers the sacrifice of the Christian religion. The Church on her part, as Spouse of Christ and in virtue of the mission received from Him, has created particular rites by which she prepares the faithful for a

---

[36] *Summa theol.*, III, 69, 2.   [37] St. Thomas, *Summa theol.*, III, 62, 5.

worthy participation in the liturgy of the Lord. The liturgy of Jesus Christ celebrated by the Church, and the liturgy of the Church as preparation and disposition for the liturgy of Jesus Christ, together go to make up liturgical worship, the liturgy properly so called.

Be it noted, finally, that the determining principle by which we shall be able to know which rites, concretely existing, have a truly liturgical character, is simply the fact of their having been instituted as such by Christ or by the Church. On the part of our Lord we have the sacrifice, which is essentially an act of public worship, and the sacraments. The Church has instituted the rites which accompany the celebration of the liturgy of Jesus Christ or dispose people to it, the various sacramentals, and in general the forms of public prayer.

The acts of the priesthood of Jesus Christ are universally and unchangeably acts of the Church's public worship, because such is the will of the Lord in instituting them. The forms of public worship of ecclesiastical origin, on the other hand, may vary in content, expression and extension, because they are always subject to the present will of the Church. It is up to the Church alone to determine the rites or the formulas which officially represent her public prayer and which can actually unite us to the liturgical acts proceeding from the priesthood of Jesus Christ, thus forming with them a single cultual unity: the complete public worship of the mystical Body of Christ.

We can now repeat the wider concept of liturgy, which in the beginning of this chapter we took from St. Thomas: "the divine worship according to the rite of the Christian religion." And we can repeat the more precise definition of Pius XII: "The liturgy is the worship rendered by the mystical Body of Christ in the entirety of its Head and members."

5 THE LITURGY,

THE CHURCH'S PUBLIC WORSHIP:

CHARACTERISTICS OF LITURGICAL ACTION

The theological concepts sketched in the preceding chapter throw light on the notion of liturgy, the Church's public worship. They help us understand *what* the liturgy is. From them we can deduce the laws that determine its structure and govern its action. These laws, which we are going to analyze, can give us an understanding of *what* the liturgy is *like*.

Each one of the doctrinal principles on which liturgical action is based casts its own reflection on the liturgy's way of being and stamps a particular modality on its internal development and its external manifestation. The influence of the doctrinal principles on the forms of worship gives rise to certain characteristics which become the essential features, as it were, in the appearance of liturgical action. By reason of them, the liturgy is what it is: the Church's public worship, in accordance with the demands of its very nature and of the positive will of Jesus Christ.

Other, accessory touches can be added, and from these the various rites will take on more variety and color. They will be the tints in which the liturgy is colored throughout an era or a region, and they will reflect the religious ideal, the culture, the taste or the historical vicissitudes of the Church in those circumstances of place or time. By reason of these accidental features, the liturgical inheritance which forms the patrimony of our present Church displays a wide range of values in its content and its form.

Even prescinding from the great difference in the characteristics proper to the Eastern liturgies and those distinctive of the Western, and limiting ourselves to our Roman liturgy, we can find enough variety in it alone: sober rites such as those that are typically Roman, and prolix rites such as those that come from Gaul; severe and profoundly theological forms of a St. Leo or a St. Gregory, and the far-fetched symbolism of the last period of the Middle Ages; dogmatic precision of the age of the great scholastics, and the more sentimental forms of the age of decadence.

Sometimes elements of diverse origin and of the most varied character are found gathered together and even superimposed in one and the same rite. Every era has left signs of its passing in the liturgy, whose vitality does not allow it to stagnate or to be foreign to the spiritual stirrings of any country or of any age.

But in the midst of this variety of content and expression there is something unchangeable, something which always remains and which comes to be a sort of substance of the liturgical forms. It is the complexus of the characteristics derived immediately from the doctrinal principles; for in these principles our Christian liturgy has its reason for being, and from these principles each one of the rites and formulas of which the liturgy is composed receives its own personality and its own physiognomy.

The system of substantial and constant laws which translate into practice the requirements of certain theological truths, forms a sort of canon, to which every rite and formula of the liturgy must subject itself in order to attain its intrinsic perfection.

Something similar to that which holds, for example, in the sphere of art, holds also for the liturgy. The styles and the subjective appreciations of beauty may vary as much as they want; but in all eras and in any style whatsoever, only those artistic manifestations which correspond to the objective canons of beauty will measure up to the concept of true works of art. The objective canons of beauty are transcendental and perennial, because they coincide with the very laws of being.

As far as their internal structure is concerned, the liturgical rites and formulas must also obey canons or laws which flow from the very nature of Christian worship as shown by theological analysis. In their outward composition and form they may present the most varied aspects without essentially altering the inner harmony. Yet the more faithfully the accidental forms reflect the intrinsic perfection of the liturgical action, the more perfect will be the whole.

Not all the elements of which our present liturgy is composed have the same value or the same structural perfection. In our liturgical books we come upon magnificent pieces, perfect in content and form. But there are others that leave much to be desired.

The criterion for evaluating the degree of perfection of the elements of public worship is not at all the antiquity of its composition, as is sometimes supposed. To use that criterion would be to lapse into a senseless archeologism. Ancient things are not always the best, nor is everything modern to be condemned. In all ages there can be good things and bad.

It is also true, however, that in the liturgy, as in the art and the literature of every country, there have been epochs, the golden ages, in which a maximum of perfection was reached because of a greater understanding and assimilation of the corresponding canons of structural arrangement. It is precisely in these canons that the proper criterion must be sought for judging the perfection of a rite or a formula.

This must be taken into account when there is concern with creating new liturgical rites or adapting the already existing ones to present needs.

It is not enough, for example, that the text of a Mass have all the proper elements, even if these imitate previous formularies. The text will not become what it is supposed to be, until each one of its parts expresses adequately the finality in worship that belongs to it according to the aforesaid canons governing all liturgical action.

The same advice holds for attempts to modernize the liturgy or bring it up to date. Not everything that calls itself modern art can be considered a realization of beauty, any more than the servile imitations of past or archaic styles can be so considered. The true artist is the one who has made the canons of beauty a part of his very being, and knows how to give them concrete, contemporary expression.

The authentic liturgist is not just the one who knows the rubrics and the jurisprudence of public worship; nor is he the archeologist or the historian who dedicates himself to investigating the monumental and documentary sources of the liturgy and knows what has been the process of the liturgy's formation and development. In the most proper acceptation of the word, a liturgist is one whose mind and spirit have become imbued with the essential laws of liturgical worship, so that he knows how to enlighten the Church's public prayer by those laws, whether the aim be to appreciate and savor the spiritual riches contained in liturgical prayer, or to inform with the authentic liturgical spirit the new forms of worship which present-day Christian life demands.

From the theological principles set forth in the preceding chapter we shall seek to deduce the principal laws that preside over the concrete actualization of the Church's public worship.

1. The Twofold Finality of the Liturgy

Because it is worship, the liturgy has *per se* a latreutic purpose: its whole reason for being is found in the individual and social duty of glorifying God. Being Christian worship, it attains its purpose by virtue of the priestly action of Jesus Christ. Christ's sacrifice, the Mass, constitutes, therefore, the center

of the liturgy; more than that, its essential act. Hence in the Eastern liturgies
the celebration of the Eucharistic sacrifice is called simply *the liturgy*.

This priestly action of Jesus Christ confers the name of liturgical, the
character of worship and the eminently latreutic aim on the rites which the
Church celebrates around the sacrifice or in the direction of the sacrifice, as
preparation for it, explanation of it or continuation of it, and by which the
Church adds something of her own to embellish and perfect the priestly
action of the Lord in a human and extrinsic way.

Such are, in the first place, the rites accompanying this action and immediately related to it, namely those that go to make up the liturgy of the
Mass from the offertory to the end of the canon.

Participating also in this primary character of sacrifice are: the Divine
Office, which has the aim of extending to the whole day, in a mystical way,
the essential glorification offered to God in the Mass; and also those sacraments and sacramentals which have been instituted to make the celebration
of the Mass possible or more worthy, and in which is imitated the essence of
the sacrifice, namely the consecration of creatures to God. We refer to the
various consecrations or constitutive blessings through which persons or
things are dedicated to God in relation to the sacrifice; thus, the various
ministerial orders, the consecration or blessing of churches, altars, sacred
vessels and ornaments, etc.

In all these rites the motive for the liturgical action is the tribute of glory
and praise to God. In them, as is proper to every act of worship, the Christian
will find his own spiritual perfection. But this effect is not sought for its own
sake; it is only a consequence of the objective consecration or the voluntary
subjection to God.

But Jesus Christ, who by His Passion procured simultaneously the glory
of God and the redemption of mankind, wanted both effects to be produced
through His priestly action in the Church, and to that action He linked the
objective and efficacious application to souls of the fruits of His redemptive
death. Hence the Eucharist, besides being a sacrifice, is also a sacrament;
besides giving glory to God, it effects the sanctification of men. By their
intimate relation with the sacrifice of the cross and with the Eucharist, all
the other sacraments obtain the ability to sanctify, since they apply to us the
power of Christ's sacrifice and dispose us for participating in the Eucharist
and receiving it.

Thus the sacraments give Christian worship its sanctifying value, and the
liturgy acquires a new finality, the soteriological purpose in relation to men,
just as its latreutic purpose ordains it directly to the glory of God.

This twofold orientation of the liturgy is derived from the Eucharist, which
therefore occupies the center of liturgical worship by a twofold claim. From
the Eucharistic sacrifice proceed in the first place the liturgical acts which
are directed to God as tribute of glorification and of praise; from the Eucha-

rist, greatest of the sacraments, proceed the other sacraments and in general the liturgy's means of sanctification, and to the Eucharist they are directed.

The four ends of the Eucharistic sacrifice—two tending to God and two looking towards man—are explained and combined according to this law of the twofold finality of the liturgy.

The excellence of the divine being, contemplated in itself, gives rise to the act of adoration, supreme end of the liturgy. The excellence and the dominion of God as manifested in His communications to creatures move us to give thanks. These are the two ends, latreutic and eucharistic, which tend immediately to the glorification of God; perhaps with the twofold shading indicated to us in the epistle to the Ephesians, where it describes the magnificence of the divine plan which directs everything to praising the glory that God has in Himself, *in laudem gloriae ipsius* (Eph. 1:12, 14), and also to praising His glory in so far as it shines forth in creatures: the glory of His grace: *in laudem gloriae gratiae ipsius* (Eph. 1:6).

The other two ends, on the other hand, tend to the sanctification of man, asking God's grace and gifts for him and expiating his sins.

The four ends of the Eucharistic sacrifice, well tied together and mutually subordinated in this way, give balance and harmony to the whole liturgical system. The other rites similarly will offer us a mixture or combination of the latreutic aim and the aim of sanctification, with predominance of one over the other according to the nature of each liturgical action. This predominance will have a marked effect on the structure of the various rites and will assign them the place they are to occupy in the harmonious arrangement of the liturgical organism, at the summit of which stands the latreutic action of the sacrifice of Jesus Christ, giving unity and coalescence to the whole.

Let us fix our attention for a while on the principal rites, beginning with the Mass. Here we find three principal parts. The central and most important part consists properly of the offering of the sacrifice. In this part, therefore, the idea of adoration in all its aspects predominates almost exclusively. The other two parts, in more direct relation with the sanctification of the faithful, are respectively a preparation for the act of sacrifice and a sacramental application of that act.

By examining individually each one of the three parts of the Mass, we shall be able to see how its own particular structure is determined by the suitable ordering of the two finalities to correspond to the character of this part of the Mass in relation to the supreme end of the sacrifice.

The first part is aimed at disposing the faithful, through faith and grace, for participation in the common sacrifice. Faith is aroused and enlightened by the readings from the Old and New Testaments and by the explanation of the word of God, all of this being directed toward a better understanding of the mystery being celebrated on this day. Grace is implored by all the means of purification and all the prayers rising up to God in this part of the Mass, whose purpose is eminently one of educating and disposing.

But there are also elements which at the same time prepare for a higher, latreutic purpose. The readings alternate with canticles of adoration and praise. The collects always begin with an invocation, which is an explicit acknowledgment of some aspect of the divine excellence on which the prayer is trustingly based. This whole part aims to bring to life, through faith, the mystery which is soon to be renewed and in which the faithful are to take part sacramentally; and it is enclosed between two songs of divine glorification: the *Gloria in excelsis Deo,* song of praise, and the *Credo,* song of faith as acceptance of the teaching that has been received and thanksgiving for it.

The second part—offertory and consecration—is directed exclusively to God, and everything in it has a latreutic character. If anything is asked of God, the purpose in view is primarily the worthy celebration of the sacrifice and its acceptance on God's part; although there are some allusions to the faithful people, that the impetratory power of the sacrifice may cause God to look on them with complaisance. The latreutic aspect receives splendid expression in the preface, with which the offertory part concludes. It forms a magnificent triumphal arch leading us into the Church's great priestly prayer, which in turn is concluded and summed up in a solemn doxology.

The prayers that go to make up the third part of the Mass, beginning with the *Pater noster,* refer again to the Christian believer, to whom the Lord will give Himself as Eucharistic sacrament. The Church's communion banquet will be the consummation of the common sacrifice of the whole Body. In this part the aspect of petition and the aim of sanctification reappear and reach a new intensity. From the *Pater noster* on, the Church's prayer keeps becoming more insistent and more concrete with a view to obtaining a pure and worthy reception of the Eucharist and a thorough assimilation of its fruits. This movement toward the particular and the concrete, which characterizes the third part of the Mass, shows itself clearly in the three prayers preceding the celebrant's communion. As a résumé of the different aspects prominent in the two preceding parts, the prayers now recited present a typical mixture of the divine and the human, closing with the offering of the whole to the most holy Trinity as the "homage of our service."

It is from this ordered variety and combination of objectives and of proportions that the celebration of the Mass acquires its richness of liturgical content, its strength of expression and the beauty of its organic unity. Every passage in the Mass has its particular meaning and its special character in relation to the place it occupies and to the purpose assigned, it in the whole. The beauty and integrity of the whole rite depends on the faithful adaptation of every passage to its own task.

Some texts of our present missal are lacking in ideological depth and liturgical worth because they do not adhere to this law. There are certain

Masses in which the various texts could change places without the substitution becoming noticeable: the introit could be put in place of the offertory, and the offertory serve as communion antiphon, because none of them has the proper character. In some Mass texts we note the tendency to make use of the liturgical compositions solely for the purpose of alluding to the characteristic virtues of a saint or bringing out the theme of the feast to which the Mass is dedicated, without taking into account the specific finality proper to that piece in the whole rite of the Mass. And there are texts which seem to have no other purpose than to make known the dogmatic or juridical basis of a celebration.

By contrast, in the classical Masses and in all those that are well composed, every text has its own proper value in harmony with the place which belongs to it in the Mass and which at the same time gives it the coloring proper to the mystery or the feast celebrated that day.

All that we have said about the Mass could be applied, observing due proportion, to the other liturgical rites.

Thus, the Divine Office also has a predominantly latreutic character. That is why it is called the *sacrifice of praise,* by analogy to the sacrifice of thanksgiving, the Eucharist. It is based on the psalms, hymns and canticles with which the Church praises her Lord throughout the day.

But these elements, directed to God, alternate with others that look to our welfare: the readings, the little chapters, the collects. Even these elements, however, flow into the general stream of praise by being concluded with other expressions of praise: the responsories, the versicles, the invocations.

And, as in the Mass, so also in the high points of the Divine Office we shall find some text of greater solemnity which claims our attention and reminds us what is the Church's primary attitude in face of the Lord. Such are the invitatory and the *Te Deum,* beginning and ending the office of Matins; the *Benedicite,* the *Laudate* psalms and the *Benedictus* of Lauds; the *Magnificat* with the offering of incense at Vespers; the doxologies of the hymns at all the hours; the *Gloria Patri* which concludes all the psalms and finds its way frequently into the Church's prayer, to keep alive in us the attitude, at once humble and sublime, of adoration.

In the Divine Office also, though proportionately much less than in the Mass, the various passages have their special function and should therefore maintain their proper character.

This is true in particular of the antiphons. They should give the tone to every psalm not only musically but ideologically, illuminating it with the light proper to that particular liturgical feast. The procedure followed, for example, in the office of the Name of Jesus is not enough: a collection of biblical texts in which the "name of the Lord" is mentioned, and a distribution of them in the office without regard for whether they are meaningful enough or whether they have any relation to the psalm they precede.

To be noted likewise is the importance and the personality of the responsories, which sum up and direct the emotions aroused in the soul by the
recitation of the Divine Office and the meditation of the mystery.

In the sacraments, on the other hand, the liturgical rites and formulas
are aimed at illustrating with variety of expression and great wealth of symbolism the sacramental effect produced in the soul by the essential action of
the rite. The faith and the good dispositions of the one who is to receive
the sacrament are thereby aroused. Again, various prayers call down special
graces of sanctification antecedent to the sacramental grace or connected with
it. The whole ritual structure of the sacraments is therefore determined by
the soteriological aim and the character of sign which is essential to them.
The latreutic aspect appears only incidentally in the invocations of the
prayers, and more indirectly in so far as the relation between the sacramental
grace and the supreme end of the Christian life is expressed.

In a similar way the sacramentals imitate the being and the structure of
the sacraments, and they constantly express and implore by their formulas
and their rites the principal effects they produce: the liberation of creatures
subjected to the spirit of evil, the obtaining of the divine favor, the preparation of the soul for receiving sacramental grace, the insertion of the material
world into the mystery of Christ. It is worthy of note that the sacramentals
which effect the most complete consecration or sanctification of souls or of
material objects, thus disposing them for worship, display their ultimate
latreutic aim more obviously in the chant of a majestic preface.

The twofold finality of liturgical actions must determine also the form
of their celebration. If the sacraments are for men, the sacrifice is for God.
Thus they are not to be celebrated in the same way.

In the liturgy of the sacraments the controlling purpose is that the faithful
be made aware of what they are going to do or receive. Every means must
be employed to bring within their grasp the meaning of what the liturgy
is doing or saying, so that they will adapt themselves more intelligently and
with better dispositions to the effects of the sacramental rites. Hence the
Church includes many admonitions and exhortations to the people, at times
establishes a dialogue with them, and more readily grants the use of the
vernacular in the formulas of the ritual.

The sacrifice, on the other hand, remains eminently directed to the giving
of glory to God. For that reason the sense of dignity and, if possible, of
majesty in its celebration must take precedence over many considerations of
a purely pastoral character. Its latreutic purpose justifies and demands the
existence of places where the Eucharistic sacrifice and the Divine Office will
be celebrated with all possible splendor as the Church's magnificent homage
to God, the Lord of all. And since the worship in many churches, although
celebrated with sufficient dignity, must be limited to its more modest forms,
it is right that in cathedrals and monasteries at least, the liturgy make use

of all its elements and display its magnificence to glorify God in the name of the Church. This solemnity in worship and this *losing of time* in order to dedicate it to God in His liturgical praise has a latreutic sense and value so much the greater as the time seems more precious for use in the work of the active apostolate and in procuring the means of subsistence.

Liturgical-pastoral action will also have to take into account the intrinsic finality of the various rites, so as to establish precisely the degree and the form of participation of the people in the liturgy. Let us turn for a moment to the three parts of the Mass.

The first, as we have seen, has a wholly communitarian purpose: the people purify themselves, pray for their needs, listen to the word of God, are instructed in the mystery being celebrated, sing canticles and make public profession of their faith; then they present themselves at the foot of the altar to offer their gifts. Up to this point everything indicates the desirability of pastoral action and of making it possible for the faithful to understand the liturgy and participate in it.

By contrast, from the singing of the *Sanctus* to the end of the canon the people assist in silence. Only from time to time do they indicate briefly and with deepest reverence their spiritual union with the priest, while he is the one who deals with God in the name of Jesus Christ and of His Church. This is the time of the mystery, which the Eastern liturgies emphasize by closing the doors of the iconostasis between the altar and the people. In the presence of God's majesty and in the most solemn moment of the *awesome liturgy*,[1] everything should point to profound adoration, and the faithful should remain united to the celebrant more by the attitude of their spirit than by the material recitation of the formulas.

After the *Pater noster* the participation of the people becomes more active again. The aspect of sacrifice yields to that of Eucharistic banquet, of brotherly *agape*, and for that reason the liturgical celebration must tend to bring out the communitarian sense of unity, of communion, symbolized by the kiss of peace as immediate preparation for receiving the Sacrament.

2. The Priesthood of Jesus Christ
Made Present and Active

The whole worship of the Christian religion is centered in Jesus Christ. His priesthood is perfect, eternal, unique. He is the necessary and universal Mediator between men and God. His worship is the only worship acceptable to the Father, and from it all of men's acts of religion receive their supernatural value.

These theological principles have a powerful influence on the internal structure of the liturgy. For the liturgy is nothing but the process of making

---

[1] *Shumboio dqurobo* (deacon's book of the Syriac liturgy) (Sharfet, 1931), p. 15.

present and active the priesthood of Jesus Christ. Through the liturgy Christ's presence is continued in the world and the action of His priesthood extends to us.

Thus the Eucharist occupies the center of the Christian liturgy, since it is precisely the real presence of Christ and of His priestly action in the Church. All the other liturgical rites will be grouped and organized around the Eucharist, and their relative importance will depend on their greater or lesser connection with the Eucharist, from which they will receive proportionately the power of communicating the presence of Christ and of transmitting His priestly action.

The presence of Jesus Christ and of His mystery in the liturgy

The presence of Jesus Christ in the Church is perpetuated above all through the *Eucharist*. By means of the Eucharist, the Lord makes Himself constantly present among us with a presence that is substantial, real, personal and permanent.

The Church knows that in renewing the Lord's sacrifice she not only celebrates the memorial of the Passion but possesses Jesus Christ whole and entire, the complete and living Christ, in whom subsist all the mysteries of His mortal and suffering life and of His present glorious life, recapitulated and contained in His Eucharist. Thanks to this fact, it is not only at Easter but also at the celebration of every one of the Lord's feasts that the Church celebrates the Eucharist, convinced that Christ is once more making Himself present with the particular power of that mystery. Thus all men throughout the centuries will be able to be contemporaries of Christ and sharers of His mysteries.

This does not mean that the various mysteries of the Lord are made present again in the Eucharist with the same physical entity they had when they were realized in history. The Lord's Incarnation, His Epiphany, His Ascension took place only once, at a determinate time and with particular circumstances, which passed, as all things dependent on time pass. But the subject of those actions, Jesus Christ, God and Man, remains and is made present in the Eucharist in His present state, which is the state of glory at the right hand of the Father. His actions, which in their historical realization are past, remain in their power and transcend space and time because they are actions of the Man-God, actions of the Word through His humanity.

In the person of Jesus Christ, present in the Eucharist, there subsists as actual and perennial the power of His mysteries, which is given us physically through the sacrament. Thus the same mystery of Christ, commemorated by the Church in every feast with His Eucharist, becomes present again with its efficacy, which is communicated to the Church and to souls. This power puts them in relation with the same historical fact, the same mystery, from which it is derived itself.

Through this Eucharistic presence, Jesus Christ takes possession of man and draws him effectively to the action of His mystery. In the Eucharistic liturgy as on the cross, the Lord's word is perfectly fulfilled: "When I am lifted up, I will draw all to Myself" (John 12:32).

A clear manifestation of this truth is seen in the feasts of the saints commemorated in the course of the liturgical year. Every one of the saints received in abundance and welcomed with love and faithfulness this presence of Christ in his life and this force of attraction which Christ has. Grace was shaping them inwardly to the mystery of the Lord which they were imitating in their deeds. For this reason the life of the saints was a moral renewal of Christ's presence in the Church, and becomes such a renewal again when the liturgy celebrates their respective solemnities, thus bringing out more vividly that aspect of the mystery of Christ which the particular saint assimilated and embodied more especially in his life.

By its character of sacrifice, the Eucharist renews and signifies under a special title the Paschal mystery of Jesus Christ: His Passion, His Resurrection and His Ascension, the three aspects of His complete sacrifice. In virtue of this presence of the Lord's Passion in the Eucharist, all the other sacraments are directed to it and have their consummation in it.[2] For all the sacraments have their reason for being in the fact that they sanctify man by signifying the Passion of Christ and making it present in a certain way in the souls of the recipients, through the infusion of the grace derived from it and through the prefiguration of the glory which is the consummation of the Paschal mystery.

In each sacrament, according to its own character, is found a profound symbolism which relates the sacramental grace proper to that sacrament to an aspect of the Lord's Passion.

Baptism is the Paschal sacrament *par excellence*. The whole liturgy of the Easter Vigil tends to express the Paschal mystery of Jesus Christ and of the newly baptized as two aspects of the same reality. The neophytes of the early Church were immersed materially in the water of the baptismal font; but with a deeper spiritual reality they were immersed in the death of Christ, to come out of the water reborn to a new life, the glorious life of the risen Christ.

St. Paul wrote to the Colossians, "You were buried together with Christ in baptism, and in Him also you rose again" (Col. 2:12). And to the Romans, "Do you not know that all we who have been baptized in Christ Jesus have been baptized to share in His death? With Him we were buried in baptism to share in His death, in order that, just as Christ rose from the dead through the glory of the Father, so we also may live a new life" (Rom. 6:3-4). For St. Thomas, this immersion of the neophyte in the Passion of Christ is so effective that he goes so far as to write, "Christ's Passion is communicated

[2] St. Thomas, *summa theol.*, III, 65, 3; 63, 6; 73, 3.

to every baptized person as a remedy, as if he himself had suffered and died."[3] He finds the reason for this compenetration in the unity of the mystical Body: "The sufferings of the Passion are communicated to the baptized person in so far as he becomes a member of Christ, as if he himself had borne that pain."[4]

Moreover, through the baptismal character the new member of Christ receives a first and fundamental configuration to the priesthood of the Head, which makes him enter fully into the worshipful aim of the sacrifice of Christ and of Christian society. By virtue of the baptismal character, the whole orientation of the new Christian's life will be in the direction of our Lord's sacrifice, through the reception of the Eucharist and of the sacraments which dispose him for it, through participation in the Church's sacrifice as a member of the Church, and through the moral imitation of Christ's sacrifice by a holy life, offered and consecrated to the worship of God in the fulfilment of his duties. The practice of the Christian virtues, the obligations of one's state in life, social and family relations, the individual's personal activity, and in an eminent way the religious state, can receive, thanks to the effect of the baptismal character, a relation with the sacrifice of Jesus Christ, and hence a value as worship; their worship-value is made operative by means of faith, which is the principle of all worship.

Confirmation, which is considered theologically as the sacrament that completes and perfects baptismal grace, has been associated to baptism liturgically as a completion and perfection of the Paschal mystery. In its theological symbolism it shares the symbolism contained and expressed in baptism, although it also has its own meaning, by which it is related in a special way to the Passion. For confirmation is the sacrament of fulness, and hence, according to St. Thomas, "those who receive it are conformed to Christ, in as much as He was full of grace and truth from the first instant of His conception,"[5] a fulness attributed to the Holy Spirit, who anointed Christ's humanity hypostatically by the presence of the divinity, to make Him the perfect victim and to communicate the fulness of the priesthood to Him with a view to His immolation.

Now in the sacrament of confirmation the Christian also is anointed; and by the grace of this sacrament, attributed especially to the Holy Spirit, he receives a conformation to the fulness of perfection of the humanity of Christ, a conformation aimed at disposing the Christian to bear witness to the Resurrection of the Lord Jesus (cf. Acts 4:33; 1:8; 2:32) before the Church and before the world.

Hence this same sacrament of confirmation produces in the Christian, by means of the sacramental character, a new configuration to the priesthood of Christ, which confers on him a true ministry in Christian worship:[6] the

---

[3] St. Thomas, *Summa theol.,* III, 69, 2.
[4] *Ibid.,* ad 1.
[5] St. Thomas, *Summa theol.,* III, 72, 1 ad 4.

[6] St. Thomas, *Summa theol.,* III, 65, 3 ad 2 and ad 4.

public office of confessing faith in Christ officially;[7] and this precisely by the immolation of his own life, whether in a bloody way by martyrdom, or in an unbloody way as a confessor of the Christian faith by the "sacrifice of confession" of which St. Augustine speaks.[8]

Penance not only applies to us the benefit of Christ's death as remission of our sins, but by its sacramental rite represents and signifies in its own way the Lord's Passion. On the cross, Christ, who was taking upon Himself the sins of the world, was judged by the Father. In the person of the Son the world's sin was judged, with a judgment of strict justice which required the death of the Son, and at the same time of infinite mercy which forgave the sins of the world. In the sacrament of penance this judgment is extended to the sinner, who bears his own sins, already judged once in the person of Christ crucified, and receiving now in this second judgment the verdict of absolution won by the satisfaction which the Lord gave. As an act perfective of the matter of the sacrament, the penitent will accept the performance of some satisfactory act by means of which he will be able to associate himself physically to Christ's sufferings, into which he has already entered mystically through the judicial rite of penance.

Extreme unction has a special connection with the sacrament of penance with regard to its primary effect, which is the healing and strengthening of the soul weakened by the results of sin. Its relation to penance is analogous to that which obtains between confirmation and baptism.

The Fathers and the doctors of the Church have seen in extreme unction a consummation of the purifying work of Jesus Christ. The Council of Trent summed up the Church's traditional doctrine in this way: extreme unction "has been regarded by the Fathers as the sacrament consummative not only of penance but also of the whole Christian life, which ought to be a perpetual penance."[9]

To produce its sacramental effect, it uses an anointing, which in this case does not effect a consecration but signifies the strength, liveliness and quiet well-being the soul receives in being permeated with the power of Christ's Passion as with the smoothest of ointments. Actually the sick person bears suffering physically in his body; and the suffering, freely accepted in an act of voluntary submission to God, as was the suffering in Christ's body on the cross, is at the same time a penalty for sin and a means of redemption. The application of the oil sanctified by the merits of the Passion to the sick person who is outwardly conformed to the suffering Christ, is a symbol of the power of our Lord permeating the sick person's senses sacramentally and giving back to his spirit its original health, while it strengthens him for suffering with Christ and communicates a redemptive value to his sufferings.

By a practice begun in the ninth century, which became common by the

---

[7] St. Thomas, *Summa theol.*, III, 72, 5 ad 2.   [9] Session XIV, cap. 19.
[8] *Enarr. in Ps.* 117, n. 1; PL 37, 1495.

end of the twelfth century, the sacrament of the sick was changed into the sacrament of the dying; and this continues to be the ordinary practice of the Church. If this sacrament is considered, then, as the final purification of the Christian before he comes to the end of his time of trial, another relation to the Paschal mystery of Jesus Christ is brought out. "By the anointing of the sick," wrote St. Albert the Great in the thirteenth century, "we are configured to Christ in His Resurrection: this sacrament, in fact, is administered to the Christian just when he is abandoning this world, as a figure of the anointing which is the glory to come, where the elect will shed every trace of mortality."

According to St. Thomas, the *res* and *sacramentum* of extreme unction consists in "a certain interior devotion, which is a spiritual anointing."[10] If we take the word "devotion" in its proper sense, as St. Thomas is accustomed to using it, namely as an interior and unconditional offering rendered to God to serve Him, the spiritual anointing of this sacrament will be a strengthening of those dispositions of the will by which the Christian consecrated himself to God on the day of his baptism and now prepares to realize in his physical life what was then accomplished in his soul, namely the configuration with our Lord's Paschal mystery, his passage from the world to the Father, from bodily death to glorious life, since the last disposition to this configuration is caused by the sacrament of the sick.

We need not take much time setting forth the relation that exists between the sacrament of *holy orders* and the Lord's Passion, since in this sacrament everything tends to configure the ordained one with Jesus Christ the Priest, for the precise purpose of conferring on him the power to represent Christ's sacrifice and renew it sacramentally in the Church. The grace and the character proper to this sacrament not only signify a particular aspect of the Passion, but transform the recipient into an instrument of Christ's priesthood, with the faculty of exercising publicly in the Church Christ's power of offering sacrifice and of sanctification.

Finally, the sacrament of *matrimony* is intended to signify the love of Christ toward His Spouse the Church (Eph. 5:32). His love, unique, indestructible, faithful to the death, was manifested wonderfully on the cross. The Fathers see the Church being born on the cross from the opened side of our Lord, prefigured in Adam. Christ crucified, dying for love of His Church, is the profound supernatural reality symbolized and represented in the sacrament of matrimony. Hence derives the Pauline doctrine, which teaches that the husband is the head of the wife, and that the duty of faithfulness is incumbent especially on her. This is expressed also by the Roman ritual in the prayer for the blessing of the wedding ring. Through the grace of this sacrament, the union of the two partners in one flesh will be a new

[10] St. Thomas, *Summa theol., Suppl.,* 30, 3 ad 3.

manifestation of the mystical unity that has made Jesus Christ and His Church a single Body.

As liturgical rites, therefore, the sacraments are instruments of the priesthood of Jesus Christ, which communicate to us the power of His sacrifice, signifying that sacrifice and making it present in a certain way in the soul of the recipient. That is why St. Thomas calls them "relics of the Lord's Passion."

The *sacramentals*, though in a more remote way than the sacraments, cooperate in renewing the presence of Jesus Christ in the Church and in the material world. For they also, in imitation of the sacraments, are ordained basically to the Eucharist and share in its power to signify and to sanctify. The sacramentals which have as their principal aim the removal of the obstacles opposing the presence of Christ and of His action, are related to the Eucharist more in its character of sacrament. Those which confer a positive disposition and a dedication to the divine service resemble the Eucharist more in its character of sacrifice.

When the dedication to the divine worship is more profound, the Church usually expresses it with a sacramental of anointing, which symbolizes more vividly the consecration of the humanity of Jesus Christ. It is in the symbolism of anointing that the Fathers have found an adequate comparison to explain the intimate penetration of the person of the Word into the humanity of Christ when the Word assumes that humanity and consecrates it as His own possession.

St. Gregory Nazianzen writes, "He is called Christ because of His divinity, since the divinity is like an anointing in relation to the humanity, not by its operation as in the other *christi* or anointed, but by the sanctifying presence of the Anointer."[11]

St. Augustine refers more explicitly to the anointing of baptism when he comments on Christ's fulness of grace and applies to it the words of the Acts of the Apostles, "God anointed Him with the Holy Spirit" (Acts 10:38): "He was anointed not with a visible oil but with the gift of grace, which is signified by the visible ointment with which the Church anoints the baptized. But Christ was not anointed by the Holy Spirit when the Spirit descended upon Him at His baptism in the form of a dove; for at that time Christ chose rather to prefigure His Body, that is, His Church, in which the members receive the Holy Spirit especially at baptism. But Christ is to be understood as being anointed by that mystical and invisible anointment when the Word of God was made flesh."[12]

And when in explaining the effects of baptism the Fathers come to consider our interior consecration to God and our configuration to Jesus Christ, the Anointed, they find a convenient image in the sacramental of anointing

[11] St. Gregory Nazianzen, *Orat. theol.*, 4, 21; PG 36, 132.

[12] St. Augustine, *De Trinitate*, 15, 26, 46; PL 42, 1093.

added by the Church to the essential rite of baptism. St. Prosper of Aquitaine, for example, says that every Christian is sanctified by the anointing in baptism to make him understand that he is made a sharer in the priestly and royal dignity of Jesus Christ.[13] And St. Augustine, "Not only has our Head been anointed, but His Body also, that is, we ourselves."[14] For through baptism we have been anointed by the Holy Spirit, from whom we have received the holy anointing that remains in us. St. Leo the Great writes with his usual depth of thought and elegance of expression, "All those who have been re-generated in Christ . . . the anointing of the Holy Spirit consecrates as priests."[15]

Among the sacramentals of the Church which tend to actualize the presence of Jesus Christ, perhaps the most important is that which we have called the *liturgical year*. Through the liturgical year the Church sanctifies time and uses it to put us in contact with the various mysteries of the Lord. Time is precisely what separates us from those mysteries.

We have already indicated how our Lords dwells among us whole and entire in the Eucharistic presence, not only in His physical being but also in the totality of His actions, states and mysteries; for although these had their historical reality in determinate places and times, with regard to their efficacy they subsist with all their actuality in the person of the Word.

When we receive Jesus Christ, therefore, and put ourselves in contact with His holy hunmanity, there are made present to us all the actions, all the states and all the mysteries that go to make up the life of that humanity. Hence the liturgy can consider any one of them as present when it makes present through the Eucharistic sacrifice the person of Jesus Christ in whom they subsist. This is the "today" which the Church repeats with so much solemnity, as an echo of the "today" of eternity. Thus on any day of the year, as far as the presence of Christ in the liturgy is concerned objectively, we shall be able to celebrate simultaneously all the mysteries of the Lord, since all are present.

But if this physical presence suffices for the liturgy to be able to fulfill its mission of praise or adoration, it is not enough to enable the liturgy to satisfy its soteriological mission. The presence of the mysteries of Christ is effective in sanctifying us only when we become configured to them, applying to them our spiritual powers, intellect and will, as immediate subjects of faith and of charity. And since our powers are so limited, it follows that they cannot be applied simultaneously to the totality of the mysteries of Christ which are objectively present. We must concentrate our whole spiritual activity and apply it to only one facet of the mystery of Christ. Then we shall be able to conform ourselves better to that mystery and receive its power to greater effect.

[13] St. Prosper of Aquitaine, *Liber sententi-arum*, 346; PL 51, 482.

[14] St. Augustine, *Enarr. in Ps.* 26, enarr. 2;

PL 36, 200.

[15] St. Leo, *Sermo* 4 *de Natali ipsius;* PL 54, 148-149.

The Church has come to the aid of these limited faculties of ours with the sacramental of the liturgical year. She has distributed throughout the natural year the celebration of the various mysteries of our Lord. In each one of these celebrations she centers all our attention and our spiritual activity on one concrete mystery, illustrates it with her teaching, disposes us by her prayer and her rites to conform ourselves to it and, uniting her action to ours, makes the whole a sacramental through which, when we receive Jesus Christ in the Eucharist, that mystery with its special efficacy is made present to us in a particular way.

Here is how Pius XII in his encyclical *Mediator Dei* has described the liturgical year: "The liturgical year *is Christ Himself who is ever living in His Church*. Here He continues that journey of immense mercy which He lovingly began in His mortal life, going about doing good with the design of bringing men to know His mysteries and in a way live by them. These mysteries are ever present and active . . . in the way that Catholic doctrine teaches us. According to the Doctors of the Church, they are shining examples of Christian perfection, as well as sources of divine grace, due to the merit and prayers of Christ; they still influence us because each mystery brings its own special grace for our salvation."[16]

The *Divine Office* is another most important sacramental which, helped by the grace of the liturgical year, makes the mysteries of Christ present in the Church together with His priestly action. And the reason for this is that the Divine Office is nothing but a moral extension of Christ's real presence in the Eucharist. The whole *raison d'être* of the Divine Office in the liturgy consists in preparing for or continuing mystically, throughout the day and even during the night, the celebration of the mystery which is celebrated sacramentally in the Eucharist of that day. By means of contemplation, that mystery is kept vivid in the mind of the Church, and serves as a fulcrum for rising from the Eucharist to the bosom of the Father, from the mystery celebrated in time to the glorious state of Christ in eternity.

For this is the other aspect under which the Divine Office makes our Lord's priesthood present in time. Our Lord now exercises it personally as sacrifice of praise in the presence of the Father, assisted by the elect who have already reached the goal. The end of praise—the latreutic and Eucharistic end—will be the only one that persists in the heavenly liturgy. But, as long as some of His members are still in the militant state, our Pontiff in heaven does not stop interceding for us. Through the Divine Office the Church imitates and extends on earth this priestly action, essentially one of praise and also at the present time one of propitiation and impetration, which Jesus Christ is exercising in glory.

The actualization of the priesthood of Jesus Christ, brought about by the liturgy, is the basis of the latreutic and sanctifying efficacy of the rites of the Church's public worship.

[16] *Mediator Dei*, n. 165.

The efficacy *ex opere operato* is explained by the fact that the same Jesus Christ works through those rites which, like the sacrifice and the sacraments, constitute His liturgy and are a continuation of His personal action. "This occurs at the consecration where in the very act of transubstantiation, accomplished by the Lord, the priest who celebrates is 'putting on the person of Christ.' . . . In truth the action of the consecrating priest is the very action of Christ, who acts by His minister."[17] The action of this minister is required only to prepare materially the elements which constitute the sacramental sign and which are capable of renewing the presence of Christ and of His power, and by his ministerial intention to unite that material action with the action of Christ, who continues to be the principal cause of the sacraments. The sacraments, therefore, are not the work of man but of Jesus Christ, and from Him they receive their ever-operative power, which flows spontaneously and obtains its effect infallibly if the one who is to receive the sacraments does not thwart the effect by placing a moral obstacle in its way.

The sacramentals, on the other hand, do not have the efficacy of a divine action, as do the sacraments. They do not constitute the liturgy of Jesus Christ, but that of His mystical Body, from which they derive an efficacy similar to that of the sacraments. The sacramental theology of the last few centuries, preoccupied with the conditions for the validity of the sacraments and limiting itself to the consideration of their essential elements, has contributed no little to lessening the appreciation of the sacramentals and of liturgical action in general.

As we know, we can distinguish two classes of sacramentals: those which accompany the use of the sacraments; and those which, independently of the sacraments, effect sanctification by virtue of the action of the Church.

While always respecting the essential content of the sacraments, the Church as their administrator has gradually come to clothe them and accompany them with venerable rites, until she has built up around them a liturgy extremely rich in content and in form. By these rites, which at the same time bring out the dignity, the symbolism and the content of the sacraments and instruct and dispose the faithful for their worthy reception, the Church's sanctifying action prepares for and cooperates in the production of the effect of the sacraments, to the point of forming a single action with them.[18]

---

[17] Allocution of Pope Pius XII to the Congress of Pastoral Liturgy, *The Assisi Papers,* p. 229.

[18] "Actions which are aimed at certain proper and determinate effects are distinguished according to the number of their effects. . . . But if they are aimed at one effect, so that one will cause a disposition or remove an obstacle, another will perfect, and another will adorn that which is perfected, *the whole is considered one integral action,* as is evident in the works of craftsmen. Hence, since the sacraments are certain hierarchical actions, according to Dionysius, aimed at effects that have to do with salvation, when several sacramental actions are aimed at one effect, one as achieving, another as disposing, or removing an obstacle, or adorning in some way, then the notion of sacrament is found essentially in that one which brings about the principal effect, while the rest are not called sacraments of themselves, but *sacramentals,* as being accessory to the sacraments." St. Thomas, *IV Sent.,* d. 7, q. 1, a. 1, ql. 1 c.

The other sacramentals are rites by which the Church extends her ritual action beyond the administration of the sacraments, while imitating their structure as signs and as instruments. By means of these sacramentals the Church draws down the blessing of God upon the faithful, and also upon certain material objects in behalf of those who use them in a spirit of faith and devotion.

Both kinds of sacramentals produce *ex opere operantis Ecclesiae* the effects which they signify outwardly. In other words, what is said of the sacraments with respect to Christ's priestly action is to be applied to the sacramentals in relation to the ministerial action of the Church, who works through them in as much as she is the depositary and the administrator of our Lord's merits and His priestly power. The efficacy of the sacramentals is based, therefore, on the union that exists between Jesus Christ and the Church, and on the decree by which He made her the administrator of His priesthood, the power of which is made present by the action and the prayer of the Church.

The ultimate consequence to which we are led by this liturgical law we are analyzing is that, as in every living organism, the Body can grow only in the measure in which it possesses and assimilates the vital action of the Head. For this reason, the growth of the mystical Body is linked in the first place to the liturgy, which makes present in a sacramental way Jesus Christ, His mystery and His priesthood, and thus transmits the vital influence of the Head directly and effectively to the members and confers on them the maximum power of assimilation.

The outward forms of the liturgy show the influence of this essential character. In almost all its prayers—the exceptions are very few—the liturgy addresses the Father through Jesus Christ; in all its rites it invokes in some way the mediation of the Lord, the efficacy of His Passion and of His mystery; every infusion of grace, every invocation of the divine favor, and every imprecation against the power of evil, is sealed by the liturgy with the sign of the cross, which has become the normal sign of every blessing. The cross of Christ presides over all places and objects connected with worship.

The altar of the sacrifice occupies the pre-eminent and worthiest place in the church, where everything is built and arranged with the altar in mind. The Church has composed one of her most beautiful rites for the consecration of the altar; she covers it with cloths, adorns it with flowers, envelops it with incense, honors it with signs of reverence, shows her devotion to it with the frequent kissing of the altar which she prescribes in the rubrics; so that the cross and the altar, by their immediate relation to the sacrifice of Christ, are the two great devotions of the liturgy, after the Eucharist. For this reason the Pope stated that the altar, because of the sacrifice offered on it, is more important than the tabernacle, in which there is the permanent presence of the Lord but not a permanent sacrifice.[19]

[19] *The Assisi Papers*, p. 233.

The theological depth of the christology of the liturgy can be seen also in the name with which the liturgy usually designates Jesus Christ. For the liturgy He is above all the Lord, the *Dominus* of scriptural and patristic tradition. This is the name which best expresses the character of our relations with Christ. Without detracting from the loving intimacy of His presence, it always keeps the sense of profound reverence and adoration which we owe to the Only-begotten of the Father. As Head of the Church, as Author of our redemption, as high Priest of our worship, He is entitled in the first place to our respect and veneration. And these are precisely the aspects under which the liturgy refers to Jesus Christ.

The liturgy does not exclude tender outpourings of ardent love at certain times, as for example in many of the responsories for feasts of our Lord. But even then it maintains a humble attitude of loving reverence, far removed from the more familiar forms of address prompted by a sentimental piety. It would be hard to find expressions more ardent and more tender than those which the liturgy addresses to the Lord during Advent or on the feasts of the Nativity and the Ascension. Only an enlightened contemplation of the mystery and an intense mystical life can have produced many of these texts. But the greater the love is, the greater also is the reverence; for charity in the liturgy is the fruit of an objective contemplation of the mystery in all its wholeness and depth.

Thus, for example, when the liturgy celebrates Christmas, it does not ignore the more human and tangible aspect, which is usually as far as popular piety goes: it enters into a pleasant dialogue with the shepherds and expresses amazement that animals should see the newborn Lord lying in a manger. But paramount over all other considerations in the texts of the Masses and of the Office is the theological depth of *the mystery of the Word made flesh*. Here is how a responsory of Christmas day describes that feast: "The true God, the Only-begotten of the Father, has come down from heaven; He has entered the Virgin's womb, that He may make Himself visible to us, putting on the human flesh that has come down to us from our first father; and He has come out through a closed door, God and Man, Light and Life, Creator of the world."[20]

3. Communitarian Character of the Liturgy

Since the liturgy is the worship that proceeds from the mystical Body of Christ, it can also be called the worship of the Christian community. The different members of this body, though united organically in tending to a common end, still have their own personalities, their individual lives and destinies and their particular relations with God.

[20] *Descendit de caelis Deus verus, a Patre genitus, introivit in uterum Virginis, nobis ut appareret visibilis, indutus carne humana protoparente edita: Et exivit per portam clausam Deus et homo, lux et vita, conditor mundi.* Monastic Breviary, 4th responsory of the 1st nocturn.

Every Christian on his own account may pray and worship God. Many Christians may even gather together to perform an act of piety in common: recite the rosary, make the way of the cross, etc. But these religious exercises are not liturgical acts, even if they be conducted in church with a priest presiding. They will always be acts of private piety, despite the collective form they may take on. The worship that these Christians render to God is the worship of one or more members, but not the worship of the whole Body.

The liturgy is the public worship of the whole mystical Body. Even when its celebration is entrusted to a particular individual and is carried out in a private way—as in the case of a priest who recites the Divine Office privately —the liturgical act will not cease to be a public act and to constitute a religious act of the whole mystical Body, represented *officially* by that member. Where a liturgical act is celebrated, there the whole mystical Body is present, the whole Christian community. Where there is not official representation of the whole Church, there cannot be a liturgical celebration.

This throws light on two new essential aspects of liturgical worship; it is: 1) the worship of the whole Christian community, 2) represented officially. The liturgy, therefore, by reason of the subject who performs it, has a communitarian character and a hierarchical character. Let us now examine the first of these.

The communitarian character of the liturgy answers to the natural need of a social worship. We may say that in a remote sense it is based on that need. But we find its proximate reason for being in the positive will of God. As Creator of nature, God made man social; as Author of the supernatural economy, He chose to give His relations with men a collective character, which diminishes in no way the spiritual personality and the moral responsibility of the individual, but rather qualifies them, introducing them into the divine plan of salvation in community and ordaining them to the Church's structure and her destiny.

The will of God is made explicitly manifest in the sacred Scripture, and particularly in the story of His relations with mankind.

It is manifested already in the first man, who was appointed head of the human race by God, not only because the whole human race was to descend from him, but because in him we were all represented in the trial, which was to be a trial not of the personal loyalty of Adam but of the loyalty of mankind, all associated, in Adam, in the sin of the first man. And because in Adam we all sinned, in him also we received the announcement of a redemption which would have a communitarian character, just as the trial and the fall had had.

For the realization of His redemptive plan, God chose a people, to whom He gave a law and made promises. Salvation was to come from the fulfilment of the promises on God's part and from submission to the law on man's part. All this, however, was tied in with the fact of a man's forming part of the chosen people; and to this end God instituted a rite, a sacrament of the Old Law, circumcision, which realized and signified outwardly the integration into the people of God.

But this complexus of realities was only a figure. The perfect fulness of the divine promises was fulfilled in Jesus Christ, who, according to an expression of St. Paul, "gave Himself for us that He might cleanse for Himself an acceptable people" (Tit. 2:14); that people which, according to the words of St. Peter, is "a chosen race, a royal priesthood, a holy nation, a purchased people," and consists of us, "who in times past were not a people, but are now the people of God" (1 Pet. 2:9-10).

This will of God, which has determined His relations with mankind and has given them a communitarian aspect, determines, as a result, the character of our relations with Him. Hence the liturgy will have to be communitarian by a twofold title; for in actuating the mystery of Christ it continues the divine communications and carries through our return to God. In the liturgy everything is related to the community and everything tends to the perfection of the community. The individual can be a minister of the liturgical action only in so far as the Church associates herself with his acts and confers a collective value on them. And when the individual is the immediate object of the liturgical action, as he is in the sacramental rites, the liturgy itself makes orientation to the community an essential quality of the very sanctification it confers on him.

We are children of the liturgy, and we cannot help bearing its image impressed in our spirit and our life. By the liturgy's sacramental action our birth to the divine life is at the same time an incorporation into the Christian community. And our insertion into the community is so profound that it determines our spiritual physiognomy, our concrete vocation in time and the degree of our final glorification in eternity. In every organism, each member receives its own entity and its characteristic notes according to the place it is to occupy in the body and according to the specific function that belongs to it in relation to the whole, just as, for example, in a mosaic every little piece is chosen by the artist according to the color and the form corresponding to the place in which it is to be put within the whole design.

Our personal holiness, according to God's plan, is ordained to the total perfection of the mystical Body: it is to be the concrete revelation of one facet of the mystery of the Lord. The Christian life that we lead, then, is not aimed solely at individual perfection, but at contributing to the definitive perfection of the Church, to the beauty of the Body of Christ. This explains the reason for that mystery which St. Paul hints at: that "to each one of us grace was given according to the measure of Christ's bestowal . . . for building up the Body of Christ" (Eph. 4:7, 12).

This measure is limited for each one; with it each Christian realizes only a partial aspect of the total sanctity of the Church. But this partial perfection has been preordained by God as a part which has its place in the perfect harmony of the whole. The total perfection of the mystery of Christ can be achieved only by the combined contribution of the Christian community. Only the Church, considered as mystical Body or as people of God, constitutes the *pleroma,* the fulness of the mystery of Christ.

The liturgy is supposed to be preparing in time this fulness which will be achieved in eternity. For this reason the structure of the liturgy is essentially communitarian and has its center in the Eucharist, which is really the sacrament of community.

In the Eucharist the organic unity of the members is most real, because they are united sacramentally to the Head, who gives them life and coordinates them in the unity of one and the same Spirit. Hence the Eucharist is typically called *communion,* and through it the other sacraments receive their ecclesiastical character. Even outwardly, the celebration of the Eucharist manifests its communitarian character in the collaboration of all the members to perform the common act of worship. Some read; some sing after another has intoned; some offer their gifts; others prepare the gifts that have been offered and place them on the altar; the celebrant consecrates; the faithful communicate; and in the variety of offices and actions the unity of the liturgical action shines forth wonderfully.

We could say the same of the Divine Office celebrated in choir, and of the administration of the sacraments or of the sacramentals with the collaboration and the concurrence of clergy and faithful, as required by the various liturgical rites.

Very meaningful also, in the Mass, is the rite of the kiss of peace, which obliges us to re-establish and strengthen the bonds of charity that unite us to the community before being united sacramentally with the Lord.

The same communitarian sense pervades all the formulas of the Mass and the various prayers of the liturgy. In all of them the subject is in the plural, even when the request is for an individual grace, because in all cases it is the community that turns to God, almost always to state to Him the desires or the needs of the Christian people.

The rules that govern ecclesiastical chant are based on this law: the chant of the liturgy must be the chant of the community, which does not permit the personal effulgence of any soloists, unless they have received with the public office of chanter the official mission of representing the whole Church in the loftiest expression of her sentiments before God.

When individualism became prevalent and even crept into the Church's public worship, many rites lost their meaning, having been deprived of the communitarian spirit that animated them, while on the other hand certain deviations toward the predominance of the individual over the community were being introduced into the liturgy and were sowing the seed of its decadence.

Thus, for example, the rubric that obliges the celebrant to recite for himself the texts which one of the sacred ministers is reading or which the choir is singing, gives evidence of a scrupulous preoccupation with celebrating the entire Mass individually, prescinding from what the other ministers are doing, and destroying the unity of the liturgical action. Thanks be to God, the new liturgical rites recently reformed and promulgated by Pius XII—harking back to their original purity and their communitarian spirit—have removed these anomalies.

We might point out other anomalies, some of which have already been indicated by the Pope in his encyclical *Mediator Dei* or by the new rules emanating from the Sacred Congregation of Rites.

We would indicate, for example, the practice of distributing or receiving communion without taking account of the collective act of the Mass, so that many Christians have come to think of communion as an act of mere individual devotion. Hence also has come the equivocal expression of *offering communion* for some particular intention. Properly speaking, communion is not offered; it is received as participation in the sacrifice which has been offered.

And even among the faithful who follow the Mass with their missals, it is quite a common practice to close the missal in order to prepare for communion or to make one's thanksgiving, thus separating oneself from the common prayer of the Church to shut oneself up in a devout individualism, precisely in connection with the sacrament of ecclesiastical unity. In the encyclical *Mediator Dei* the Pope recommends a thanksgiving after communion—we shall treat of this later—but mentions twice that this private prayer should be said when the Mass is over, not immediately after receiving communion, when the better prayer continues to be that of uniting ourselves to the public thanksgiving of the Church. Here are the Pope's words: "When the Mass, which is subject to special rules of the liturgy, is over, the person who has received holy communion is not thereby freed from his duty of thanksgiving; rather, it is most becoming that, *when the Mass is finished,* the person who has received the Eucharist should recollect himself . . . ."[21]

We might mention also, as contrary to the communitarian character of the liturgy, the multiplication or the habitual celebration of votive Masses or Requiem Masses for purely personal reasons, without regard for the sense of the Church's common prayer on the particular day. The mind of the Church on this point can be seen clearly from the recently simplified rubrics, which expressly forbid the daily Mass of the dead on the days left free by the suppression of the privileged octaves. Here the words of Cardinal Lercaro at the opening of the seventh Italian Week of Liturgical Studies, held at Oropa, are significant: "And the attentive reader of the decree has not failed to notice the check put upon the invasion of votive Masses, above all of the

---

[21] *Mediator Dei*, n. 123.

Requiem Masses; a check which must have been hoped for by every soul hungry for the spiritual food which the liturgy offers every day in its formularies, and desirous especially of living the mystery of Christ in the liturgical cycle."[22]

Very significant also is the provision of the decree *Maxima redemptionis nostrae mysteria* for the reform of Holy Week, which recognizes officially a new way of reciting the Divine Office which is not choral recitation or private recitation but recitation *in common—in communi*—and is equivalent in practice to choral recitation. By this regulation the Church wants to make it easy for those priests who do not have the obligation of choir to gather together for the common recitation of the Divine Office, sharing in the same ritual privileges that are attached to the choral recitation. This provision indicates well enough what is the mind of the Church: to foster in so far as possible, even in the outward celebration, the communitarian character of the liturgy.

Another important provision which points up this orientation of the Church is found in the instruction attached to the aforesaid decree: the permission to celebrate low Masses in the afternoon or evening of Holy Thursday. The only reason which justifies this provision according to the instruction is a pastoral motive of a communitarian nature, not the personal devotion of the celebrant.[23]

The point is not that the communitarian sense of the liturgy disagrees with personal devotion; rather, it regulates personal devotion according to a just measure and moderates its indiscreet or excessive manifestations. We have stated this and we shall insist on it again: the liturgical community does not presume to nullify the individual, nor does it want to take away anything of his personality. On the contrary, it augments and elevates his personality, because it ordains his individual good to a higher common good.

The Christian who duly appreciates the communitarian sense of the liturgy does not consider himself dispensed from the individual activity of his spirit, dispensed from turning to God and from living the Christian life in practice; but he knows how to find the perfect complement of this personal activity in collaboration with other Christians, so as to form all together the social act of public worship, objectively superior in being and perfection to any religious act whatsoever of an individual nature.

These notions are quite simple and obvious; but during the centuries of decadence of the liturgical spirit they were obscured and almost lost, so that today they appear to many as new ideas. They are hard for these people to conceive accurately, their minds being influenced as they are by other ideas that have to be dislodged because they unduly occupied the place of the correct notions. The result may easily be that these people will give these

[22] Discourse published in *Rivista Liturgica*, 1955, p. 192.

[23] *Ordo Hebdomadae Sanctae Instauratus:* decree, II, 5; instruction, III, 17.

notions a value that does not belong to them: either they will receive them reluctantly and look askance at them because the ideas seem to them erroneous or exaggerated, or on the other hand they welcome them so gladly that they attribute to these ideas an import broader than they are meant to have, and make them something which they are not. Hence the Holy See must be very insistent in bringing back into line those who fall short on the one side and those who exceed on the other. But in this way light is shed, and the true meaning of the concepts related to the liturgy stands out ever more clearly.

Pope Pius XII took a particular interest in describing precisely, on various occasions, the communitarian sense of the essential act of liturgical worship, the holy Mass. And since the errors or the conceptual inaccuracies in this matter are usually manifested in practice and in concrete deeds, the Holy Father spoke of concrete facts so as to clarify the theologico-liturgical doctrine. It is worth our while to try to gather together the principal concepts of this doctrine.

First of all we must take into account the fact that, when we speak of the communitarian sense of a liturgical action, we may be referring to its entity as worship together with the public and official representation which that entity presupposes, or we may be referring to the concrete form in which this act of worship is actually being celebrated. By definition, every liturgical act has intrinsically a public, social and collective character, because it is an act celebrated officially in the name of the whole Church. But in its concrete celebration it may take on a collective form or a private form, according to whether the community of the faithful actually take part in it or whether they are not physically present.

We must distinguish also between those acts which the priest performs formally as a priest and which are therefore properly his own in so far as he is an official minister of public worship, and have always a collective value by reason of that which he represents, and those other acts of worship which the priest performs, not precisely as a priest, but in as much as he is a Christian and forms part of the faithful people.

Taking account of these distinctions and applying them concretely to the celebration of holy Mass, we shall see that every priest who celebrates a Mass, whether he does it solemnly and with a great concourse of the faithful taking an active part in it, or whether he celebrates privately and without a congregation, is performing an act of public and collective worship because, in any case, he is renewing the sacrifice of Christ, who offers Himself in the name of the whole Church whenever He offers Himself to the Father.

On the other hand, if a priest simply assists at Mass, he is not performing the sacrificial action proper and exclusive to the priest, but is limiting himself to participating actively in the offering of the sacrifice just as one of the faithful.

If we confine ourselves solely, therefore, to the priestly and representative value of the action of the priest in celebrating the Mass, and compare it with that of the priest merely assisting at Mass, even if he receives communion, we shall obviously have to conclude that the first action surpasses the second, just as the action of Christ in offering His sacrifice surpasses the action of the Christians admitted to participation in it. This is the concept expressed so many times by the Pope with the incisive statement that the celebration of one Mass at which a hundred priests assist devoutly is not equivalent to a hundred Masses celebrated by a hundred priests.

These notions of ours would be incomplete, however, if we did not take into account another aspect of Christ's sacrifice. It is this: Jesus Christ not only offers Himself to the Father as Head of the Church, but also unites with Himself His whole mystical Body; so that, as we explain in another place, the Mass is the sacrifice of the whole Church, in as much as the Church forms a single reality with its Head. Hence St. Thomas can state that, if the *res et sacramentum* of the Eucharist is the physical Christ, the *res tantum* of this sacrament is the mystical Christ, so that the Eucharist of itself is the sacramental sign of ecclesiastical unity.[24]

In as much as it is Christ's personal sacrifice, the Mass is always most perfect in its being, in its value as sign and in its realization, because it always makes present in a real and actual way the sacrificial action of Jesus Christ, and it always achieves what it signifies, namely the immolation of Christ, which took place as an absolute sacrifice on the cross. On the other hand, there is not always the same perfection in the realization of the role that belongs to the Church in offering the sacrifice of the mystical Body, nor in the demonstrative value of the Eucharist as a sign of ecclesiastical unity.

For, although it is true that every time a Mass is celebrated, Jesus Christ unites the whole Church to His sacrifice, still the members of the Church do not always assent consciously and actually to this oblation which Christ makes in the name of all of them. It follows that the realization of the sacrifice in the part that belongs to the Church is susceptible to greater or lesser perfection, according as the actual union of the Christians to the sacrifice of Jesus Christ is more or less real and conscious. Hence we can say that whatever contributes toward effecting the active participation of the ecclesiastical community in the holy Mass increases the integral perfection of the sacrifice of the total Christ.

Moreover, the character of the Eucharist as sign requires that the ecclesiastical unity signified have the most perfect reality possible, precisely because of the Eucharist. For this reason also, the sacrifice of the Mass acquires a greater perfection when it unites the community of the Christians who form the Church, not only by their simultaneous material presence in time at the hour of the sacrifice, but above all by the fusion of their spirits and wills

[24] St. Thomas, *Summa theol.*, III, 67, 2; 73, 3, 4, 6; 80, 4.

with the mind of the Church and thereby with Jesus Christ, who is uniting us to His sacrifice.

This signification of ecclesiastical unity by the Eucharist, and also the reality of our active, conscious and willing participation in Christ's sacrifice, are so important that they can influence, and do in fact influence, the order of things in the rite of the Mass and the provisions for the outward form of its celebration.

Actually Christ has left it up to the Church to arrange the celebration of His sacrifice. In doing so, the Church takes account of the nature of this sacrifice, the elements that go to make it up, its purpose, its value as sign, as well as the nature of the men for whom the sacrifice of the cross is renewed on earth throughout the centuries.

For a due appreciation of the whole value of the Mass and an equitable determintaion of the laws that are to regulate its celebration, all these elements must be taken into account, as in fact they are taken into consideration by the Church.

If we were to pay attention only to the entitative value of the priestly act of sacrifice, we should obviously have to conclude that it is incomparably better to celebrate the Mass than to limit oneself to assisting at it. Again, if we were to confine ourselves to the value of the Mass or of Eucharistic communion as worship or as sanctification, we should have to desire the greatest frequency for it, to the point of celebrating the Mass many times a day or receiving communion as many times as possible.

But the Church knows that Jesus Christ has willed His sacrifice to be renewed throughout the centuries not because of the entitative value of the sacrifice, which, being infinite, transcends space and time and is not increased by repetition, but rather to adapt the application of its fruits to our limited and "successive" or "step-by-step" way of being. Hence, when she had to determine the frequency of the Eucharist, the Church based her decision above all on the details of human life. Now by reason of the succession of day and night, of work and sleep, all of man's individual and social activities are renewed and recommenced in the space of time that we call a day. Consequently, the Church has decided that our worship also should be renewed every day with the celebration of holy Mass and that, just as we must daily procure our material bread, so also the reception of the Eucharistic food would be a daily act.

Any further multiplication would imply a failure to recognize that Jesus Christ has chosen to give His sacraments a human quality by synchronizing them with the rhythm of man's life, and a failure to take into account our limited capacity for assimilation, which of itself sets bounds to the quantity of food that can be taken to advantage.

Yet the Church does not hesitate to modify the general rules on the celebration and reception of the Eucharist whenever the particular application of one of its fruits makes a change necessary or expedient, and whenever she wants to bring out some one of the realities signified by the Eucharist.

Thus, to emphasize one of the aspects and especially to reap one of the fruits, the Church permits communion to be administered again, as viaticum, to one who had communicated that same day, before taking sick or being injured. Likewise, for reasons of an historical-symbolic nature, which have now become a very clear manifestation of the threefold aspect of one mystery, she permits each priest to celebrate three Masses on Christmas day. And she does the same on All Souls' Day to bring out more effectively the communion of love that unites the Church on earth with the Church suffering in purgatory. And we might also mention the bination and trination of Masses in places where there are not enough priests to give due attention to the needs of the faithful without these measures.

What the Church never does is to allow greater frequency in the use of the Eucharist for reasons of personal devotion; that is why the Council of Trent uprooted the abuses on this point which "devotionism" had introduced into the celebration of the Mass.

On the contrary, with the aim of bringing out the eminently communitarian and hierarchical sense of the Mass, the Church sometimes forbids the individual priests to celebrate. Thus she decrees that on Holy Thursday and Holy Saturday there be only one Mass in each church and the other priests do not celebrate, so that they may join the faithful in assisting at the Mass and may communicate at this community Mass.

Thus on the day on which the institution of the Mass and of the priesthood is commemorated, the Church wants to see all considerations of an individual nature superseded by the ecclesiastical idea of the unity of the mystical Body in subjection to the hierarchy and in dependence on the Lord's Eucharist, and she wants this concept of unity and of community to be manifested outwardly also, by a single sacrifice, a single hierarchical head, a single assembly of the faithful, a single communion.

And on Good Friday, to signify still more visibly the identity of the sacrifice of Jesus Christ on the cross and on the altar, she suppresses the celebration of the Mass, while she accentuates and makes present mystically the historical act of the sacrifice of the cross by the solemn chanting of the gospel text of the Passion, and desires the whole Christian community, priests and people, to take part in it spiritually by the adoration of the cross and sacramentally by the Eucharistic communion.

Outside of these dates established in the liturgical calendar, there may be times when incidental reasons warrant a modification of the Church's general rules. It is up to the Church to determine when these times are.

This is what Pius XII did when he declared that on the occasion of liturgical congresses it is quite acceptable to have only one of the priests celebrate the Mass, with the other priests attending and receiving communion from the celebrant.[25] If all the priests celebrated their individual Masses on these occasions, the great number of those so celebrating would obviously entail improvisation of a great number of altars which might be lacking in reverence, and undue haste in the successive celebrations at each altar. The reverence that should surround the act of sacrifice indicates abstention from celebrations which could not have the proper outward dignity, while the assistance of those attending the congress at a community Mass increases its splendor as an act of worship and puts more emphasis on its ecclesiastical meaning. On the other hand, there is no reason to fear that this procedure would do any harm spiritually to the priests; for they will know how to appreciate in due measure the communitarian aspect of the Mass and the spiritual fruits of an intense active participation, without slighting or underestimating the sacrificial and public value of private Masses.

The solution may be better for those of the Eastern rites, since the practice of concelebration is habitual among them. Concelebration obviates the inconveniences of a great number of private Masses lacking that outward perfection which would accrue to them from the realization of their communitarian meaning, and it enables the priests to perform the specifically priestly act of consecrating the Eucharist and offering the sacrifice to the Lord. In these concelebrated Masses each one of the concelebrating priests performs fully the priestly action of Jesus Christ, who, as the Pope said,[26] instead of acting through only one minister, acts through many priests simultaneously.

In concelebrations it is possible also to observe more clearly the ecclesiastical character of the hierarchy which forms a college—the priestly college—around the bishop or the hierarchical head who presides over the whole action and carries out its external solemnity, while the assistance of the faithful makes the communitarian sense of the liturgical action more vivid and real.

4. Hierarchical Character of the Liturgy

The Church, the community, is not a mere aggregation of individuals; it is an organic and organized body. This supposes a coordination and even a subordination among the various functions of the different organs. That is to say, there must be a gradation among the many members, determined by the different functions to be performed in attaining the common end.

Be it noted that this gradation or hierarchy does not primarily establish the members in a greater or lesser dignity, but first of all assigns them an office, a mission to be fulfilled. The social importance of this mission will determine the dignity of the one who is to perform it. Thus it is not the personal rank but the office in relation to the community that establishes the various degrees of the hierarchy.

[25] Allocution of Pope Pius XII to the college of cardinals and to the bishops on the occasion of the proclamation of the feast of the Queenship of Mary; *A.A.S.*, 1954, p. 670.

[26] *The Assisi Papers*, p. 229.

For a correct concept of the hierarchy, it is very important to be precise about its essential communitarian purpose. This precision has special importance in the field of action of the liturgy, in which the hierarchical degrees are often called *servitus,* and the exercise of the hierarchical power is called *servitium,* and those who rank high in dignity receive the name of *servi.*

To determine more exactly the place occupied by the hierarchy in the community of the Church, it helps to distinguish two aspects under which ecclesiastical unity is realized. They are: community of life; community of means for obtaining and maintaining this life.

The community of life proceeds from the communion (common union) with God through Christ in the unity of the mystical Body. It is the life of grace, which God communicates to souls and which, begun in this life, will enjoy a perfect existence in the next.

The other basis of ecclesiastical unity is the community of means for arriving at the life of grace and for maintaining it and increasing it. This implies an imperfect state of growth, of subjection to time, of adaptation to our present way of being, and will come to an end when the Church has perfectly attained her end, that is, when she has achieved the fulness of the mystery of Christ in the glory of the Father.

In this community of means we find the ecclesiastical organization with all its institutions: the deposit of faith, the law and the precepts, the sacraments and all the means of worship and of sanctification. It is here that we must locate the hierarchy.

The hierarchy therefore implies in the Christian community a stage of imperfection in the process of formation of the mystical Body of Christ. Like the other institutions in the organization of the Church, the hierarchy is necessary in so far as the Church does not yet possess the divine life with full interiority and definitive perfection; together with everything that has the character of a means, it will cease when God is all in all things.

For the members of the Church living on earth, the fountain of living water does not yet gush spontaneously from their interior: it must be communicated to them from without. Hence arises the necessity of external means to put the soul in contact with God. These are principally the sacraments and the hierarchy. The sacraments are the material instrument of this mediation. The hierarchy, in contact with God through the grace received for this ministry, makes effective application to souls of the instrument which is sacramental causality. This is the proper office of the priest as minister of Jesus Christ.

Actually in applying to the liturgy the foregoing notions on the ecclesiastical hierarchy, we must distinguish between the two forms of worship which the Church possesses: the worship instituted by Jesus Christ and the worship established by the Church herself.

Christ instituted His sacrifice and the sacraments; that is to say, a worship of which He is personally the unique and true priest, but which the Church celebrates in obedience to Christ's command, forming with Him a single subject of the work of worship. We might say that it is the worship whose celebration devolves upon the Church from her Head.

The other kind has its origin in the Body itself of the Church; it is the worship which proceeds from the ecclesiastical community and raises itself to God.

This distinction is found insinuated in the definition of the liturgy given us by Pius XII when he distinguishes between "the public worship which our Redeemer as Head of the Church renders to the Father" and "the worship which the community of the faithful renders to its Founder, and through Him to the heavenly Father."

The hierarchical priesthood is minister of both kinds of worship, but by different titles. It exercises the first kind, to use the expressions of St. Thomas,[27] "in the person of Christ" *(in persona Christi)*; the second, "in the person of the whole Church" *(in persona totius Ecclesiae)*.

As for the worship that comes from on high, namely the worship instituted by Jesus Christ, the priest is nothing but His minister. Christ is the true celebrant; the priest acts in His name and as His representative. That this representation may be real and effective, Christ endows His minister with a configuration to His own priesthood, the priestly character of the sacrament of holy orders, conferred for the exercise of a communitarian function of worship.

Under this essential aspect of his priesthood, the minister of Jesus Christ depends absolutely on Him, not on the community. The exercise of his priesthood is oriented to the community, but he has not received from the community in any way, even by reason of the concept of representation, the hierarchical entity of his priesthood. For the community is not the priest of this worship of Jesus Christ, but only the terminus or object of His sacramental action. It cannot give what it does not have, therefore, nor confer a representation of something which it is not.

Very clear on this point is the teaching of Pius XII in the encyclical *Mediator Dei,* which he himself underscored and summed up before the sacred college of cardinals and the Catholic bishops in his allocution of November 2, 1954. In this doctrine he censures the error of those who "assert that the people are possessed of a true priestly power, while the priest only acts in virtue of an office committed to him by the community. . . ." The priest, because he represents the person of our Lord Jesus Christ, "goes to the altar as the minister of Christ, inferior to Christ but superior to the people. The people, on the other hand, since they in no sense represent the divine Redeemer and are not a mediator between themselves and God, can in no way possess the sacerdotal power."[28]

[27] St. Thomas, *Summa theol.,* III, 82, 5 and 6.

[28] *Mediator Dei,* nn. 83, 84. Allocution of November 2, 1954; *A.A.S.,* 1954, p. 668.

More recently, in the discourse to the Assisi congress of pastoral liturgy, the Pope once more expressed his thinking on this point: "This occurs at the consecration where in the very act of transubstantiation, accomplished by the Lord, the priest who celebrates is 'putting on the person of Christ.' The consecration . . is the central point of the whole liturgy of the sacrifice, the central point of the 'action of Christ whose person is put on by the priest-celebrant' or the 'concelebrating priests,' in the case of true concelebration. . . . In truth the action of the consecrating priest is the very action of Christ, who acts by His minister. In the case of a concelebration in the proper sense of the word, Christ, in place of acting by one minister only, acts by several. . . . That there may be concelebration in the proper sense, it does not suffice to have and to manifest the intention of making one's own the words and actions of the celebrant. The concelebrants themselves must say over the bread and the wine, 'This is My Body,' 'This is My Blood'; otherwise their concelebration is merely 'ceremonial.' "[29]

A different way of speaking is permissible when the concern is with purely ecclesiastical worship, that is, the worship established by the Church, whether to accompany the celebration of the essential rite of the sacrifice or the sacraments, or in the sacramentals instituted by the Church, or again as prayer of the Spouse, that is, to use the very words of the Pope, as "the worship which the community of the faithful renders to its Founder, and through Him to the heavenly Father."

Here the celebrant of this worship is "the community of the faithful," that is, the Christian community in as much as it constitutes a moral person, a subject of rights and of actions. It is the Church, considered rather as Spouse of Jesus Christ than as His Body.[30]

As president of the assembly of the faithful and as representative of the community in the liturgical celebration, the minister of the Church acts in the name of the community, and from it receives his investiture in the hierarchy, though not by delegation of the community but by institution of the Church itself. And, since the Church's liturgy is often united to Christ's to form a single cultual unity, the Church usually confers the highest degrees of its hierarchical representation on the same persons chosen by Christ as ministers of His worship. Thus the sacramental priesthood includes at the same time both the ministry that comes to it from Jesus Christ and that which the Church confers on it.

[29] *The Assisi Papers*, pp. 229-230.

[30] "The word 'Church' is understood in two ways. For sometimes it designates only the Body which is joined to Christ as its Head, and only in this acceptation does the Church have the nature of a bride; and in this context Christ is not a member of the Church, but the Head exerting influence on all the members of the Church. In another way, 'Church' is understood as indicating the head and the members joined . . . . But when the Church is spoken of in this way, 'Church' means not only bride, but bridegroom and bride, as being made one by a spiritual union." St. Thomas, *IV Sent.*, d. 49, q. 4, a. 3 ad 4. Cf. Yves M. J. Congar, O.P., *Lay People in the Church* (Westminster, Md.: Newman Press, 1957), p. 199.

The Church has also established other ministers of purely ecclesiastical worship, to whom she entrusts certain secondary ministries such as public readings, certain services about the altar, the liturgical chant, particular blessings and exorcisms, the custody of the faithful and the keeping of order in the church, etc. Such undoubtedly are the subdiaconate and the minor orders, which have varied in number and in duties with the passage of time. The Church sometimes entrusts the official representation of herself and a part of her public worship to seculars, either in a permanent way, as is the case with the Divine Office for nuns, or in a temporary way, like the fact of being a witness of matrimony in the name of the Church in the absence of the priest, etc.

Every ecclesiastical ministry is based on a title which legitimizes the official representation of the Church in performing this ministry. In the offices entrusted in a stable manner to the laity, the title is based on a juridical fact which confers the corresponding canonical deputation. Thus, in the case cited of the Divine Office entrusted to nuns, the title which gives them the canonical mission of praying officially in the Church's name is the monastic profession.

Ordinarily, however, the representation of the Church in acts of worship carries with it a spiritual principle, which is a grace conferred through a sacramental rite connected with the deputation to the respective liturgical ministry. And since all the acts of worship are ordained to the priestly act of sacrifice, the rites which confer the power to perform these acts of worship are also considered as a participation in the rite through which the priesthood is conferred, namely the sacrament of holy orders; and thus these ministries are also called sacred orders, by extension. Those who are delegated to the various liturgical ministries receive the corresponding ministerial grace through these sacramentals instituted by the Church for this purpose. The dignity of these rites and the grace conferred through them is greater in proportion as the office to which they delegate is closer to the priestly office and more directly ordained to the Eucharistic sacrifice.

Thus the hierarchy of orders is established. Founded on the positive will of Jesus Christ, it ascends from lower ecclesiastical ministries, communicated by a sacramental of the Church, up to the priesthood-sacrament. By the grace of this sacrament the priests receive the greatest ministerial power, that of being "ministers of Christ and dispensers of the mysteries of God" (1 Cor. 4:1), with a twofold sanctifying power, that of consecrating the Eucharist and that of sanctifying souls for that same Eucharist and for the life of the Church.

The power of offering the Eucharistic sacrifice with the consecration of the bread and the wine is the principal and primary power; that of sanctifying men is secondary and subordinate to the first. The first can exist without the second; the second can exist only with a view to the first. The power over the Eucharist is the basis of the reality of the priesthood; the different duties connected with the power of sanctifying the faithful establish the difference between presbyterate and episcopate in the same priesthood.

These two grades of the priesthood are not adequately distinguished from each other, because they coincide in their full power with regard to the Eucharist. As St. Thomas teaches, the episcopate is not superior to the presbyterate or simple priesthood in so far as the relation to the true Body of Christ is concerned.[31] The presbyterate really possesses the power of consecrating and offering the Eucharist, which is the supreme and most divine power, above which there cannot exist any other greater power.

The hierarchical pre-eminence of the bishop over the simple priest proceeds from the fact that it is he who is deputed in a special way to the social function of sanctifying and governing the people of God. This mission gives a particular character to the priesthood of the bishop and constitutes him in a new kind of hierarchy, distinct from the hierarchy of orders based on the power of consecrating the Eucharist. This is the hierarchy of jurisdiction, which endows him with the power of ruling and governing the Christian people with divine authority.

The social aim of the bishop communicates to his priesthood, within the limits of his jurisdiction, a fulness in the exercise of the priestly power which concerns the sanctification of the faithful. Thus, just as the priesthood of the presbyter or priest is wholly centered in the Eucharist, and only secondarily includes the duty of sanctifying men, to dispose them for the worthy reception of the Eucharist, so the priesthood of the bishop accentuates this second aspect, to the point of constituting a specific aim of his rank in the hierarchy, for which reason he receives the full power of acting "in the person of Christ" on the mystical Body.[32] This hierarchical fulness is a mission of fatherhood over the Church, which he is to sanctify and govern.

Hence, within the power of holy orders, those ministries of sanctification which imply fatherhood and fulness are reserved to the bishop.

First of all there is the communication of the priestly grace through the sacrament of holy orders, and the fulness of the Christian life through the sacrament of confirmation. To him alone belongs also the faculty of consecrating and sanctifying everything related to the use and administration of the Eucharist in the ecclesiastical community, as for example the consecration of the holy oils, of a church, of an altar, of the sacred vessels, the blessing of vestments, etc.

As far as the power of jurisdiction is concerned, the bishop has by divine right the faculty and the mission to govern with fulness of powers and as representative of our Lord that portion of the Church which has been entrusted to him, and even the whole Church of Jesus Christ if he is the

---

[31] St. Thomas, *Summa theol., suppl.,* 29, 6 ad 1; 40, 4 and 5.   [32] St. Thomas, *Summa theol.,* III, 82, 1 ad 4.

bishop of Rome, the pope, who holds the highest place in the hierarchy of jurisdiction.

With the union of the two powers, that of holy orders without reservation and that of jurisdiction, the bishop is visible head and spiritual superior of his Church. He is "like a prince in the Church, like a prince of the whole ecclesiastical order," writes St. Thomas.[33]

The priest, on the other hand, although he is equal to the bishop in the possession of full power over the Eucharistic body of our Lord, with the consequent secondary power of sanctification, lacks the power of jurisdiction. This can be conferred on him only by the Church as participation in the episcopal or papal jurisdiction. And even the sanctifying power received with the priestly character, in so far as it refers to the sanctification of the faithful, is his only in potency, in an imperfect and incomplete way.[34] For the Church retains some of these powers of sanctification and reserves them to the bishops; and she conditions the exercise of others upon a further deputation by the bishop, who directs them concretely to the good of the faithful. In this way the priest is granted a participation in the hierarchical mission of the bishop, superior and head of the Christian community.

The bishop is head of the Christian community by the fulness of the sanctifying power for the sanctification of the faithful; he is its superior by his mssion of governing. In virtue of this last title, the bishop's principal office is that of directing the people of God to their supernatural end and effectively promoting the common good of Christian society. The bishop must determine and regulate the use of the forms of liturgical worship, orient and stimulate the manifestations of the religious life of his people, be vigilant to preserve the deposit of faith, enlighten with the light of revelation the souls of the faithful, and further the application of Christian principles in all the manifestations of human activity within the territory of his jurisdiction. To this end he is possessed of the necessary legislative, judicial and coercive powers.

By reason of his being a head, which is the formal constituent element of every society, by reason of his hierarchical power as superior and by reason of the fulness of his powers—all this having been received from Jesus Christ and being exercised in His name—the bishop is the nucleus around which is formed a Church in miniature, the diocese, which realizes in a limited and particular extension everything that is predicated of the universal Church, mystical Body of Christ. The bishop is Christ's immediate representative among the faithful; he is the Christ of his diocese.

The bishop, who forms with his diocesan clergy and people a unity of organized Christian life, is the living and complete representation of the mystery of the Church. His church, the cathedral, is the visible symbol of

---

[33] "Est quasi princeps in Ecclesia, quasi princeps totius ecclesiastici ordinis." St. Thomas, *Summa theol.*, III, 65, 3 ad 2; 82, 1 ad 4.
[34] St. Thomas, *Summa theol., suppl.*, 40, 4.

this ecclesiastical unity in Christ. We need only recall the beautiful expressions repeated every year by the liturgy on the anniversary of its dedication. Its altar, its baptistry, its *cathedra,* its choir, are the compendium and the expression of the Church's liturgical life.

The cathedral sums up the whole life of the bishop and of the Christian community gathered around him. This building, which in the course of the centuries has sheltered so many generations of faithful and of shepherds, and has been witness of the most sublime acts—individual and social—of the religious life of the diocese, is a powerful reminder of the constant presence of Christ in the diocese and a sign of the communion of the faithful among one another and of their union with Christ.

The cathedral, according to the mind of the Church and the spirit of the liturgy, is, and should be in practice, the splendid center of the Christian life and the liturgical activity of the diocese, while all the other churches are an extension and a limited imitation of the religious and cultual intensity of the cathedral.

Above the bishop there is only the pope, who holds the highest place in the ecclesiastical hierarchy, since his episcopal powers of priesthood and of jurisdiction are not limited to the territory of his diocese of Rome, but extend to the whole word, uniting under his shepherd's crook all the faithful, all the priests and all the bishops, and thus giving unity to the whole Church of Christ. To the pope belongs in an absolute and universal way whatever is ascribed to the bishop with regard to the spiritual and hierarchical rule of his diocese. Hence the pope is the vicar of Christ, the visible head of the mystical Body, the supreme ruler of the Church.

This hierarchical organization, essential to the Church, is marvelously reflected in the liturgy and exerts a powerful influence on its makeup. Without priesthood we would not have the Eucharist; without a bishop there would be no Church; without the pope, the unity and universality of the mystical Body of Christ would not exist.

It is impossible to conceive of the liturgy except as an ordered hierarchical action which, through the various ministries proper to each step, from the vestibule of the church to the altar, brings the faithful to the Eucharist, to unite them all in Christ in the unity of the Christian family. The union of the Christians with the pope, through the union with their own bishop, establishes the union of the Church with Jesus Christ. No one can reach Him except through the hierarchy; so that whoever separates himself from the hierarchy no longer forms part of the Church and separates himself from Christ.

Hence, before putting us into sacramental contact with our Lord in the Mass, the liturgy reaffirms our communion with the hierarchy; and as a sign of this communion the canon of the Mass has us pronounce the name of the pope and that of the bishop, through whom we form a single praying family, with all the orthodox and those who profess the same faith, the universal faith which proceeds from the Apostles: *catholicae et apostolicae fidei cultoribus.* The rite of the breaking of the host is nothing but a reminiscence of the *sacrum fermentum,* which was at the same time a symbol of the unity of the sacrifice celebrated in all the churches and a sign of communion with the hierarchy.

The two characteristics of the liturgy which have been set forth up to this point—community and hierarchy—are inseparable. They complement and support each other as the material and the formal element of a single organism. Pope Pius XII said, "The contributions which the hierarchy and the faithful bring to the liturgy are not added as two separate entities, but represent the collaboration of members of the same organism which acts as a single living unit."[35] The community would not form a body, a Church, if the hierarchical element did not specify it and confer supernatural unity and vitality on it. Nor would the hierarchy have any reason for being, without its intrinsic ordination to a mission to be fulfilled within the community.

The liturgy always brings out this hierarchical quality, just as it always presupposes the communitarian character. Only the pope, for the whole Church, and the bishops, for their respective dioceses and within certain limits, can legislate on liturgical matters. Liturgical acts must always be presided over and directed by an official minister of the hierarchy. In her places of worship the Church assigns the sacred ministers a post of honor next to the altar, and distinguishes among them also the different degrees of the ecclesiastical hierarchy, assigning to each one the seat that befits his rank: the throne or the *cathedra,* the chairs of the choir, or mere stools. Each order has its appropriate vestments, its own honors and its own duties in the liturgical service.

The liturgy is fond of mutual signs of respect, governed by an orderly recognition of dignity and function. Mutual respect and reverence to the hierarchy constitute one of the most solid foundations of liturgical ceremonial. The majority of the ceremonies have no meaning if they are not informed by this spirit.

For the liturgy, there is always a great distance between the hierarchy and the people, despite the intimate compenetration it establishes between the two. Even in addressing God it does not forget this distinction of classes, which is founded not on dignity but on service of God and community. "Hanc igitur oblationem *servitutis nostrae* sed et *cunctae familiae tuae*" says the priest before the consecration, as he designates the common Victim by the laying-on of hands. And after the consecration he makes the same affirmation of a hierarchy again: "Unde et memores, Domine, *nos servi tui* sed et *plebs tua sancta.*"

But, granted the validity of this distinction, the fact remains that the

[35] *The Assisi Papers,* p. 226.

hierarchy is *for* the community. Both together form the Church and are the proper subject of liturgical action. This was clearly expressed by Pius XII: "The liturgy is a vital function of the Church as a whole. . . . To this unique liturgy, each of the members, whether invested with episcopal power or belonging to the body of the faithful, brings all that he has received from God, all the resources of his mind, his heart, his achievements." "If the hierarchy communicates by the liturgy the truth and the grace of Christ, it is for the faithful, on their part, to accept these whole-heartedly, and to translate them into living realities. Everything which is offered to them, the graces of the sacrifice of the altar, the sacraments and sacramentals, they receive not in a passive manner in allowing them simply to flow into them, but in collaborating in them with their whole will and all their powers, and especially in participating in the liturgical offices or at least in following their unfolding with fervor. . . . It is in this unity that the Church prays, offers sacrifice, sanctifies itself, so that it can be asserted with good reason that the liturgy is the work of the whole church."[36]

For this reason, the people cannot remain absent in the designation of their shepherds. In ancient times they intervened actively in the election or designation of their bishops and priests. Let us recall, for example, the elevation of St. Ambrose to the episcopate. And the Roman Pontifical still recalls this popular intervention when it suggests that the faithful give their own opinion before the ordination of the new priests: "Dear brethren, since the captain and the passengers of a ship have the same reasons for feeling secure or the same motives for fear, those whose cause is a common one should be of the same opinion. Not without good reason, therefore, did the Fathers establish that the people also should be consulted about the election of those who were to be raised to the service of the altar."

The unity of action between the hierarchy and the community shines forth constantly in the exercise of the liturgical ministry. The priest or the bishop speaks to God in the name of the Church, but the community makes the spirit of this prayer effectual by its interior attitude, and ratifies with its *Amen* everything the celebrant has said. Dialogue is prominent in the sacramental liturgy and in the liturgy of praise; but even in the celebration of the Mass it remains alive and incisive. The priest himself when he turns to the people to invite them to join in his prayer, calls the Mass "my sacrifice and yours." The readings in the Mass, the chants, the collects suppose the presence and the participation of the community.

Hence arises the need for the sacred ministers at certain points in the liturgical action to speak to the faithful in their own language, that the same spirit may more readily permeate all of them together. This need is given vivid emphasis and official recognition in the concessions the Church has granted in our day. It had already been recognized in apostolic times. In

---

[36] *The Assisi Papers*, pp. 225-226.

reproving some of the Corinthians for their immoderate desire to receive the gift of tongues, St. Paul based his argument on the necessity of a common prayer: "Unless with the tongue you utter intelligible speech, how can anybody know what you are saying? You would be like someone talking to the air. . . . If you give thanks to God with the spirit alone, how can he who holds the position of the uninitiated say 'Amen' to your thanksgiving, since he does not know what you say? You certainly give thanks well, but the other is not edified. I thank God that I speak in foreign languages more than any of you. But in the Church I would rather speak five words intelligibly, so as to instruct others, than ten thousand words in a foreign language" (1 Cor. 14:9, 16-19).

Even in the priest's most sublime act and the one which is most his own, the Eucharistic consecration, when everything invites the faithful to keep recollected in silent adoration, the liturgy wants the community to intervene by uniting themselves in spirit to the celebrant and giving their assent in a certain way to the action of the sacrifice.

Our Roman liturgy, the most sober in this respect, as it is in other respects, places an enthusiastic dialogue just before the canon, at the preface, that the faithful may unite themselves to the celebrant's eucharist, his thanksgiving. And as a conclusion to the canon it requires once more the *Amen* of the people, after the solemn doxology. Between these two acts of popular assent, the Roman liturgy has the priest pray silently. Perhaps the *Amens* interspersed throughout the canon indicate the existence of a different practice long ago.

But, even without the sound of words, the celebrant is continually speaking to the faithful by his actions, that they may follow the priestly prayer sufficiently and be pervaded with its sentiments. In no other part of the Mass does the priest use so many gestures. He raises his eyes and his arms to heaven, lowers them again and bows deeply, kisses the altar, extends his arms in the attitude of an *orante,* joins his hands, closes his eyes and bows his head, blesses the offerings and raises them so that the people can see them. Through this dramatic series of gestures the community can keep itself united to the silent action of the priest.

In the Eastern liturgies, despite the fact that the act of consecration is celebrated behind the iconostasis and with the doors closed so that the faithful do not see the priest, he lets his voice be heard solemnly singing the words of the consecration, to which the faithful respond with their *Amen.*[37]

[37] Perhaps in no other liturgy is the intervention of the community in the solemn moment of the sacrifice so impressive as in the Visigothic liturgy and in the anaphora of the Coptic liturgy of St. Basil. In the latter, every word of the anamnesis and of the consecration is ratified in chorus by the assembly's acts of assent, of faith and of adoration. After having recalled the mysteries of the Lord, the celebrant continues:

Priest: And He left us this great mystery of piety when He had resolved to give Himself for the life of the world.

Community: We believe it and we firmly profess that it was so.

P.: He took the bread in His holy, immacu-

We have dwelt on these two constitutive principles of the Church and of her liturgy—hierarchy and community—because these are the principles which have suffered most from the harmful influence of individualism. As these two principles became less operative, the liturgy lost its vitality, and the divorce between liturgy and private piety became definite. To re-establish the desired purity of the liturgy and to make it once more not only the official prayer of the Church but also the effective prayer of the Christian community, it is necessary to reappraise and coordinate the hierarchical sense and the communitarian character of the Church's public prayer, as in fact the Church is already doing in the current liturgical reforms.

We can see in numerous provisions of the restored Holy Week this desire to reunite the priestly action and the participation of the community in the unity of the liturgical rite. The dialogue between the celebrant and the faithful is re-established, and the distance which separates the nave from the altar is shortened. Henceforth, in these rites, the Christian people can become aware that the great distance which exists between them and the priesthood and hierarchy is not a distance that divides, but rather a distance that unites all in the ordered arrangement of the mystical Body. Henceforth, they can understand that they, the Christian people, are not strangers to the mysterious rites the priest is celebrating at the altar; rather, he is performing those rites precisely because of the people. Hence the new rubrics provide that certain rites be performed in such a way that the people can have a good view of them: the blessing of the palms, the blessing of the baptismal water, even if the traditional *benedictio ad fontes* has to be omitted. And the Holy Father in his important discourse on pastoral liturgy chose to allude to the venerable Roman practice of celebrating the Mass facing the people.[38]

late, blessed, life-giving hands.

C.: We believe that it really happened thus.

P.: And He raised His eyes to heaven, to You, God His Father and Lord of all. He gave ✠ thanks. He blessed ✠ it. He sanctified ✠ it.

C.: Amen, amen, amen. We believe it, we acknowledge it, and we glorify Him.

P.: He broke it and gave it to His holy and pure disciples, saying, "Take it and eat of it, all of you. This is My body, which is broken for you, and given to many for the remission of sins. Do this in memory of Me."

C.: We believe that it was really so. Amen.

P.: In like manner He also took the chalice after having eaten and mixed water and wine in it. And He gave ✠ thanks.

C.: Amen.

P.: And blessed ✠ it.

C.: Amen.

P.: And sanctified ✠ it.

C.: Amen, amen, amen, amen. We believe this also and we acknowledge it and we praise Him.

P.: And He tasted it and gave it to His holy and pure disciples, saying, "Take it and drink of it, all of you. This is My blood of the New Testament, which is poured out for you and will be given for many in remission of sins. Do this in memory of Me."

C.: Amen. We believe that it was really so.

P.: "Every time you eat this bread and drink this chalice, you are proclaiming My death, acknowledging My Resurrection and making a memorial of Me until I come."

C.: Amen, amen, amen. We proclaim, O Lord, Your death, we acknowledge Your Resurrection and Your Ascension, we praise You, we bless You, we give You thanks and we invoke You, Lord our God. Etc.

Joseph Aloysius Assemani, *Codex Liturgicus Ecclesiae Universae*, book 4, part 4: *Missale Ecclesiae Alexandrinae*, part 2, *Anaphora S. P.N. Basilii Magni* (Rome, 1754; reproduced by Hubert Weller, Paris, 1902), pp. 53-56.

[38] *The Assisi Papers*, p. 234.

5. Sacramentality of the Liturgy

In this section we shall not give the words *sacrament* and *sacramental* the precise sense in which we have used them up to now. *Sacramentum* is one of the words used very frequently by the ecclesiastical writers, but with a meaning which is very inexact and fluctuating.[39] The proper meaning given it today by theology was not established definitively until the twelfth and thirteenth centuries. In accordance with this terminology, we have called those rites *sacraments* which were instituted by Jesus Christ and which signify and cause grace. By analogy, *sacramentals* are the rites instituted by the Church, which, while signifying a spiritual reality, produce their effect by the merit of the Church's own prayer and action.

Tertullian, St. Cyprian, St. Hilary, St. Ambrose, St. Augustine, St. Leo used this word *sacramentum* with great frequency and with notable variety of meanings. It is hard to specify the exact sense they wished to give it in each case. The interpretation becomes more uncertain from the fact that in the time of these Fathers sacramental theology, to which they gave a noteworthy impulse, was still far from its definitive evolution and determination.

The fondness of some of these writers for symbolism and for allegorical interpretations adds still further to the imprecision of meaning of the sentences in which the word *sacramentum* is found, or the Greek word *mysterium,* which in certain cases is equivalent to it. Much abuse has arisen from the theological imprecision in some expressions of the above-mentioned Fathers, because of their excessive symbolism and the doubtful meaning to be attached to the words *mysterium* and *sacramentum;* and these expressions have been given an interpretation that is more poetical than true.

For the ecclesiastical authors before the centuries of the great theologians, *sacramentum* usually designates, aside from other acceptions not very frequent, the oath of initiation to a secret doctrine or institution, or one of the sacred truths or actions whose meaning transcends what the words or the gestures express, or the rites which are used as sensible sign of an invisible spiritual reality. In general, and prescinding from ideological shadings, the most frequent acceptions of *sacramentum* imply a sensible reality which is related in some way with a hidden or transcendent spiritual reality. These are the first rudiments of the concept which the scholastic theologians will elaborate and define later on.

In describing the present law of the sacramentality of the liturgy, we are taking the word *sacrament* and its derivatives in this broader acception used by the Fathers, as involving a communication by God through a sensible medium. By this law we want to indicate, therefore, that Jesus Christ and the Church have established as a general rule of their respective worshipful actions the use of outward and sensible means to obtain effects in the super-

---

[39] Cf. Joseph de Ghellinck, S.J., *Pour l'histoire du mot "Sacramentum,"* vol. I, *Les Anténicéens* (Louvain, 1924).

natural order. With this understood, we can state that the liturgy is an essentially sacramental worship.

This quality of liturgical worship corresponds to God's plan and to the nature of man. God wishes to communicate Himself to us in order to raise us to Him. God's communication to us and our union with Him are possible only in the spiritual order. The divine nature can be shared only by a spirit, and cannot be understood except as object of the intellect and the will. But God's communications, although they raise our nature to a supernatural order, do not alter the natural use of its faculties. Moreover, our elevation to God has to be achieved in a way that befits the life we are living. Hence it follows that the normal actuation of our spiritual faculties, even in the supernatural order, presupposes the use of our senses. We love only what we know as good, and we know only that which has first passed somehow through our senses, the proper object of which consists in material beings.

Adapting Himself to our way of being, God has chosen to make use of material creation and of bodily actions to raise us to participation in His divine life. God hides His power under forms perceptible to the senses, through which the human spirit discovers God and is divinely transformed into His being and His operations.

This law is verified in an eminent way in Jesus Christ. In His humanity there is realized the maximum communication of the divinity to a creature, which is raised to the divine order in the most perfect way possible, so that this humanity subsists in the person of the Word and Christ's actions receive a theandric value. Hence Jesus Christ is the great sacrament, the sacrament of sacraments, exemplary and efficient cause of all sacramentality. His humanity is the *res sacramenti* which at the same time hides and manifests the divinity.

He was a sacrament during His mortal life: Simeon already proclaimed Him a *sign* of contradiction. The same bodily reality as seen by some was a cause of scandal and of blindness, "that seeing they may not see," as Christ Himself declared; while as seen by others, namely in humility of heart, it was a revelation of the divinity: St. Peter's acknowledgment, "You are the Christ, the Son of the living God" (Matt. 16:16); St. Paul's joyful announcement, "The grace of God our Savior has appeared to all men" (Tit. 2:11); and the enthusiastic beginning of the letters of St. John, "I write of what was from the beginning, what we have heard, what we have seen with our eyes, what we have looked upon and our hands have handled: of the Word of Life. And the Life was made known . . . which was with the Father, and has appeared to us" (1 John 1:1-2).

After His Ascension into heaven, Jesus Christ continues to be the great sacrament of the whole Church. His humanity continues to be for us the revelation of God and the instrument of our divinization. "Knowing God under a visible form, we are drawn by Him to the love of things invisible," sings the Church in the preface of Christmas. And in that of the Epiphany: "When Your only-begotten Son appeared, clothed in our mortal substance, He restored us by the new light of His own immortality."

This is the concept which the liturgy of Christmas repeats in various prayers. Thus, in the secret of the first Mass, when offering God the oblations for the sacrifice of that night, it asks "that in virtue of this sacred exchange we may be found like to Him in whom our nature is united to You." And in the secret of the second Mass it asks again that "just as He who today is born as Man shines also as God, so also these fruits of the earth may communicate to us that which is divine."

These two liturgical texts show us another aspect of the sacramentality of Jesus Christ: His continuity in the Church. The sacramental value of Christ's humanity has found its complement in the Church, which, according to St. Cyprian's expression, is the *sacrament of unity, which lives forever and gives life to the people of God.*

If the Incarnation, the sacrament of Jesus Christ, finds its fullest reason-for-being in Christ's priesthood, since it is through His Incarnation that He unites to Himself and conforms to Himself the whole worship of the Christian religion, it is logical that this worship imitate and continue the sacramental makeup of its exemplary and principal cause.

The continuation of Christ's real presence and of His sacrifice in the Church, the Eucharist, is the greatest of the sacraments of the Church, and everything that prepares for it or is related to it will have a sacramental character. This applies not only to the sacraments instituted by Jesus Christ but also to the Church's sacramentals or to any other rite more or less related to the Eucharist.

Everything in the Church that has the nature of worship imitates the kind of existence exemplified in Jesus Christ: it is an object or action perceptible to the senses, which hides, symbolizes, reveals and communicates a supernatural, sanctifying reality. Thus these things are not mere symbols which foster certain psychological-religious attitudes; they are actions of Christ or of the Church, made present and perceptible by external rites.

The same thing can happen now to these sensible rites as happened to the humanity of Christ: they can either be a stumbling-block or an object of indifference, or they can be welcomed with humble faith and sincere charity. When Christ put His fingers into the deaf mute's ears, or anointed the eyes of the man born blind with clay formed by His own saliva, or let His healing power pass through a contact with the hem of His garment, He was inaugurating the manifestations of His theandric action, which were to continue by means of the rites of the Church's liturgy.

Not all the objects or actions of the Church's worship contain and communicate in the same way and in the same degree the sanctifying power which comes to us from Christ's humanity, but in all of them the law of sacramentality is fulfilled.

Every feast of the Church in which any mystery of Jesus Christ is cele-brated can be called a sacrament, because through ritual texts and actions it puts us in touch with the theandric power of Jesus Christ which flows from that mystery. Thus the fathers, and especially St. Leo, speak to us of the *sacramentum incarnationis, sacramentum passionis, sacramentum resur-rectionis, sacramentum paschale, sacramentum ascensionis*, etc., referring to the corresponding mystery of the life of Christ as well as to its sacramental renewal in the liturgical celebration.

The Church itself, its priesthood, its hierarchy are sacraments because of the supernatural power communicated through realities of a sensible order. If God communicates His gifts to us and we are able to reach Him, this happens only by means of churchmen and Church institutions, by means of the priests and the human beings who constitute the hierarchy. God has willed that the normal means by which His action should reach and trans-form our spirit should be contact with the lowliness of material objects or bodily actions and with the natural defects of actual persons.

One of the sacraments used most by the liturgy is the sacred Scripture, which corresponds doubly to the patristic concept of sacrament.

The Scripture is a sacrament in itself, as the word of God. To make His thoughts known to us and reveal to us the inscrutable realities of His being, of His inmost life, of His relations with creatures and of His redemptive plan, God has made use of limited human concepts, and of speech, still more limited because it is closer to matter and more subject to it. Scripture reflects the manner of thinking and of expressing oneself which is peculiar to men whose minds are formed according to the culture and the mentality of a certain era and a particular country. Moreover, it is subject to all the limita-tions of an individual psychology. Yet such is the vehicle of the Word of God: it contains and communicates the divine Light of revelation, which has been and will continue to be Life for all those to whom God wants to communicate Himself.

Like the sacrament of the cross of Christ, the sacred Scripture will con-tinue to be a scandal to the Jews, foolishness to the gentiles, but power and wisdom for the elect (1 Cor. 1:23-24), who do not seek in it persuasive argu-ments of human wisdom, but the manifestation and the power of the Spirit, that their faith may not rest on human wisdom but on the power of God (1 Cor. 2:4-5).

Aside from this sacramental value of its own which belongs to the word of God, a value that is always operative, the liturgy in certain cases endows it with another meaning, adapted to its aim of worship. We are not concerned here, properly speaking, with any of the meanings of sacred Scripture com-monly admitted by the exegetes, but rather with an adaptation of the sacred text, which is employed to express, with the manifold richness and super-natural capacity of the word of God, some aspect of the liturgical mystery. We might say that the Church, with motherly solicitude, nourishes her children on the spiritual food of the sacred Scripture, after having assimilated and prepared it herself according to the needs of the moment.

A deep insight into this meaning is the fruit of an intense supernatural and liturgical life. But the meaning is sufficiently within the reach of all who with an open mind let themselves be instructed by the teaching which the Church imparts in connection with worship. If this meaning is not taken into account, no satisfactory explanation can be found for many scriptural texts used by the liturgy. On the other hand, one who strives for an insight in the light of this sacrament is readily enlightened with the most brilliant irradiation of the mystery of Christ, and thereby introduced into a tranquil contemplation and raised even to the sublime heights of the mystical life.

The various passages which make up the proper formularies of each Mass, as well as the antiphons and the responsories of the Divine Office, are usually very rich in liturgical content. Even the psalms themselves take on a special coloring according to the feast that is being celebrated and the antiphon that accompanies them. Notice for example what very different meanings the psalm *De profundis* has in the morning Office of the Dead and at Vespers of Christmas. The introit of Easter Sunday—to choose one among many similar cases—which so vividly and so gently makes us relive Christ's sentiments as He presents Himself victorious to the Father after the drama of the Passion, although taken from Psalm 138, receives its depth of theological concept and its beauty of expression from the liturgical sacrament.

Perhaps in no other place does this meaning show itself so constant and so fruitful as in the antiphons of the *communio,* which are usually illuminated by the brilliant light of the sacramental presence of Jesus Christ. Each of them expresses a speech of Christ to the Church, with particular connotations for the priest or the faithful who have communicated, or else their speech to the Lord, as a reciprocal kiss of Eucharistic union.

The charm which attracts us to some commentaries on the liturgy, which makes us particularly fond of them and keeps our interest ever alive—we refer especially to Cardinal Schuster's *Liber Sacramentorum*—is due more to a vivid perception of this sacramental meaning of the texts than to the author's historical erudition.

The liturgy loves and teaches us to love the gentle deference by which God is willing to use such human means to communicate the divine life to us. By its teaching function the liturgy tends to stimulate our awareness of the profound meaning of its formulas and its rites and our spiritual enjoyment of its supernatural content.

Note that we are speaking of rites, not of ceremonies. The liturgy is essentially ritual, that is, sacramental; but it is not a ceremonial, except in a very secondary way. The rites form the very structure of the liturgy; without rites, the liturgy would not exist; which is equivalent to saying that, according to God's actual plan, without rites there would be no communication of divine life to the Church. The ceremonies, on the other hand, are nothing but the outward ordering of the rites, and therefore they can be modified or changed without modification or change in the formal content of the liturgy. To sacrifice the rites to the ceremonies would be an absurdity and would lead to a courtier-like formalism; by contrast, many ceremonies could be suppressed without having the rites lose any of their symbolic and sanctifying value.

These considerations make evident—as we have indicated elsewhere—the ignorance or the error of those who confuse liturgy with ceremonial, and who worry to the point of scrupulosity about the smallest rubrical details concerning reverences, order of movements, combinations of persons, problems of occurrence and concurrence, etc., and then fail to appreciate the sacramental value of the rites—not their history, perhaps, but their theological meaning, their supernatural content. In this consists the knowledge of the liturgy; for, although as a social act it needs laws and rules for its external order, the liturgy is first of all the worship of God, the renewal and contemplation of the mysteries of Christ, the divine communication of supernatural life.

6. The Liturgy, Temporal Center of the Unity of the Divine Plan

When St. Paul describes the plan of the divine economy, he shows us a vision of solemn grandeur: "to reunite all things in Christ, those of heaven and those of earth; and when all things are made subject to Him, then the Son Himself will be made subject to Him who subjected all things to Him, that God may be all in all things" (Eph. 1:10; 1 Cor. 15:28).

This plan conceived by the divine wisdom displays a magnificent perfection in its intrinsic unity, although its realization was to be achieved in three great stages. The first two, after creation, would take place in time, the third would have its perfect fulfilment in eternity. The first would have the character of a preparation, and would be like the shadow of a light to come; the second would give place to the realization in time and in image; the third would consummate God's plan in the heavenly manifestation of the truth, now freed from all veils.[40]

Christ is the center and the cause of the unity of the whole plan; He is the Alpha and the Omega; He who was, He who is and He who will be. His first coming marks the end of the shadows and inaugurates the period of the reality hidden in mystery and under images or figures; His second coming will mark the end of time, and will establish the clear vision and the

---

[40] Cf. St. Ambrose, *In Ps.* 38, 25-26 (PL 14, 1051-1052); *De Officiis*, I, 48, 238 (PL 16, 94); St. Thomas, *Summa theol.*, I-II, 101, 2.

perfect union in eternity. Between these two comings of the Lord the second stage develops, that of the veiled realities, that of the Church's sacramental life, that which forms the central nucleus and brings the shadows into relation with the light, that which realizes the figures and gives them their complement, that which initiates in mystery the realities of the parousia and of the life to come.

The three stages share in the aim of worship which is common to the whole, and each of them is characterized by its own particular manner of giving worship to God. Thus we have a ceremonial and figurative worship, a sacramental worship, and a worship of apocalyptic splendor. Our sacramental worship, like our stage of realization in mystery, brings the two extremes into relation with each other. The two extremes are inserted into the eternity of God the Creator and God the Consummator; and our sacramental worship constitutes the center of unity, in time, of the whole divine plan.

Our liturgy, therefore, constitutes a synthesis of the three stages, since the most diverse and the most distant elements of the three stages find a harmonious coordination and a perfect unity in our liturgical rites. It would be impossible to understand our liturgy fully without taking into account this twofold projection against the remote past and the parousia which is the object of our hope. In general, we can say of our liturgy what St. Thomas said of the sacraments, namely, that they were a commemoration of past things, a demonstration of present things and a forecast of things to come.[41]

Every year we are reminded of this presence of the past and of the future in our liturgy by the fact that the annual celebration of the mysteries of Christ is bracketed between two liturgical seasons, Advent and the last weeks of the time after Pentecost. The special purpose of Advent is to recall the era of promises, of figures, of expectation; while the last weeks after Pentecost foretell Christ's second coming, the parousia, the heavenly worship.

The meaning of the three stages with regard to worship and their mutual relationship of unity are synthesized in an image, which calls to mind the threefold and unique communication of God to men: the image of Jerusalem, that Jerusalem which is kingdom, city and temple, which exists in a place on earth as the earthly Jerusalem and is built in heaven, blessed vision of peace, as the heavenly and imperishable Jerusalem. Between these two, and linked with them by the grace of Christ, is the Church. "The Church," writes St. Augustine, "begins with this earthly Jerusalem, from which it is destined to pass on to the enjoyment of God in that heavenly Jerusalem: it begins from the one below and ends in the one above."[42]

The texts with which our present Jerusalem, the Church, sings her own glory on the Lord's Epiphany are taken from the prophet Isaias: *Surge,*

---

[41] St. Thomas, *Summa theol.,* III, 60, 3.   [42] St. Augustine, *Enarr. in Ps.* 147; PL 37, 1929.

illuminare, Ierusalem, "Arise, be radiant, Jerusalem!" To grasp the full import of this text, we must have in mind the vision of that magnificent Jerusalem, restored in all its splendor and lording it over those who had enslaved it, as the Israelites who were contemporaries of the Deutero-Isaias in exile dreamed of it; and, at the same time, the supernatural magnificence of our Jerusalem, enlightened by the brightness of Christ's countenance in His royal Epiphany and gathering within her pale all the people of the earth; and, again, the glory of the heavenly Jerusalem, resplendent in the glory of the Lamb, brilliant with the lustre of the saints.

The same must be said of the vision of hope which Jerusalem offers us on the fourth Sunday of Lent: "Rejoice, Jerusalem; Jerusalem which is built as a city; the Jerusalem which is above, which is free, which is our mother."

The Jerusalem of the Old Testament was the religious and political center of the chosen people. Everything related to it, as theocratic nation or as temple of the glory of Yahweh, now has its perfect realization in the Christian people, in the royal priesthood and the liturgy of the Church, which in turn initiates that kingdom which will have no end, the new Jerusalem adorned as a bride. From this it follows that we in our liturgy can recite the texts of the Old Testament in all truth and in their deepest meaning, without their being out of date or anachronistic; in fact, they are most pertinent when pronounced by Christian lips.

Many psalms, especially the historical ones, would have no meaning if they merely commemorated past events in the life of the Israelite people. What is told historically about the people of Israel is but a figure of that which is current and perennial in the Church. To pray with the liturgy we must know how to penetrate through these figures and find Christ in the Church and in the splendors of His glory. St. Augustine in his *Enarrationes in Psalmos* shows himself particularly clear-sighted in finding this christological and ecclesiastical meaning in the foreshadowings of the Old Law.

The Office, the Mass, the sacramental liturgy are full of these recollections of the Old Testament and these allusions to the heavenly liturgy, which perfect and complete the significance of our rites and our prayers.

The texts of the Old Testament, abounding in messianic hopes, which form the liturgy of Advent, have their full and contemporary meaning in the Christian longing for the final union with Christ with the vision of His countenance and inclusion in His glory, which is begun and progressively increased with the present renewal of His mysteries.

The penitential texts of Lent, with the severe reproofs of the prophets to the people of Israel and with their predictions of messianic redemption and of divine mercy, were written with us in mind, without losing any of their historical character.

The cries of the just man suffering persecution, as we read them in the Masses and Offices of Passiontide, although they were pronounced or written by David, Isaias, Jeremias and other personages of the Old Testament on particular occasions in their life, are the cry of Jesus Christ confronting His Passion. And the lamentations which Jeremias puts on the lips of the Jerusalem of his day, humiliated by her enemies and desolate in the face of her own destruction, were never so true as on the lips of the suffering Christ or of His mystical Body, the Church, as she contemplates the sufferings of her God and Lord.

The same texts that served to extol the Pasch of the Jews now glorify Christ, our Pasch, and celebrate our common passage from the world to the Father.

Every year in the Easter Vigil the Church by means of the deacon sings in the solemn praise of the paschal candle, "For these are the paschal festivities, in which the true Lamb is slain with whose blood the doorposts of the faithful are consecrated. This is the night on which You first caused our fathers, the children of Israel led out of Egypt, to pass dry footed through the Red Sea. This is the night, then, which dissipated the darkness of sin with the brightness of the pillar of fire. . . . This is the night on which the bonds of death are destroyed and Christ rises victor from the depths. . . . O truly blessed night, which alone merited to know the very hour when Christ rose from the depths!"

It is interesting to note that the liturgy here is not merely recalling historical facts more or less related to the Lord's Resurrection; its intention is rather to connect them and make them present as figures and anticipations of the full reality which takes place in the celebration of the paschal liturgy. Similarly, one of the collects of this night says, "O God, whose ancient miracles we see still shining in our times, for that which You did for one people by the might of Your right hand in delivering them from the Egyptian persecution You perform for the salvation of all nations through the water of regeneration; grant that the whole world may cross over to become children of Abraham and partake of the dignity of the people of Israel."

Many of the texts read or chanted in the different Masses, and especially the antiphons for the communion, though taken from the books of the Old Testament, are illuminated by the veiled splendor of the heavenly liturgy which is begun and shared in the mystery of the Eucharistic communion of Christ sacrificed and glorious. In various Eastern liturgies the anamnesis extends from the creation all the way to the parousia, so that in the celebration of the liturgy there is explicit mention of this presence of the whole work of God, centered in the work of the Redemption.

Symbol and synthesis of this unity of prayer in the different periods of worship is the hymn of God's glory which is repeated unchangingly year in and year out across the ages from eternity to eternity. It is the trisagion which befits God's honor: the "Holy, Holy, Holy, Lord of the armies; the whole earth is full of Your glory!" which Isaias heard sung by the Seraphim (Is. 6:2-3), which was repeated in the Kedushah of the synagogal liturgy, which constitutes the hymn of the glory of God by which the Church unites her voice to the angelic voices, and which in the heavenly liturgy is the canticle of the four living beings who surround the throne of God and who never rest day and night, saying, "Holy, Holy, Holy is the Lord God all-powerful, who was, who is and who is coming" (Apoc. 4:8). Some martyrs, who before their torments had the privilege of being consoled by the anticipated vision of the glory that awaited them, likewise heard this canticle from the heaven that was opened to them: "Before the door stood four angels, who clothed us with white garments on our entrance. And we went in, and we heard the voice of many saying 'Hagios, hagios, hagios!' unendingly in unison."[43]

Our liturgy, therefore, is the presence of the Old Testament and of the glory to come, in the mystery of the present reality. "All these things happened to them as a type, and they were written to warn us, upon whom the final age of the world has come" (1 Cor. 10:11). And our Lord Himself assures us that His kingdom is within us (Luke 17:21). Actually the celebration of our liturgy in time takes place simultaneously with the celebration of the heavenly liturgy in eternity.

This force of attraction and of cohesion which characterizes the liturgy extends to the whole universe, which in one way or another is drawn to Christ through the liturgy. Man with his twofold nature, his faculties and his activities; material creation in all its forms; the angelic world in a particular way—all have their part in our Christian rites.

Material creatures have their part in the liturgy at least in so far as the liturgy praises God in their name, communicates to them the sanctification that comes from Christ and introduces them into His universal kingdom.

The presence of the angels is evoked very frequently in our liturgical acts, either to invite them to come as ministers of our purification or as guardians of our acts of worship against the stratagems of the enemy, or to unite ourselves to them in their mission of divine praise, or to make them messengers who will carry God's blessings to us and present our prayers and the offering of our sacrifice to God.

This meeting of all the beings of the universe, this concurrence of space, of time and of eternity in the celebration of our liturgy does not take place in a disordered, chaotic way. Rather, they are assimilated and inserted in a perfectly ordered arrangement, which is adapted to our nature. Concretely, this concurrence is brought about in the great sacramental of liturgical time, and develops according to three different cycles: the daily, the weekly and the yearly.

The daily cycle sums up Christ's redemptive work and the progress of our Christian life by following the course of the sun's light. Every liturgical

---

[43] Martyrdom of SS. Perpetua and Felicitas and of their Companions, XII; *Actas de los Mártires*, p. 431.

hour has a particular relation with some mystery of the Lord. At Matins, Christ is considered as the resplendent light desired during the darkness of the night. This light is gloriously displayed at Lauds with the rising of the sun, which speaks to us of resurrection; at Prime it shines to illuminate the works of our day; at Terce it is the fire of the Holy Spirit which enkindles our charity; at Sext, with the full light of midday, it reaches the zenith to give warmth and life to our good works; and at None, with its unfailing rays, it transmits to us that grace which will never let our Christian life reach a twilight. At Vespers the absence of the sun's light gives us the occasion for preparing and lighting the lamp and for offering our Lord the sacrifice of our light, participation in the perennial light of Christ, who will watch over our sleep and free us from nocturnal fancies and from the horror of darkness, as we ask at Compline.

The weekly cycle has the function of summing up periodically the work of creation. Every day the hymns of Vespers remind us of the works of God's goodness and of His creative power. In the different hours, the ordered, periodical distribution of the psalms introduces into our liturgy the varied themes of the prayer of the Israelite people and of the Christian people, recalling the manifestations of the divine attributes, the relations of God with His people, the predictions of the mysteries of Christ, the correspondence of men, very fluctuating in character, with the work of the divine benevolence.

The yearly cycle introduces into the liturgy every year the whole work of God, summed up in His two great supernatural gifts: His words, the Bible; and His Word, Christ. The annual reading of the various books of the sacred Scripture and the renewal of the mysteries of our Lord form the basis of the liturgical year.

With the threefold cycle, time is sanctified and comes to be a vehicle of grace; through it we have the concrete realization of our acts of worship, the transcendent presence of the whole work of God, of the whole mystery of Christ, and the inclusion of the universe and of human history in the Christian mystery.

Thanks to the arrangement of the liturgy, the time brings us at every moment its opportune message with relation to worship: it puts us in contact with a particular aspect of God's communications to men and arouses in us the corresponding tribute of praise.

We are pleased to express this idea in the words with which Monsignor Montini, archbishop of Milan, presented the *Calendarium Ambrosianum* of 1957: "What finer way can there be of looking forward to a period of time than to know how much of that time we are going to spend in speaking with God, and how we are going to do it? Time runs on an eternal thread; our instant joins the immovable 'always' of God. Such is the plan of this primary activity, prayer, to which the life of priests and religious is consecrated; perhaps some of the laity accompany them in the course of each day's Divine

Office. This is a plan that keeps track of every hour; in it, day and night have their obligations established in advance; and every rhythm has its own particular spiritual tonality: feasts and ferias alternate; Christ, the spiritual sun, marks the times of day and night and describes in our spiritual cycle the orbit, ever new and ever wondrous, of His Life, source of mysteries of grace and source of examples; then Mary and the saints form the crown. Yes, this is the 'crown of the year of God's goodness.'"

The Church's threefold cyclical plan includes all the facets of the divine economy, both in the natural and in the supernatural order, and distributes them in time in an orderly way, so that all and each of them are opportunely renewed in our life, communicating their content of grace to us, and prompting our corresponding worshipful attitude.

Hence is derived the particular significance attached to the circumstance of time in many liturgical acts. The Church has made time so important in the meaning of her prayer that this meaning is lost in great part if one prescinds from this circumstance of time in saying the liturgical prayers. For every period of the year, every day, every hour, has its particular character which puts definitely within our reach and adapts to our condition as men subject to time, the transcendental realities which are the object of the divine economy and of the Church's liturgy.

St. Thomas, reflecting the practice observed in his day, writes, "It has been reasonably established that God be praised in various ways according to a suitable distribution of times and places. And therefore, just as the Divine Office is to be celebrated in a suitable place, so also it is to be done at the proper times. And this would not be possible if one were obliged to recite at another time the hours which had been omitted at their proper time. This might lead to the absurdity of having to say *Iam lucis orto sidere* ('The morning sun is risen now') at the hour of Compline, or of having to recite the office of Passion Sunday in Paschaltide. Hence it does not seem that he who has failed to recite some part of the Divine Office should be obliged to recite those hours which were omitted, but rather that he should make up for them with something that has a relation to the divine praise."[44]

The discipline introduced by the recent restoration of the Holy Week has applied this principle to the Office of the sacred triduum by abolishing, in public recitation and for those who assist at the proper celebrations of those days, the parts corresponding to the time taken up by the celebration of these liturgical actions. Thus Vespers of Holy Thursday and Good Friday, Compline of Holy Saturday and Matins of Easter Sunday have been dropped.

If in the performance of liturgical worship it is proper to adapt the circumstance of time to our concrete and "step-by-step" way of being, at the same time it should not be forgotten, as far as its spiritual entity and its signification are concerned, that the liturgical action, realized by concrete

---

[44] St. Thomas, *Quodl.* 3, q. 13, a. 29.

and material means, surpasses all bounds of space and time to reach the immensity and the eternity of God. And this it does, not only in so far as God is the end to whom our worshipful action is directed, but also because He penetrates and informs our action through the priestly action of His incarnate Word and by the operation of His Spirit, who unites us to Christ in time, so as to fulfill our liturgy and consummate our union with God in eternity.

Thus the Church by her liturgy continues in space and in time the mystery of the Lord, the priestly action of Jesus Christ, whose priestly acts, performed historically and renewed mystically in time, persist henceforth unfailing and perennial in eternity, perfecting in the splendor of glory the marvelous unity of the works of God. By reason of the eternal priesthood of Jesus Christ in the celebration of the heavenly liturgy, God receives with pleasure the liturgy that is still celebrated on earth with the imperfection proper to earthly things, and accepts as perfect the worshipful homage of the creatures who, through Christ's priesthood, reach the highest peak of their perfection and their beatitude.

Before the throne of God, Jesus Christ eternally celebrates His liturgy, His and that of the Church: the unique liturgy, inaugurated by Him on earth, continued by His Church in time and consummated in eternity. Hence St. John in the sublime visions of the Apocalypse was able to contemplate the glory of heaven as the celebration of a solemn liturgy. In it there is no temple, because the Lord God almighty, with the Lamb, is its temple (Apoc. 21:22). There on the very throne of God, standing upright as one who is performing the sacrifice and at the same time as the one who is immolated, is the Lamb (Apoc. 5:6).

Around Him, that is, around our High Priest, is gathered the assembly of the elect: the angelic ministers of God; the Church, Body of Christ, and even the whole of creation, ransomed by His blood; all sharing the one liturgy of Jesus Christ. "I saw, and I heard the voice of many angels . . . and the number of them was thousands of thousands" (Apoc. 5:11). "After this I saw a great multitude which no man could number, out of all nations and tribes and peoples and tongues . . . clothed in white robes and with palms in their hands" (Apoc. 7:9). "And they cried with a loud voice, saying 'Salvation belongs to our God who sits upon the throne, and to the Lamb!'" (Apoc. 7:10).

And the voice of the universe echoes the Church's liturgy: "And every creature that is in heaven and on the earth and under the earth, and such as are on the sea, and all that are in them, I heard them all saying, 'To Him who sits upon the throne, and to the Lamb, blessing and honor and glory and dominion, forever and ever!'" (Apoc. 5:13).

7. Objectivity of Expression in the Liturgy

Liturgical worship is eminently objective in character. That is to say, it adapts its internal structure and its means of expression to the requirements of the object toward which it tends, not to the subject, whose duty it is to be directed and educated by the liturgy up to the point of conformity with the object of worship. The liturgy is a way that leads to God through the regulation of worship. God Himself has chosen to indicate the principal landmarks of this route, and has left it to the Church to supplement these indications by completing the sketch of the whole road. He who wants to follow this road cannot be wandering according to his fancy. To reach the desired goal, he must submit to the itinerary already established by God and by the Church.

The liturgy, then, is objective because in its purpose, in its structure, in the determination and ordering of its means of worship, it corresponds to the positive norms given by God and specified by the Church, and obligates the subject to adapt himself to these objective norms in offering his tribute of worship, prescinding from his own personal inclinations. With the adaptation of the subject to its objective norms, the liturgy effectively achieves its twofold aim of worship and sanctification. For the subject of liturgical action is not the individual as such, but Jesus Christ or the Church; the individual acts as their minister or as a member of the Church. The individual dispositions are necessary only in so far as they are required in order to act as a human person in conjunction with the Church or in her name. For this reason the sacraments duly administered, that is, adapted to the objective rules that govern their administration, have the power to produce their effect and do produce it, even aside from the question of the faith or the state of grace of the one who administers them.

Similarly, the Church's public prayer has its efficacy as worship before God, independently of the individual dispositions of the praying subject, as we shall see in the next chapter.

Whoever wants to take part in liturgical prayer must attune his personal individuality to the proper subject of public prayer, which, as we have said, is no other than the Church. He will have to enter into the mind and the will of the praying Church, therefore, adapting his own mind and his own will to the Church's to bring them into definite conformity with the objective norm of liturgical prayer.

Before we can achieve this adaptation of the individual to the spirit of the Church's prayer, we must know the Church's attitude of worship in every concrete case, an attitude which has to be shown by some external means. We have this medium in the outward forms of the liturgy: its gestures and especially its words. It follows that the liturgical forms, the expression of the Church's prayer, also share in the objectivity of the liturgy, since they are nothing but sensible manifestations of the concrete adaptation of the Church, the praying subject, to the objective norms of public and official prayer. Thus the liturgical formularies are on the one hand an expression of the

Church's thought, while on the other hand they constitute the objective norm to which the individual's mind must be conformed if he is to be integrated with the subject of liturgical prayer.

All this is not achieved without effort. It is always a hard thing to overcome one's own inclinations and psychological dispositions and adapt oneself to someone else's mind and will. Moreover, the external formulas to which we must subject ourselves present their own difficulty, since they must express in a way perceptible to the senses the most elevated concepts of a supernatural order and the most refined feelings, with formulas that are brief and concise. These requirements of content and of expression have to be embodied in a particular style of liturgical formulas. Hence we must know their principal characteristics in order to get a better and quicker grasp of their meaning.

By reason of their primarily dogmatic or doctrinal content, the formulas of the liturgy have a theological and conceptual character. From all that we have set forth in the preceding chapters, it can readily be deduced that the Church's prayer is directed particularly to the intellect, to communicate the knowledge of the divine mysteries and to unite the mind to God by a living and enlightened faith. The profound concepts of the supernatural life demand expressions packed with thought, which cannot be understood without a mental effort. The difficulty of expression is still greater because these divine truths are given us in mystery, by means of images and analogies, in which it is often hard to distinguish what is present reality and what refers to the next life.

Aside from this, we must take into account that the greater part of the texts employed by the liturgy are taken from the sacred Scripture, the reading of which is already difficult on account of its style, its theological concepts, and especially the wealth of content of its spiritual meaning. To this biblical sense must be added still another meaning, the one given the scriptural texts by the liturgy when it uses them to express the mystery of Christ renewed sacramentally in the Church.

Thus, for example, the words which the Church puts on the lips of the risen Christ in the introit of Easter Sunday acquire a new meaning very different from that which the same words have in Psalm 138, from which they have been taken. And those other words of the same Psalm 138, "How weighty are Your designs, O God, how vast the sum of them!", upon passing into the liturgy through the Vulgate translation, are changed into the following text, used many times on the feasts of the Apostles: "But to me Your friends, O God, are made exceedingly honorable; their principality is exceedingly strengthened."

As for the texts composed by the Church, and especially the collects of our Roman liturgy, the Church customarily uses short, concise forms, in harmony with the Roman temperament, which involve a greater density of concept and a greater intensity of attention. The very words used sometimes have a depth of meaning that goes far beyond what the words express; it is in the context that the correct interpretation of the text must be sought.

Let the following petitions, taken from some collects of our missal, be considered under this aspect:

illius salutaris capiamus effectum, cuius per haec mysteria pignus accepimus;[45]

in illius inveniamur forma, in quo tecum est nostra substantia;[46]

quae nunc specie gerimus, rerum veritate capiamus;[47]

mentes nostras et corpora possideat doni caelestis operatio: ut non noster sensus in nobis, sed iugiter eius praeveniat effectus;[48]

oblatio nos, Domine, tuo nomini dicanda purificet; et de die in diem ad caelestis vitae transferat actionem;[49]

ut quod agit mysterio, virtute perficiat.[50]

The apparent obscurity of the texts and the difficulty of interpreting them seem to be an obstacle to liturgical prayer. And so they are for one who does not strive to penetrate beyond the surface but is content with a superficial contact with these formulas, reciting them because he has to, and not putting into the recitation the effort of a proper mental preparation which would be rewarded with the spiritual understanding of the text. When the soul has become accustomed to the style of the liturgy, and with careful, attentive labor has investigated the content of its formulas in study and in prayer, it will find in those formulas a light so resplendent and at the same time so gentle that it indicates the presence and action of God, and fills with life and warmth those phrases apparently so dry and cold. The liturgical texts are then an abundant source of doctrine, and effect a solidly theological spiritual formation.

At the same time the soul will also perceive in them the delicacy and intensity of feeling which they contain and arouse. St. Augustine writes in his Confessions, "How I wept with emotion to hear the sweet sound of Your Church singing hymns and canticles! Those sounds flowing into my ears instilled the truth into my heart, so that a feeling of piety glowed there and the tears came to my eyes, and the flow of tears was good for my soul."[51] In the formulas of the liturgy, however, the emotions are affected only in the measure in which the intellect has penetrated the mystery and assimilated the truth contained in it. And this is a guarantee of the solidity of our spiritual formation.

If the liturgical texts are conceptual by reason of their content, they take on characteristics of universality by reason of their intention. That is to say,

[45] Postcommunion of Tuesday of the first week in Lent.

[46] Secret of the midnight Mass of Christmas.

[47] Postcommunion of Ember Saturday in September.

[48] Postcommunion of the fifteenth Sunday after Pentecost.

[49] Secret of the second Sunday after Pentecost.

[50] Secret of the second Sunday after Easter.

[51] St. Augustine, *Confessiones*, IX, VI; CSEL 33, I, 1, p. 208.

being intended to determine the prayer of all the members of the Church, they are devoid of anything that would imply a particularism.

When a prayer springs spontaneously from the soul, it reflects the soul's psychological state: it becomes a verbal image of what that soul is, thinks and feels in its present state, under the influence of determinate physical and moral circumstances. If that prayer were put into writing and given to others to recite, it would not be said with the sincerity and the depth with which it was conceived, except in the case of another person whose personal circumstances all coincided with those of the person who composed the prayer. The more the persons differ psychologically and morally from each other, the less sincere and spontaneous will be the recitation of that formula. For this very reason, not all the prayers that are found written down are to everyone's liking, nor can everyone profit from them in the same way.

Actually, whenever anyone recites a prayer composed beforehand, he takes that formula as a model for the spirit and as a guide in the ascent to God. He who finds himself spiritually distant from the concepts and the sentiments that inspired it will have to make a tiring effort to adapt himself to them. Perhaps this effort will facilitate the penetration of the mind by the ideas expressed; but it will be most difficult to make one's own emotional state coincide with the state supposed by that prayer, which basically ought to be helping the intellect and the will to be united to God, if everything is not to be reduced to a sentimentalism which will never rise to the status of prayer. This accounts for the superficiality and the ineffectiveness of prayers in which sentiment predominates.

The liturgical formulas, therefore, being written to direct the prayer of all the Christians, must be devoid of all personalism, reducing the role of sentiment to the minimum and granting the more important place to thought. Only thus can they be taken as the common prayer of the community and as the particular prayer of each person: the individuals, conforming themselves to the objective doctrinal content of the liturgical prayer, will be able to invest it with the emotions and sentiments that flow spontaneously from their actual psychological state, and thus the prayer will become more alive for them.

The Church teaches us to follow this practice when she has us recite identical psalms on occasions which presuppose very diverse spiritual attitudes; for example, the psalm *De profundis* in the Office of the Dead and on Christmas day.

And if the sobriety of sentiment in the liturgical formulas permits a person to adapt himself to them in any spiritual state whatsoever, the effort to penetrate the ideas expressed in the formulas raises the mind to the level of the great supernatural truths and provides a solid education for the spirit of the Christian who prays with the Church.

The universality of the liturgical formulas presents three principal facets.

The texts of the liturgy must be universal in the doctrinal order, in the moral order and in the affective order.

As for the doctrine expressed in the formularies of the liturgy, these, taken as a whole, should contain the totality of religious truths and of the aspects of the mystery of Christ; and everything should be distributed in proper proportion, that every one of the truths may gain entrance into the Christian's mind to inform it and may there occupy precisely the place and the importance which correspond to it objectively.

Private prayer can and usually does dwell on one or another point, that which most affects the individual who is praying. The devotions ordinarily proceed in this way: they fix on a particular truth or a sacred event or a religious idea for which the soul feels a preference and on which it dwells almost exclusively so as to draw from it the light it contains and convert this truth or idea into a nurture and a guide for the spiritual life.

Thus, for example, the devotion to the Passion of Christ, or to the Heart of Jesus or of Mary, or to the sorrows and joys of St. Joseph, fixes the soul's attention on these particular facts, that it may contemplate them, savor them and imitate the example they propose. This way of praying is easy and within reach. But it has a serious drawback: if one devotion comes to predominate in the life of a Christian, the result is a one-sided development of his spiritual life, which thereby becomes unbalanced and rather shallow. This danger is aggravated when the devotions are more concrete, more closely tied to the senses and more often repeated; for by absorbing the spiritual activity in one particular point, they prevent its being applied to other aspects just as necessary or even more necessary for the complete formation of the spirit, since those devotions are inadequate for the full nourishment of the interior life; unless they be used only as a point of departure to open up new and broader horizons of supernatural life.

Because of their particularism, devotions as we are now considering them can also be the occasion of another danger, that of deforming the very object of devotion to which they are attached, since by paying excessive attention to it they destroy its proportion with the rest of the Christian life.

If we dwell too much, for example, on the consideration of the divine mercy or of the divine justice or of any other particular attribute of God, we expose ourselves to imagining the divine nature in a human way and as if these attributes were contrary to one another; and thus we may form a false idea of God, to the obvious detriment of our spiritual life.

So it is also with the Eucharist. Even though it occupies the center of the liturgical life, and the Church's worship without it would have neither efficacy nor reason for being, if we consider it in itself, segregating it from the whole of the liturgical life and making it the object of a particular devotion, we shall end by deforming it. No doubt this devotion will highlight its entity as sacrifice, or perhaps still more as sacrament and as presence of

Jesus in the tabernacle. But by particularizing and insisting on one or the other of these facets more intensely than the Church herself is used to doing, the devotion attributes undue proportion to these aspects of the Eucharist, at the expense of their objective importance itself. For the value and the dignity of the Eucharist cannot be duly appreciated except in the vital organism of the Christian life, as presented and lived by the Church. The practical consequences of such a particular devotion will be, if nothing else, to disfigure the real concept of the Eucharist and to disturb the balance of the organism of worship instituted by the Church; just as would happen in the human organism if all vital interest and activity were centered in the heart, even though the heart may be considered as the most important organ of our body.[52]

On this point Pope Pius XII spoke very clearly. Here are the principal concepts: first of all the unity of Eucharistic worship in the diversity of its aspects: "It is one and the same Lord who is immolated on the altar and honored in the tabernacle and who pours out from there His blessings. . . . The person of the Lord must occupy the center of worship, for it is that which unifies the relations of the altar and the tabernacle and gives to them their meaning."

Jesus Christ is the cause of the unity of Eucharistic worship; He is also the cause of the difference in importance of the various aspects of the Eucharist, since not all of them have the same connection with His person: "The person of the Lord must occupy the center of worship. . . . The Lord is in some respects greater than the altar and the sacrifice. . . . The altar surpasses the tabernacle because on it is offered the sacrifice of the Lord. The tabernacle, doubtless, possesses the *sacramentum permanens;* but it is not an *altare permanens,* because it is only during the celebration of the holy Mass that Christ offers Himself in sacrifice on the altar—not after, nor outside of, Mass. In the tabernacle, on the other hand, He is present as long as the consecrated species remain, without, however, offering Himself perpetually. One is fully justified in distinguishing between the offering of the sacrifice of the Mass and the *cultus latreuticus,* the supreme form of worship offered to the God-Man hidden in the Eucharist."

We should like to emphasize that the Pope is here touching on the theological reason underlying the diversity of value as worship attached to the altar and to the tabernacle, in other words to the sacrifice of the Mass and to the adoration of the Eucharist: the sacrifice is an act of Jesus Christ, who offers Himself to the Father, and therefore the Mass is an act of infinite value

---

[52] In this respect it is interesting to notice the Church's insistence on maintaining the prohibition of Masses, whether sung or low, before the Blessed Sacrament exposed, or, in certain cases of liturgical law, their restriction. See the reply of the Sacred Congregation of Rites to the *Dubium* whether these Masses could be permitted or at least tolerated. Making explicit exception of two privileged cases, the Sacred Congregation replied on July 27, 1927: "In the negative to both." *A.A.S.,* 1927, p. 289.

as worship; while the latreutic worship offered to the Lord hidden in the Eucharist is always an act of ours, that is, a human act, very limited in its value and its dignity as worship, often an act of private devotion, though it may sometimes have a liturgical-ecclesiastical character.

Hence the Pope proceeds, "A decision of the Sacred Congregation of Rites, dated July 27, 1927, limits as much as possible the exposition of the Blessed Sacrament during Mass; but this is easily explained by the desire of keeping habitually separate the act of sacrifice and the worship of simple adoration in order that the faithful would clearly understand their proper character."

After stating specifically that to be content with the sacrifice of the altar while having a lesser esteem for the presence and the action of Christ in the tabernacle would be to belittle the importance of Him who performs the sacrifice, the Pope concludes that the center and the reason of Eucharistic worship is found in the offering of the Mass which renews the sacrifice of Christ: "It is first of all by the sacrifice of the altar that our Lord makes Himself present in the Eucharist, and he is in the tabernacle only as a 'memorial of His sacrifice and Passion.' "[53]

It is important, therefore, not to separate two things which by reason of their origin and their nature should remain united. But it is important also to attribute to each one the value and the emphasis which correspond to each one's nature, to the will of Christ in instituting the Eucharist and to the degree of connection with our Lord's person and His worshipful action.

To return to our theme: the liturgy, by its universality in the doctrinal order, always preserves a just measure so as to avoid the disadvantages of a personal evaluation or of leaning to one extreme or the other for purely subjective reasons. As the Pope says in the discourse just quoted, the whole deposit of the faith and the whole truth of Christ contained in the Scripture and in tradition is found in the liturgy, so that it is hard to think of a Christian truth that is not expressed there in some way. This does not mean that the liturgy always considers all the truths in the aggregate. Rather, it distributes them in an ordered way throughout the liturgical year and in accordance with the variety of its rites, so that they succeed one another, and the interest awakened by one truth, however great it may be, is put aside opportunely by another truth which comes to occupy the place it held in our consideration.

The mystery of Christmas, for example, for which we have been prepared throughout Advent, is the object of the liturgy's consideration for some weeks, during which various feasts occur to point up the different aspects of the Lord's manifestation. But, although the contemplation of the mystery of the Nativity might be prolonged with positive spiritual profit for the life of the Church and of souls, Septuagesima comes at its due time, separating us from the spiritual joys of Christmas and leading us to the consideration of sin

[53] *The Assisi Papers*, pp. 233-234.

and its consequences. And thus the liturgical seasons succeed one another in an orderly way and with just proportion, and with them the various aspects of revealed truth and of Christian doctrine.

In the moral order, too, the liturgy avoids particularism. The liturgy is interested in the development of a normal, sane Christian life, without turbulence; and for this life it is always offering the proper food: the means which communicate grace and the truth which nourishes the spirit; and it leaves them to produce their fruits of virtue at the opportune time.

Adapting itself to our way of being and providing for the needs that are common to all Christians, the liturgy at certain periods is rather insistent on some particular moral aspect of the Christian life, but always with a universal tone. It does not descend to details or propose concrete applications, which might be useful and suitable for some, but perhaps have the opposite effect on others. The details remain the proper object of each one's initiative, as applications of the moral attitude produced by the liturgical acts.

Just as it has done for doctrine, the liturgy fosters certain responses of the moral life at the different times of the liturgical year: hope and desire during Advent, compunction during Lent, spiritual joy and purity of life in Paschaltide, etc. It thereby gives the norm of conduct to which all Christians should model themselves, and leaves to the particular initiative or to the virtue of each one the choice of means and the intensity of the response.

Of interest in this respect is the following page of Guardini, which we quote in its entirety:

"Liturgical action and liturgical prayer are the logical consequences of certain moral premises—the desire for justification, contrition, readiness for sacrifice, and so on—and often issue afresh into moral actions. But here again it is possible to observe a fine distinction. The liturgy does not lightly exact moral actions of a very far-reaching nature, especially those which denote an interior decision. It requires them where the matter is of real importance, for example the abjuration at baptism, or the vows at the final reception into an order. When, however, it is a question of making regular daily prayer fruitful in everyday intentions and decisions, the liturgy is very cautious. For instance, it does not rashly utter such things as vows, or full and permanent repudiation of sin, entire and lasting surrender, all-embracing consecration of one's entire being, utter contempt for and renouncement of the world, promises of exclusive love, and the like. Such ideas are present at times, fairly frequently even, but generally under the form of a humble entreaty that the suppliant may be vouchsafed similar sentiments, or of an encouragement to ponder upon their goodness and nobility, or of an exhortation on the same subject. But the liturgy avoids the frequent use of those prayers in which these moral actions are specifically expressed."[54]

---

[54] Romano Guardini, *The Spirit of the Liturgy,* trans. by Ada Lane (London: Sheed & Ward, 1930), pp. 23-24.

In formulating its petitions also, the liturgy displays a character of universality. As a general rule the prayers of the liturgy do not ask for graces of a particular order. In the administration of the sacraments and of the sacramentals it goes more into detail and asks God for those gifts which ought to be the effect of the sacramental rite or which dispose the recipient for it. Composed for the spiritual or material good of individuals, the formularies of the ritual partake more or less of this particularity of aim. Yet they are very sober in their expression and do not usually descend to personal details. Something similar must be said of the collects of those votive Masses which are aimed at obtaining some special grace. Aside from these cases, the petitions formulated by the liturgy ask God for graces of a general order, applicable to all Christians in their different states and conditions.

Taking as a basis the collects of the missal, we see that on some feasts the petition is directed to obtaining the fruits proper to that liturgical solemnity. On Christmas night, for example, we ask that "as we have known on earth the mysteries of the light of the Lord, we may also enjoy His happiness in heaven."[55] On Epiphany day we ask God that, "having already known You by faith, we may be led even to contemplate the beauty of Your majesty."[56] On the feast of the Ascension we pray "that we, who believe that Your only-begotten Son, our Redeemer, ascended this day into heaven, may ourselves dwell there in spirit."[57] For Pentecost we ask the grace to "savor what is right, according to the same Spirit, and to rejoice always in His consolation."[58] The collects of many ferias of Advent and of Lent and of the Sundays after Easter make us ask, in a similar way, for the graces proper to those liturgical seasons.

On other feasts, however, and ordinarily on the ferias and Sundays of the whole year, only a grace of a general character is asked for. The petition proper to Easter Sunday is the following: "help us and grant fulfilment to the desires which You Yourself have implanted in us."[59] Here are the supplications made on some of the Sundays after Pentecost: "pour into our hearts the tenderness of Your love, that, loving You in all things and above all things, we may obtain Your promises, which surpass all desire;"[60] "implant in our hearts the love of Your name and grant us an increased religious sense, that You may nourish what is good in us, and with zealous care preserve what has been nourished;"[61] "we humbly implore You to remove all that may be harmful, and grant us everything that will be helpful;"[62] "grant us the spirit of thinking and doing always what is right, that we, who cannot exist without You, may be able to live as You would have us;"[63] "let the

[55] Collect of the midnight Mass of Christmas.
[56] Collect of the feast of the Epiphany.
[57] Collect of the feast of the Ascension.
[58] Collect of Pentecost Sunday.
[59] Collect of Easter Sunday.
[60] Collect of the fifth Sunday after Pentecost.

[61] Collect of the sixth Sunday after Pentecost.
[62] Collect of the seventh Sunday after Pentecost.
[63] Collect of the eighth Sunday after Pentecost.

ears of Your mercy be open to those who humbly implore You; and, that You may grant their desires, make them ask for that which pleases You;"[64] etc.

The same thing is true of the feasts of the saints. On many of these feasts, and especially the most ancient ones, the prayers are offered for the most general kind of needs: "that by their intercession we may feel the effects of Your protection;"[65] "that we may rejoice in the power of her advocacy with You;"[66] "graciously grant us protection against all adversity;"[67] "may the testimony borne to Your name by Your saints be our defense, and by its merits win for us the support our frailty needs;"[68] "grant that Your Church may love what he believed and preach what he taught;"[69] "through his intercession, graciously bestow on us the fruits of Your accustomed mercy;"[70] etc.

In other collects, the grace implored is related to some prominent aspect of the life of the saint who is being venerated. This is more likely to occur in the later collects, which usually mention, moreover, the saint's characteristic virtue, ideal of life or favorite motto. For example: "O Lord, who said, 'Unless you become like little children you shall not enter the kingdom of heaven,' grant, we pray You, that we may follow the footsteps of the virgin St. Therese in her humility and simplicity of heart so as to win the everlasting award;"[71] "O God, disburser of heavenly gifts, who united a wonderful innocence of life with an equal spirit of penance in the angelic youth Aloysius, grant by his merits and his prayers that we who have not followed him in his innocence may imitate him in his penance;"[72] "O God, who by means of Your confessor St. Joseph have been pleased to provide a new help for Your Church in forming the young in piety and knowledge, grant, we pray You, that after his example and through his intercession we may so act and teach as to win the eternal reward;"[73] etc. Even among the ancient collects, some are found which follow this structure: "God all-powerful, who gave blessed Lawrence the strength to overcome his fiery torments, we pray that You grant us the grace to extinguish the flames of vice in ourselves."[74]

As can be seen, even the collects that enter into greater detail always maintain a discreet tone and confine themselves to suggesting a certain particular order of graces.

The profundity of concept and the universality of expression which we

[64] Collect of the ninth Sunday after Pentecost.

[65] Collect of the feast of SS. Primus and Felician, June 9.

[66] Collect of the feast of St. Agnes, January 21.

[67] Collect of the feast of St. Martin, November 11.

[68] Collect of the feast of SS. Nazarius and Celsus, July 28.

[69] Collect of the feast of St. Bartholomew, August 24.

[70] Collect of the feast of St. Augustine, August 28.

[71] Collect of the feast of St. Therese of the Child Jesus, October 3.

[72] Collect of the feast of St. Aloysius Gonzaga, June 21.

[73] Collect of the feast of St. Joseph Calasanctius, August 27.

[74] Collect of the feast of St. Lawrence, August 10.

have seen, are mirrored in the literary style which regulates the composition of the liturgical formulas. We shall confine ourselves concretely to the style of the collects of the missal, because they are the most characteristic formulas from this point of view. They are usually composed of sentences that are short, concise and well proportioned in their elements. The words they use, chosen with careful attention and propriety, are elegant, classical, symmetrical and rhythmical.

As a general rule, the collects are composed of three dominant ideas: an invocation (for example: *Omnipotens sempiterne Deus*), a statement of the motive on which our petition is based (for example: *de cuius munere venit, ut tibi a fidelibus tuis digne et laudabiliter serviatur*) and the petition properly so called, which constitutes the purpose of the collect (for example: *tribue, quaesumus, nobis: ut ad promissiones tuas sine offensione curramus*). It should be noted that the second part, the statement of the motive of the prayer, is usually omitted when the collect would become too long.

In the best written collects this threefold structure forms a little oratorical composition, divided into two parts, protasis and apodosis, with one or two incises in each of them. Thus the four members (sometimes three) form one whole period. In the formation of this oratorical period, in the collects that correspond to the golden age, the threefold rule established by Cicero is observed, that is: the *compositio,* or competent selection and harmonious combination of words; the *ordo,* or distribution of words according to the rules of oratory; and the *numerus,* or combination of accents to form a rhythmical or metrical cadence. The application of these rules readily distinguishes the collects of classical composition by their harmonious cadence and their sense of proportion.

Let the following collects, for example, be considered. The rhetoric is exemplified in the Latin, a rather literal English translation being added as an aid to those who do not read Latin:

1 *Omnipotens sempiterne Deus,*
2 *da nobis fidei, spei et caritatis augmentum:*
3 *et, ut mereamur assequi quod promittis,*
4 *fac nos amare quod praecipis.*[75]

    1 All-powerful, eternal God,
    2 give us an increase of faith, hope and charity;
    3 and, that we may be worthy to attain what You promise,
    4 make us love what You command.

---

[75] Collect of the thirteenth Sunday after Pentecost.

1 *Mentes nostras, quaesumus, Domine,*
2 *lumine tuae claritatis illustra;*
3 *ut videre possimus quae agenda sunt,*
4 *et quae recta sunt agere valeamus.*[76]

> 1 Our minds, we pray You, Lord,
> 2 enlighten with the light of Your brightness,
> 3 that we may be able to see what we should do
> 4 and have the strength to do what is right.

1 *Praesta, Domine, fidelibus tuis:*
2 *ut ieiuniorum veneranda solemnia,*
3 *et congrua pietate suscipiant,*
4 *et secura devotione percurrant.*[77]

> 1 Grant, Lord, to Your faithful
> 2 that the solemn observance of the fast
> 3 they may enter upon with fitting piety
> 4 and carry through with steadfast devotion.

1 *Hostias, Domine, quas nomini tuo sacrandas offerimus,*
2 *apostolica prosequatur oratio:*
3 *per quam nos expiari tribuas, et defendi.*[78]

> 1 The offerings, Lord, which we present, to be consecrated
>   to Your name,
> 2 may the prayers of Your Apostles accompany;
> 3 and grant that by their prayers we may obtain pardon and
>   protection.

On the other hand, the collects composed in times of decadence are characterized by the lack of doctrinal depth, of sobriety and universality in expression, and of rhythm, order and proportion in their literary composition.
Let the foregoing examples be compared with the following collects:

Deus, in cuius passione, secundum Simeonis prophetiam dul-
cissimam animam gloriosae Virginis et Matris Mariae doloris gla-
dius pertransivit: concede propitius; ut, qui transfixionem eius
et passionem venerando recolimus, gloriosis meritis et precibus
omnium Sanctorum Cruci fideliter adstantium intercedentibus,
Passionis tuae effectum felicem consequamur.[79]

---

[76] Prayer over the people, Wednesday of the
first week in Lent.
[77] Collect of Ash Wednesday.
[78] Secret of the feast of the Apostles SS.

Peter and Paul, June 29.
[79] Collect of the feast of the Seven Sorrows
of the Blessed Virgin Mary, Friday of Passion
Week.

O God, in whose Passion the sword of sorrow foretold by Simeon pierced the most sweet soul of the glorious Mary, Virgin and Mother, grant in Your mercy that we who reverently call to mind her anguish and suffering may, through the glorious merits and intercession of all the saints who faithfully stand by the cross, obtain the blessed fruit of Your own Passion.

Omnipotens sempiterne Deus, qui unigenitum Filium tuum mundi Redemptorem constituisti, ac eius Sanguine placari voluisti: concede, quaesumus, salutis nostrae pretium solemni cultu ita venerari, atque a praesentis vitae malis eius virtute defendi in terris, ut fructu perpetuo laetemur in caelis.[80]

All-powerful, eternal God, who appointed Your only-begotten Son the Redeemer of the world, and willed to be appeased by His Blood, grant, we beseech You, that we may so honor by our solemn service this the price of our redemption, and by its virtue be so defended from the evils of our present life on earth, that we may enjoy its fruit forever in heaven.

Offerimus tibi preces et hostias, Domine Iesu Christe, humiliter supplicantes: ut qui Transfixionem dulcissimi spiritus beatae Mariae Matris tuae precibus recensemus, suo suorumque sub Cruce Sanctorum consortium, multiplicato piissimo interventu, meritis mortis tuae, meritum cum beatis habeamus.[81]

We offer You our prayers and oblations, Lord Jesus Christ, humbly imploring that, even as in our prayers we recall the piercing of the most sweet soul of Your blessed Mother Mary, so through the merits of Your death and the multiplied intercession of Your Mother and her holy companions at the foot of the cross, we may share in the reward of the blessed.

Omnipotens aeterne Deus, qui creasti et redemisti nos, respice propitius vota nostra: et sacrificium salutaris hostiae, quod in honorem nominis Filii tui, Domini nostri Iesu Christi, maiestati tuae obtulimus, placido et benigno vultu suscipere digneris; ut, gratia tua nobis infusa, sub glorioso nomine Iesu aeternae praedestinationis titulo gaudeamus nomina nostra scripta esse in caelis.[82]

All-powerful, eternal God, who created and redeemed us, graciously regard our prayers, and accept with a favorable and

---

[80] Collect of the feast of the Most Precious Blood, July 1.

[81] Secret of the feast of the Seven Sorrows of the Blessed Virgin Mary, Friday of Passion Week.

[82] Postcommunion of the feast of the Most Holy Name of Jesus.

benign countenance the sacrifice of the saving victim, which we
have offered to Your majesty in honor of the name of Your Son,
our Lord Jesus Christ; that Your grace may be poured out upon
us and we may rejoice to see our names written in heaven under
that title of eternal predestination, the glorious name of Jesus.

What we have said, referring to concrete examples in the collects of the
missal, could be applied in due proportion to the other liturgical texts, at
least in so far as it refers to their general characteristics: conceptual character,
universality and sobriety of expression. As to their exact composition—internal
and external—every class of liturgical piece has its own particular rules. A
collect, an antiphon, a preface, a responsory, each occupies a place of its
own within the liturgy, and must be composed according to special rules
which govern its content and its form of expression.

These laws regulate the more external and accidental part of liturgical
worship, but they complete its perfection. The integral perfection of a work
of art is to be found, basically, in the details which complement and bring
out its essential perfection. The liturgy, which embodies the priesthood of
Jesus Christ and of the Church, as tribute of praise to God on the part of
redeemed mankind and the regenerated universe, not only has perfection in
its divine content and in its intrinsic value as worship, but should even be
displayed outwardly with that objective beauty and that human perfection
which are worthy of adorning the priestly work of the mystical Body of
Jesus Christ.

6   THE INDIVIDUAL CONTRIBUTION

TO THE CHURCH'S PUBLIC WORSHIP

In the preceding chapter we dwelt particularly on the external element of public worship. The rites and formulas employed by the Church in the liturgy would not have any value if they were not an outward, sensible expression of an interior, spiritual worship which gives them religious value and supernatural worth. We have already indicated this as the general norm and the essential principle of every act of worship expressed in a way that is perceptible to the senses.

But when it comes to applying this principle to the Church's liturgy, a difficulty arises. For there are various subjects involved in the act of worship: Jesus Christ as Head of the Church, the Church herself as mystical Body of Christ or as His Spouse, and finally each one of the Christians who go to make up the unity of the Church. Whose role is it, then, to contribute the interior and spiritual element? In other words, who is to animate with a vital and personal action the external rites determined by the Church? And it may be asked further: how and in what proportion are the external rite and the interior element of the liturgy to be coordinated or mutually subordinated?

We have made a distinction between the liturgical action of Jesus Christ and that of the Church. In the first, Christ is the unique priest, both of His sacrifice and of the sacraments with which He produces in men the holiness and the grace He has merited for us by His sacrifice. Actually, however, all these acts involve also the intervention of a minister who in Christ's name performs the sacrificial or sacramental action consciously and with personal action.

Moreover, Jesus Christ offers and renews His sacrifice as Head of the Church, making the Church part of Himself. It follows that He not only merits for her the fruits that accrue from His priesthood, but also incorporates her into His own organic unity, as subject of His worshipful action. And we must keep in mind also that this Church, incorporated into the organic unity of Jesus Christ, is made up of all the Christians and each one of them. As members of the Church, they receive the sanctifying action of Christ's priesthood, not as the fateful effect of magic rites, but rather with the indescribable efficacy of a divine action that must be grafted supernaturally, but vitally, onto a human nature, which accepts it and thereby collaborates freely in the production of the sacramental effect. Thus it comes about that all these have a part in Christ's priestly action, each in his own way: Jesus Christ Himself, His minister, the Church and every Christian as a conscious member.

In the liturgical action of the Church considered as Spouse of Christ, He becomes her necessary Mediator with the Father. Here the subject of the worshipful action is the Church herself, in as much as we distinguish between the Body which carries out the action and the Head who gives it life. But in this action also the subject can be considered as multiple. For we find here: the Church as collective worshiping entity, the minister who officially performs the worshipful action in her name, and each one of the members who go to make up the Church and who by their union with the hierarchy acquire an active value as partial subjects of the total and adequate subject of worship.

In what proportion, then, are all these elements which intervene in the public worship of Jesus Christ or in that of the Church supposed to inform that worship with their own spirit, so that the external rites of the liturgy will obtain a perfect efficacy as worship?

With regard to Jesus Christ, we need not insist again that the whole value and supernatural efficacy of the liturgy proceed from the perfect and total gift by which the soul of Jesus delivers to the Father His physical being as Man-God and His mystical being as Church, as supreme and universal act of adoration and as means for consecrating all creatures in the measure which befits the place each one occupies in the plan of the divine economy. The adoring and prayerful attitude of the soul of Jesus Christ perseveres and will persevere unfailingly for all eternity, thus informing any act which the earthly or heavenly liturgy performs in His name and by His authority.

The Eucharistic sacrifice and the essential rite of the sacraments are always, in their external celebration, a sensible and social expression of the latreutic and sanctifying will of Christ's soul. Hence these worshipful actions are always efficacious in themselves, because when they are performed properly, that is, according to the will of Jesus Christ in instituting them, they are in contact with that will and are the vehicle of our Lord's personal action.

With regard to the minister, we see that his action is twofold: outwardly he must perform the sacramental rite through the two elements, material and formal, which give it the nature of sign; inwardly he must unite this sensible sign with the invisible action of Christ's will. This is the intention with which the minister acts as intelligent and free instrument, and which permits him a living, personal participation in Christ's liturgical, priestly action. This suffices to make the material, sensible rite a true act of worship and to enable it to obtain the essential effect of its divine efficacy; on the supposition, where the sacraments are concerned, that the subject receiving them does not offer any obstacle to the communication of grace. This obstacle would be the conscious and present adherence of the will to sin, which cannot coexist with the infusion of grace.

Without detracting in any way from the efficacy of Christ's worshipful action, it can be said that both the minister who acts in His name and the faithful who take part in the celebration or the reception of this essential worship, by the fact that they are members vitally united to the Head, can add something to the integral perfection or to the degree of perception of the efficacy of this priesthood of Jesus Christ. This they can do if, as intelligent beings, they bring to the liturgical action a spiritual harmony with the corresponding attitude of Christ's soul.

For example, in the sacrifice of the Mass, although it is always pleasing and acceptable to the Father because it is always the supreme act of religion offered Him by Jesus Christ, the social and representative character of Christ's priesthood will have a more perfect and adequate expression if the celebrant and the faithful who assist at the Mass participate not only by their material presence but also by successfully conforming their spiritual attitude to that of Christ's soul as He offers His sacrifice to the Father.

This takes place, in general, if a person pays attention to the celebration and to the meaning of the rites; still more concretely, with the use of the intellect and the adherence of the will. The intellect is united to the act of worship by an enlightened faith, of which contemplation is the highest index. The will concurs by the desire of participating in the liturgical action and receiving its effects, and by the surrender of itself in communion with the sacrifice of Christ or in such a way as to let itself be penetrated by the action of grace in the sacraments.

If we pass from Christ's worship to the Church's, we shall find another order and proportion in the application of the spiritual element to the liturgical action, whether the concern is with the complementary rites of the sacraments or with the whole rite of the Mass or with the Divine Office. In all these liturgical acts, by the fact of their being acts of the Church, it is up to the Church herself to place the interior act of religion which will give them their value as worship, besides performing the external rite. We say, and rightly so, that the Church prays, the Church expresses such and such concept in the liturgy, the Church feels in a certain way. But in these cases, 'who is the Church? Who is it that truly feels these sentiments or is enlightened with these concepts?

If we consider the Church as a mere aggregation of individuals, we shall not be able to determine what the Church actually thinks or feels if it does not happen that all the individuals who compose it, or at least the majority of them, or the most representative part, think or feel in the same way. In such a case we should have to say that often, and even throughout long epochs of history, the liturgical formulas did not really represent the prayer of the Church, since the majority of her members, and the most representative ones too, remained practically ignorant or spiritually far removed from the content of those formulas.

We cannot forget that the Church is an organic body, human and at the same time supernatural. Being organic and composed of human elements, it needs a hierarchy, formal principle of its existence and its unity. Being supernatural, it not only tends to a divine end but also receives in its being and its actuation the vital influx of its Head, who constantly communicates to it His Spirit, who for this reason is called, by analogy, the soul of the Church. The union of these two elements, Spirit and hierarchy, will resolve the difficulty and show us the formal content of the acts attributed to the Church. We can say, then, that the internal act of the Church's liturgical worship is placed by the Church itself in as much as it is a social unit of worship, actuated by the will of the hierarchy, who act, as such, moved by the Holy Spirit.

Liturgical action and prayer contain, therefore, the meaning they have received from the hierarchy under the uniform guidance by which the Spirit has impelled and led the Church to worship God through public prayer. In order to be able to know, for example, what is the authentic sense of a text or a rite, one must see what meaning was given it by the hierarchy who established it, and how it is incorporated into the current of doctrine and of worship which the Holy Spirit causes to circulate through the body of the Church. The objective norms of interpretation will be given by ecclesiastical tradition and by the hierarchy themselves in their official declarations.

It is the function of individuals in particular, and above all of the ministers of the Church's worship, to activate the spirit of the Church's public and official prayer. For every one of the individuals is an integral part of the ecclesiastical and worshiping community. Although no one of them is essential to the Church, which could exist and act aside from any one of them considered individually, still it would no longer exist and it would not be what it is, if it were not made up of all of them.

In order to be truly called the Church's prayer, liturgical prayer need not be recited by all and each of the faithful, nor even by the majority of them; it is enough that the minister of the liturgical action have received from the Church the power to represent her publicly and officially before God in the exercise of that act of worship.

It might even happen that the minister himself who is acting officially in the Church's name did not harmonize his spirit with what he was doing or saying; and it might happen too that those who constitute the hierarchy, considered as private individuals, were not aware of the value and the content of liturgical prayer or did not have a due appreciation for it. That would make no difference: the Church's public prayer would not thereby fail to express what it contains in reality; all that is needed is this quasi-material performance of the liturgy and a minimum of intention to do what the Church wants, in order for the liturgical rites to make the authentic and official thoughts of the whole Church rise up to God.

In this case the divine element would make up for the deficiency of the human element, according to St. Paul's expression, "But in like manner the Spirit also helps our weakness. For we do not know what we should pray for as we ought, but the Spirit Himself pleads for us with unutterable groanings. And He who searches the hearts knows what the Spirit desires, that He pleads for the saints according to God" (Rom. 8:26-27).

Such a prayer would lack the perfection of being materially the prayer of the whole Church, that is, of all its members. It is clear, however, that this imperfection is in the members and not in the prayer, which continues to gather up the worshipful activity of all of them, although it may be far removed from their worship by reason of its content and of its expression as well. This explains the Church's interest in having all of the faithful, and particularly the ministers of her public prayer, actuate and perfect the liturgical prayer and the ecclesiastical rites, adapting their individual interior dispositions to the prayer, and assimilating and expressing as their own what those rites signify.

With the union of these two elements—the outward and objective element contributed by the liturgy and the interior, subjective element, which in principle is proper to the Church and which is to be concretely actuated by the ministers and by the faithful—the liturgical act obtains its maximum value as worship. Then, truly and properly speaking, it is an expression of an interior worship, so that it becomes worship in spirit and in truth, as God desires it to be; and moreover it attains the maximum degree of its sanctifying efficacy, because it finds the intellect and the will of the faithful completely open and applied to the sanctifying content of the mystery.

If we wanted to analyze the part belonging to each of the two elements in liturgical prayer, we could say that the subjective element brings it about that this complexus of words and actions is truly and actually prayer; the objective element serves as a norm for the prayer and gives it a social and ecclesiastical character of liturgical action. Each element has need of the other, and both together constitute a single cultual reality.

The interior element, in as much as it supposes an initial and present will of the praying Church, is essential and gives liturgical prayer its principal efficacy, both as prayer and as liturgical. Hence every liturgical prayer and action has a true value as worship, because it is always animated by the Spirit of the Church, as we have indicated above, even if the minister who is actually performing it be distracted or fail to adapt his spiritual activity to the formulas he is pronouncing or the rites he is performing. The same can be said with regard to the interior dispositions with which the faithful receive the liturgical action or take part in it.

In these conditions, however, the liturgical act does not attain perfection, since for the perfection of the total effect there must be a concurrence, in due proportion, of the perfection of the principal cause and that of the instrumental cause. The minister should join to the Church's prayer his own interior attitude, which actualizes it in a vital way and communicates to it the perfection proper to a conscious instrumental action. Thus the prayer of a priest who recites the breviary distractedly does not cease to be the prayer of the Church, but suffers from the deficiency of the minister, because, even if it is true that he acts as an instrument, he does not do so as a fully conscious instrument.

The dispositions of the faithful complete the perfection of the liturgical act, giving reality and actuality to the vital unity of the praying subject.

Moreover, it is evident that the sanctifying effect of the Church's prayer on the minister himself and on the faithful is in direct proportion to the spiritual intensity with which they unite themselves to the Church's prayer, by means of a sincere assimilation of thoughts and of desires.

If the subjective element must inform the liturgical prayer, the objective element, which takes concrete form in the formulas and the rites, must direct it and orient it. Being the hierarchical and ecclesiastical element, it has the function of orienting and unifying the spiritual activity of the different subjects who concur in the formation of liturgical prayer. The objective element teaches us and prescribes for us what must be said in prayer and how it is to be said. The mind and the spirit of those who celebrate liturgical prayer or participate in it must not only bring to it the reality of an interior worship, but also conform this worship to that which the words or the outward rites signify. Only then will full unity be achieved between the subject and the object, between the individual, the minister and the Church.

We might ask still another question. Can a prayer imposed from without be sincere? Will it always be possible to obtain an attitude of spirit adapted to certain pre-established formulas?

St. Benedict, who had a profound grasp of the spirit of liturgical prayer, gives us in a short sentence the norm of this prayer: "Let our mind be in agreement with our voice." Many masters of the spiritual life would have given it to us completely inverted; that is: "Let our voice be in agreement with our mind." With this motto they would want to inculcate the idea that the external formulas of prayer should be a sincere expression of the interior devotion. This prayer, however, would not be liturgical prayer. It would be our prayer, that of each one, that which springs spontaneously from our soul and expresses what is within us. Liturgical prayer, on the other hand, is the prayer of the Church. The Church must inspire it, must take the initiative in it, giving us the content and even the external form of the message we are to carry before the majesty of God in her name.

This law of docility, of letting oneself be guided by the Church, applies above all to those who have the mission of representing the Church officially and who are ministers of public prayer; but it applies also to the faithful who in union with the hierarchy take part in the celebration of the liturgy.

Certainly the act of subjecting our mind to the text of the liturgical prayer supposes an effort of adaptation and obliges us to prefer the mind and the interests of the Church to our own spontaneous inclination and our personal tastes. But this constitutes our greatest dignity, that of being able to incarnate and give actuality to the prayer of Jesus Christ and of His Church.

As a reward for the sacrifice of our individualism and for our personal contribution, we are granted a greater degree of identity with the Church, the grace of contemplation and a superabundant, solid food for our souls, which in this way are immersed in the current of supernatural life and of divine praise that circulates between the Church and God, through our timely instrumental action. The effort of adapting our spirit to the words dictated by the Church models us on the Church, teaches us to think and feel as the Church thinks and feels in the presence of Christ and of His mystery, until the rhythm of our whole life is like an echo of the voice of the praying Church.

That the contribution of our interior worship to the liturgical prayer may be sincere and perfect, we should let ourselves be gently carried along by the text and we should pray in the Church's name. Let us briefly clarify these two concepts.

It is not morally possible, of course, to apply our mind with constant attention to every word of the liturgical text so as to animate every word of it with our sentiments. It is enough to introduce ourselves into the current of prayer, contemplation and praise with which the Holy Spirit makes the Church turn to God and which takes concrete shape in the outward forms of liturgical prayer; then we need only let ourselves be carried along.

Our vital inclusion in this current of supernatural ascent of mind may be more or less intense, according to the degree of our compenetration with the praying Church through the words she dictates for us.

Actually we can be united to the spirit of the Church through a mere material contact with the words of her prayer. This is the case with those who recite the Divine Office without understanding the text, whether because they do not know Latin or because they are ignorant of the theological concepts or the historical notions contained in the Office, or even simply because for some plausible reason they are unable to give their attention to the sense of the text or keep their attention constant. Then it is enough to have the sincere will to unite ourselves to the Church, to pray as she prays and to express her desires to God, pronouncing with devotion and reverence those words which for the most part were revealed by God with the aim of dictating to us the prayer that is pleasing to Him, and which contain also the thoughts and the feelings of the Spouse of Christ. It is the simplest form, but a sincere form, of union with the praying Church.

More vital is the conscious and attentive recitation of the texts, while we follow with the mind the immediate meaning of that which the lips pronounce, with the intention of uniting ourselves to the Church to praise God in this particular way, in the celebration of such and such a mystery which forms a sort of basis for the recitation and illuminates the various texts with its light.

Still more perfect is the participation of those who arrive, through the words, at the contemplation of the mystery, and keep their intellect and will united to it while they are examining its various aspects in the many different lights shed on it by the liturgical texts. This identification with the praying Church is so profound that it invades the whole being and spiritual activity of the one who prays in this way and establishes him in that perfect unity by which the Spirit and the Spouse are fused in one aspiration and one voice: "Come! . . . Come, Lord Jesus!" (Apoc. 22:17 and 20). This happens especially in the choral Office, where the whole sacred environment, the slow recitation, the sweetness of the chant and the Gregorian melismata point up the text and lead readily to contemplation.

The other condition for praying well in the recitation of the liturgical prayer is to pray in the name of the Church. When we recite the formulas of the liturgy, we should identify ourselves with the Church in such a way as to convert her prayer into our own.

An ambassador who feels his whole being pervaded with the mission entrusted to him will let it be clearly understood that he is in full sympathy with the official words he is transmitting, and this will win him the esteem of the persons among whom he is acting as mediator. In no way must he ever place his own personal and private inclinations before the public and official content of his message.

In liturgical prayer we must relegate our sentiments to second place, however devout they may be, and give priority to the aspirations of the Church. To these, of course, we can add ours also, since we too are part of the praying

Church. He who prays in the Church's name must prescind from himself, so as to leave all the activities of his own spirit freely at the disposal of the Church. To this renunciation of personal interest out of loyalty and love for the Church is linked the highest perfection of our prayer, which is incorporated into the prayer of the Spouse of Christ in that exceptional degree which she reserves for the minister of liturgical prayer.

When we pray thus, our spiritual attitude is sincere, even if the words do not correspond to our present psychological state. For we do not intend to express what we feel, but rather what the Church feels, striving to adapt our sentiments to hers. There are always souls in the Church whose needs, thoughts and aspirations are expressed exactly by the liturgical words we are pronouncing. Our prayer gathers up these sentiments and presents them to the Lord, after communicating to them a supernatural exaltation which perhaps those individuals do not have at that moment and which perhaps many of them would never be capable of attaining. By praying in this way we make ourselves interpreters of everything that needs to be presented to God: the outpourings prompted by sanctity in the most chosen souls and in so many good children of the Church, each of the present episodes of the stuggle between good and evil in the world and in souls, all the spiritual and bodily needs of the members of Christ, all the labors and sacrifices to establish and spread the kingdom of God.

How supernaturally beautiful and how fruitful is the liturgical prayer, for example, of a priest in charge of souls who presents to God, after having made them his own, all the desires and needs of his parishioners, whom he knows well and who are the object of his solicitude, uniting these desires and needs to those of all Christians and even of all men, whom he does not know, but who form with him and his parishioners a single Body in Jesus Christ!

This is what the liturgy presupposes when it describes Lent as the time in which "the priests, the Lord's ministers, shall pray with fasting and with weeping, and shall say, 'Spare, O Lord, spare Your people, and do not abandon Your inheritance to shame!'" (Joel 2:17). And it is only in the light of this fundamental concept of liturgical prayer that the excellence of the monastic priesthood and its fruitfulness, of universal extent, can be understood.

The practical ignorance and the neglect of the ecclesiastical character in the recitation of the Church's public prayer mark the first step, often a decisive one, on the way to a lack of esteem for liturgical prayer, especially in its choral celebration. It is accepted as a sacred duty, which is performed with devotion by reason of its very character, but without understanding of its deep meaning.

This situation gives rise to that curious paradox of the divine services being loved but proving tedious, being celebrated with devotion but becoming a burden, representing the *onus diei* which is offered to God willingly but which involves sacrificing the precious time that might be dedicated to the works of the apostolate. Under these conditions one may succeed in appreciating the Divine Office as a duty of one's state, but one cannot properly savor its content of prayer and spiritual nourishment.

This paradox is manifested clearly in the great saints who lived in the ages of decadence of the liturgical spirit and of a more accentuated individualism.

St. Francis of Assisi always advised his friars to be very faithful to the recitation of the Divine Office and, despite the exigencies of their ministry, to give preference to the choral Office; and he warmly exhorted them that all, even the priests, should participate in a single Mass, the common Mass, the conventual Mass.[1] The directive norm of the Divine Office still preserves in St. Francis the savor that St. Benedict had infused into it, but an inversion of terms already denotes a movement of regression from the collective to the individual character: "Let the clerics say the Office with devotion before God, that by their unity of mind they may please God . . . paying attention to harmony of mind, that the voice may be in agreement with the mind, and the mind in agreement with God."[2]

St. Dominic, despite his personal devotion to the Divine Office and his marked concern for the worthy celebration of the choral Office, prescribed to his friars, undoubtedly in reaction against the interminable monastic Offices of his time, "Let all the hours be said in the church briefly and succinctly, in such a way that the brethren will not lose their devotion and that their study will not be hindered any more than necessary." Here the concern is only with shortening; and, given the excesses of those long Offices which completely filled up the schedule in many monasteries contemporary with him, St. Dominic's reaction is quite understandable. Yet the tendency to abbreviate is already noticeable.

Later on, St. Ignatius will suppress the choral Office of his religious completely, for reasons of apostolate, his own personal devotion for the Divine Office notwithstanding. He himself declared that if he had followed his own taste and the inclination of his soul, he would have instituted the chant and the choir in his Company. And in the twentieth annotation of his Spiritual Exercises he advises the retreatant to choose his place of residence for the retreat "in such a way that it will be easy for him to go to Mass and Vespers

---

[1] "Moreover, I advise and exhort in the Lord that in the places where the friars stay, only one Mass a day be celebrated, according to the form of the holy Roman Church. And if there be several priests in the place, then, out of religious love, let one be content to assist at another priest's celebration; for our Lord Jesus Christ satisfies those who are worthy, whether they be absent or present." St. Francis of Assisi, *Ep.* XII, *Ad Sacerdotes totius Ordinis; Opuscoli del Serafico Patriarca S. Francesco d'Assisi* (Florence, 1880), p. 42.

[2] *Ibid.*, p. 34: *Ep.* XI, *ad Capitulum Generale*.

every day without fear that his acquaintances will be any obstacle to him."[3]

Some decades later, St. Francis de Sales already offers us a very clear example of failure to understand the ecclesiastical value of the liturgy: among the resolutions he made at the end of November, 1602, on the occasion of the retreat in preparation for his episcopal consecration, is found the following: "On festive days I will recite the rosary during the solemn Mass." And his biographer tells us that he was always faithful to this resolution.[4]

The tendency to suppress the choir Office, resulting from lack of understanding of the ecclesiastical character of the Divine Office, has culminated in our days with the necessity of suppressing or notably reducing the choral Office in some basilicas. His Eminence Cardinal Schuster wrote on October 5, 1948, "The choir is a precious grace, which the world today no longer appreciates, and therefore the Lord is withdrawing it even among the clergy." It is one of the typical paradoxes of our age of transition. While cathedrals and basilicas remain mute, as if in liquidation of a period of decadence, the Pope with his writings fosters the liturgical renewal which is once more publicizing the ecclesiastical sense of public worship; he recommends the single-minded participation of clergy and faithful in the liturgical celebrations; and he makes possible the return to a liturgy that is understood and lived.

On the other hand, when the ecclesiastical sense of liturgical prayer is lacking, the soul finds no correspondence between the liturgical texts and its own sentiments. Still unsatisfied after fulfilling his duty of the Divine Office, the priest or religious feels the need of seeking in other less substantial foods, sometimes in mere dainties, the nourishment he has not known how to find in the plentiful, varied and nutritious meal which the Church has offered him and which has passed between his lips almost untouched.

By this we do not mean that every form of extraliturgical piety should be banished. The encyclical *Mediator Dei* indicates clearly the place that belongs to this piety in the spiritual life of the Church, and we shall treat of this in the following chapter. But it is lamentable that the need of recourse to this kind of devotion derives from the fact of not understanding the meaning of the liturgical prayer and not being sufficiently pervaded with it, especially when the concern is with those to whom it has been officially entrusted; and it is lamentable that the values are thereby inverted, that which has only a secondary worth being given the dominant place in a person's spiritual life, while he does not know how to draw profit from that which the Church offers as the adequate and most efficacious means of attaining personal union with God.

[3] *Exercitia Spiritualia Sancti Ignatii de Loyola et eorum Directoria (Monumenta Historica Societatis Iesu, Monumenta Ignatiana,* series 2, Madrid, 1919), p. 246. — See note 23, ch. 3, p. 46 above.

[4] "Les jours de feste il recitera . . . le chapelet pendant la grand'messe": *Oeuvres complètes de S. François de Sales* (Paris, 1884), VI, 602. — Dom Jean de Saint-François: "les jours de feste, il disoit . . . le chapelet à la grand'messe": *Ibid.,* I, 70.

This inversion of values is manifested, for example, in some seminaries, where the recitation of the rosary and the practice of other particular devotions have a collective and official character—and there is nothing wrong in that—but where at the same time those who are ordained *in sacris* have to recite the Church's official prayer privately and on their own account, finding the time wherever they can, even with prejudice to their scholastic duties.

When the liturgical prayer is not profoundly assimilated, the plan of spiritual formation so wisely arranged by the Church is frustrated, leaving irreparable gaps in the terrain of ideology and of piety. The most profound teachings pass unobserved, unity of action is lost, and therefore a great part of the Church's efficacy as a teacher; the spiritual formation is reduced to a minimum, since there cannot be a true education without the disciple's effort to receive and assimilate the doctrine of the teacher.

As a result, the most solid practices of extraliturgical piety tend to fill the voids that are being formed in the Christian life in the measure in which the liturgy has been abandoned for lack of understanding. A substitute is sought, in new formulas of a more personal and concrete type, for that which the liturgy already possessed. When, for example, people did not know how to appreciate the Marian content of Advent, they had to have recourse to the devotion of the Mass of the Blessed Virgin. The necessity of a periodical practice of the Spiritual Exercises as a normal means of spiritual improvement made itself felt in the measure in which the meaning of the Lenten liturgy was being lost.

Often the pious practices which in the lives of many Christians have come to occupy the place that belongs to the liturgy, have been forced to have recourse to the liturgy itself, spontaneously or deliberately, imitating its forms, its methods and even its content, if they wanted to offer a guarantee of solidity and efficacy. For example, the rosary has become an individual form of popular breviary in which, as in the liturgy, the mystery of Christ is contemplated while the Hail Marys are recited in place of the psalms. We could also compare the general plan of the Exercises of St. Ignatius[5] with the liturgy's Lenten scheme of doctrine, from Septuagesima to Paschaltide.

The typical scheme of methodical prayer presents a notable parallelism with that of the Office of Matins: composition of place and preparatory prayer (invitatory and hymn); three points of meditation (three nocturns with their lessons); affections and colloquies after every point (responsories); thanksgiving *(Te Deum)*; and we can even include the preparation of points on the evening of the preceding day (first Vespers of feasts).

It is not only the lack of understanding of the ecclesiastical value of liturgical prayer that leads to an undervaluation of it in practice. Another, stronger reason, often derived from that one, though it may be independent of it, is the absence of that condition which we have indicated as the first condition

[5] *Exercitia Spiritualia S. Ignatii de Loyola et eorum Directoria*, p. 226.

necessary in order that liturgical prayer be true and perfect: to let oneself be carried along gently by the text. This condition, for that matter, is common to the liturgy and any form whatsoever of vocal prayer with a pre-established text; and we know that without it there would not be any true prayer.

For, as we have already said, vocal prayer presupposes an interior act of worship, of which it is the expression. If this interior act does not exist, there is no prayer, even though the lips pronounce the most beautiful formulas. We can state, then, that in many cases a person is not praying with the Church simply because he is not praying. And the same holds for the other vocal prayers. There is not always a worshipful attitude of the spirit corresponding to the words of prayer that the lips pronounce; and it is still more rare for the mind to strive to keep itself conformed to the sense of the text being recited.

There are many vocal prayers which only have a certain value as prayer because the one who says them has been motivated to do so by a general sense of devotion and also perhaps by the specific intention of reciting those particular formulas; but then in reciting them he does not pay attention to their meaning, and hence his intellect and his heart remain far from them. No doubt he has the intention and that attention necessary in order that it may be said that in some way he has prayed and also fulfilled the canonical obligation, when there is one. But he does lack that attentive application of the mind essential to the perfect act of religion; and the spiritual profit he will draw from the prayer will certainly be very limited, if there is any at all.

Let us take the rosary as an example. How many recite it with little or no attention, during the recitation of each decade, to the corresponding mystery, although this is precisely what constitutes the basis of this devotion! And, confining ourselves to the Hail Mary, how many Hail Marys are recited without any thought either about the fact or about the significance of the angelical salutation, which should be mystically renewed on the part of every Christian whenever he addresses the Mother of God with the angel's words!

Of course, this interior application of the spirit admits of many degrees. But here it would be enough to have that minimum degree necessary in order that the vocal prayer might be alive and lived; in other words, in order that it might be prayer in spirit and in truth. We could say that very often there is much recitation and little prayer.

And in liturgical prayer he who only recites and does not pray remains completely unsatisfied, and must seek nourishment for his soul elsewhere. No form of prayer, however, can nourish the soul if it does not apply itself to grasping and assimilating the sense of the formulas recited.

But there is this difference between liturgical prayer and the other kinds of vocal prayer. Liturgical prayer, by reason of its ecclesiastical character itself, its doctrinal profundity, the objectivity and sobriety of its formulas, satisfies only the one who penetrates its meaning with more or less intensity, that is, the one who prays by means of it. To those who only recite it, it says nothing. On the other hand, other, easier forms of prayer, of a much more subjective character, in which sentiment predominates, demand less effort at mental adaptation; and, at any rate, even when the mind does not penetrate the meaning of the texts, they awaken a certain feeling of devotion— we will not say true interior devotion—and thus produce the impression of having done something good.

In any case the spiritual profit will be incomparably less, being proportioned to the lesser effort of the mind and to the lesser depth of the truths contemplated and of the concepts expressed.

Liturgical prayer requires an intensity of application which is not satisfied with a liturgical dilettantism. If anyone should suppose that he is living by the spirit of the liturgy merely because he loves Christian antiquities or is enthusiastic about the solemnities of worship or about Gregorian chant, but did not also strive to penetrate the mystery of Christ contained in the sacred rites, it would not be long before he was disillusioned in face of the void he would experience in his own life.

The first and essential condition for praying liturgically is simply this: to pray. When a person truly prays, assimilating the spiritual food the Church offers him in the liturgical texts, his spirit remains completely satisfied and has no need to take refuge in other practices of piety. Not that he despises them or holds them in low esteem, but that he is already nourished superabundantly.

This holds especially for the ministers of liturgical prayer, since by reason of the duties of their state they are consecrated to be the men of the Church's prayer. The Divine Office, the Mass, the administration of the sacraments and of the sacramentals fill up a good part of their day. Simply by understanding and assimilating just those words which they pronounce in the Church's name, they have more food than is necessary to nourish the most intense spiritual life. This is precisely the rule of spiritual life given them by the Church on the day of their ordination to the priesthood: "Know what you are doing. Imitate what you are handling."

The sincerity of liturgical prayer does not exempt anyone from the distractions, so human, which from time to time take the spirit away from the text of the prayer. The liturgy knows this well, and takes care to help our weakness and our good will with certain brief but substantial formulas which, disseminated at intervals in the prayer, recall our attention more forcefully and put us back in contact with God.

Among these formulas the most important is the *Gloria Patri,* with which all the psalms conclude and which is so often inserted into the liturgical texts. Every time this doxology is repeated—much more when it is accompanied in choir by the corresponding bow—it offers us the occasion of intensifying our attitude of humble adoration, while offering gratefully to the Most Holy

Trinity everything that we have lived during the preceding psalm or text, or else profiting from this recall of attention to ask pardon for our distraction and to accept with sincerity in our spirit, though in a brief moment, what we have pronounced distractedly with our lips.

The frequent repetition of the *Kyrie eleison* also, and of some versicles such as the *Deus in adiutorium,* the *Dominus vobiscum,* etc., is a good means of recalling our attention and leading us to renew our compunction for having been distracted, and to renew the confident desire to be purified and to unite ourselves again consciously with the praying Church.

When a person prays truly and knows how to mold his spirit to the Church's prayer, not only does he attain to a profound life of prayer, but his mind becomes permeated with the Church's thought. He who prays with the Church and as the Church prays, identifies himself with her doctrine, with her manner of interpreting the sacred Scripture and of judging human deeds; he becomes accustomed to evaluating the realities of the natural and supernatural life according to the values which the Church sets on them; inquiring into the reasons for the rubrics and the liturgical ceremonies, he knows how to appreciate at its true worth the dignity of the persons, and he is filled with the social sense of reverence and courtesy by which the Church gives to each one the honor that belongs to him; he even refines his sensibility to discover, through liturgical worship, the transcendental sense by which the Church appreciates natural beauty, art, culture, civilization.

The crisis of the liturgical spirit has a necessary manifestation in the crisis of the ecclesiastical mentality. Thinking with the Church involves penetrating the sense of her liturgical books, of her canonical rules, of the pontifical documents, the three great sources in which is contained and from which flows the thought of the Church and her spirituality. But, just as it is not enough to pronounce the words of the liturgy or know its laws, if one does not possess its spirit, so it is not enough, either, to know the canon law and welcome the pontifical teachings, if one does not succeed in animating the letter with the spirit. Only he who is accustomed in the most personal and intimate things, that is, in his relations with God, to the subjection of his personal way of seeing and feeling, so as to see and feel as the Church does, will know how to prescind from all subjectivism in the practical life, as he must do if he is to incarnate and translate into action the mentality of the Church. He who knows how to pray in the Church's name knows how to live according to the spirit of the Church.

7 LITURGICAL SPIRITUALITY
AND CHRISTIAN LIFE

The individual contribution to the Church's public worship does not exhaust the possibilities of the Christian's interior life; rather, it develops them. The Church in her liturgy does not set out to monopolize the spiritual activity of the faithful, or even that of the ministers of her public worship; on the contrary, she nourishes their spiritual activity, educates it, orients it, infuses greater vitality into it and gives it a strong impulse toward God. The eminently social character of Christianity does not diminish the religious personality of the individual, but rather adds to it. The whole sacramental life and the pedagogical effort of the Church in the liturgy tend to increase the supernatural life of each one of the members of the mystical Body, and to make his personal inclusion in the Body and his union with Christ more vital by a progressive actuation of his faith and his charity.

The liturgy's aim of salvation and its value as education, therefore, suppose in the individual a spontaneous religious activity which, although it has to be stirred up, nourished and directed by the liturgy, does possess an individual and private character, and constitutes the basis and the measure of personal relations with God. The liturgy infuses the Christian life into souls and procures for them the substantial food common to all Christians, to nourish that life. It is up to each person to dispose himself for receiving this food, digesting it and assimilating it; and he still has the possibility of preparing other nourishment for himself on his own account.

This was the precise point made by Pope Pius XII in the above-mentioned discourse of September 22, 1956, to the Assisi congress: "By the side of the public worship, that of the community, there is a place for the private worship which the individual gives to God in the secret of his heart or expresses by his exterior acts, and which has as many variations as there are Christians, although it proceeds from the same faith and the same grace of Christ."

The private spiritual activity which Christians may exercise, even within a liturgical spirituality, is threefold. It comprises: the acts of private piety and of Christian life that are a sort of preparation for participating duly in the Church's public worship, which, as has been said, is the center of the Christian religion and life; the interior activity of the Christian which has the aim of assimilating the spiritual food received in the sacraments and in the other acts of public worship; and the acts of devotion that have no direct relation to the liturgy, but may be inspired or at least oriented by it.

The spiritual life of the Christian is not limited to a participation in the Church's public worship, even supposing that the participation in question is living and active. Nor is it enough to have a sincere private piety such as will perfect the individual relations of the soul with God. There still remains a good margin to be filled up before reaching the perfection of the Christian life. To direct individual piety and teach it to fill up this margin reserved to private spiritual activity is the task of the various systems of spirituality, which strive to lead us by the hand to the very heights of Christian perfection and of the mystical life, following the ways and the methods proper to them.

The Church, with her method of unification of human and divine activities in pursuit of the Christian ideal, extends her teachings and her peculiar style —in a word, her spirituality—even to this field of private activity.

To clarify the concepts in question, we must make it plain that the Church has never elaborated in theory or proposed explicitly as her own a systematic method of spirituality. But actually the Church has a particular way of conceiving and evaluating the mystery of God and of Jesus Christ, whether considered in itself or in relation to us; she has an exact concept of her own mission; she gives a certain value to each one of the objective and subjective means of sanctification; and in fact she acts according to such and such principles, in accordance with such and such practical rules. Thus, without presuming to offer a system, she has in practice a system of her own; though not intending to reduce things to a method, she has in fact created a method of her own, and she is putting it into practice.

From this constant practical method of conceiving and judging facts, both natural and supernatural, there results a mentality: in our case, the ecclesiastical mentality, the mentality of the Church. Thus also, from the constant practical way of turning to God and directing to Him the various aspects of the Christian life, there results a spirituality: the spirituality of the Church, the spirituality which the Church officially professes.

In this sense it could be said that the Church's public worship is nothing but her spirituality officially manifested through the formulas and the material rites that constitute the liturgy. But it is undeniably true that the Church's thinking and her spirituality officially manifested can very well be the norm of the individual Christian's thinking and of his spiritual life. Hence there may arise a real system of spirituality, which will seek to order the private spiritual life of the faithful in accord with the mentality and the spirituality of the Church as shown in the exercise of her liturgical worship.

Thus we shall have a spirituality which in the practical ordering of the Christian life will follow no other norms than those which the Church herself, as such, practices and, in this way, teaches the individual to practice. The characteristic of this spirituality will be to apply to the private life of the individual the same principles and the same norms that the Church applies in her public life.

Now the mind and spirit of the Church are made known to us officially through her public worship, her laws and the documents emanating from the Holy See (we include in these the pontifical teachings). Hence the aforesaid spirituality will draw from these three sources exclusively the doctrinal and practical rules which, according to its method, are to regulate the individual life of the Christian. Thus the spirituality to which we are referring can rightly be called ecclesiastical spirituality, in as much as it is based wholly and solely on the rules of Christian life given or practiced officially by the Church.

Yet we have called it liturgical spirituality. We are aware of the Holy Father's dictum in his discourse of September 22, 1956, that the liturgy does not embrace the whole field of the Church's activities. But among the ecclesiastical sources mentioned, the liturgy is the most important and effective as far as the ordering of the spiritual life of the Christian is concerned. For the liturgy is, of itself, the ordinary and common source of the spiritual life that issues abundantly from the sacraments and the other objective media of sanctification. Moreover, it is the celebration of the Church's public worship, for which reason it is also the best and most secure rule of every life of piety and of every relation with God.

The liturgy is also the eminently social act of the Church, which puts the hierarchy and the Christian community in close contact. Hence it teaches a due appreciation of this hierarchy and it becomes the perfect model of the virtues that govern the relations with superiors, with equals and with inferiors.

The liturgy, again, is the most universal, most popular and most efficacious means at the Church's disposal for communicating with all the faithful, and thus it becomes also the occasion best fitted for training and educating them in everything that concerns the perfection of the Christian life.

That is why we have given the name of liturgical to that spirituality which, being based exclusively on the principles of the Church, frankly adopts as its own the methods used by the Church when she celebrates her liturgy.

Nevertheless, liturgical spirituality does not presume to reduce the Christian's whole life to a worthy and enlightened participation in the acts of liturgical worship. Liturgical spirituality neither adds to nor subtracts from that which must go to make up the Christian life in one way or another. Like every legitimate spirituality found in the Church, liturgical spirituality is a pedagogical method serving the ideal of Christan perfection. Hence it must restrict itself to directing and regulating the integral content of the Christian life according to determinate and particular principles, so as to facilitate and effect the attainment of Christian perfection, that is, the perfection of charity.

For this reason liturgical spirituality in its individual applications has no hesitation at all about adapting itself to the most diverse subjective needs of individual Christians, according to the temperament, the intellectual and moral formation, the state of life of each one of them. Otherwise, it would not succeed in shaping their entire life after its own spirit. It always tends, however, to bring the mind, the spirit and the life of the individual into agreement with the mind, the spirit and the life of the Church herself, as manifested especially in the acts of her public worship.

Thus it is not only the individual acts of piety serving as preparation for the liturgy or achieving its personal assimilation that will be impregnated with the concepts and sentiments of the liturgical action, practically forming an organic unity with it. The whole spiritual life of the Christian also, the practice of the virtues and even the devotions of purely subjective character will be in harmony with the liturgy and will become a sort of individual expansion of the religious mentality which has been taking shape under the influence of the Church's public worship intensely lived.

We shall indicate the principal manifestations of the subjective spiritual life within the compass of liturgical spirituality. Before anything else, however, it must be noted that in liturgical spirituality the center and the norm of the whole private activity of the Christian is the mystery of Christ, renewed and lived in the liturgy. The greater or lesser importance the individual attributes to his acts of private piety or of virtue depends on the degree of relationship they may have with the mystery of our Lord. Moreover, in the choice of means, as well as in the way of using them, he adheres to the criterion and the procedures of the Church in her public worship.

1. Private Spiritual Activity as Preparation for the Liturgy

Remote preparation: penance and purification

Like any school of spirituality, the liturgy must concern itself first of all with getting the Christian into that state of interior purity which is necessary if he is to set out on the road of spiritual ascent to God and to become gradually more sensitive to the divine communications.

Since we are sinners, the first fruit of grace in our soul will always have to be pardon and purification. And to obtain these we must first have a humble recognition of our condition as sinners, a deep sorrow for our sins and evil tendencies, and the sincere desire of an effective return to God. This is the spiritual attitude known as compunction.

The participation in the mystery of Christ and the sacramental life, even in so far as their application to us produces of itself an effect of expiation, demand first of all that the subject prepare himself for them by a sincere feeling of compunction. Justice and propriety dictate this attitude for the one who is to present himself before the holiness of God. Compunction of soul should be habitual in the Christian, since he is to live in God's presence and in close relationship with Him, and since he so often has occasion to vivify this presence in the acts of the sacramental life.

It is not hard to obtain compunction if we seek to make the supernatural content of the liturgy a conscious part of our lives. For there is nothing that will humble us more and instil into us a stronger conviction of our condition as sinners than an abundance of grace and an intimacy with the Lord. The liturgy, as efficacious source of grace, as presence and communication of the mystery of Jesus Christ, fills the soul with supernatural light and, through this contact with God, roots it in truth. It thereby makes the Christian deeply humble and leads him to a sincere acknowledgment of his condition as a sinner and of the constant possibilities of his committing evil.

Moreover, the repeated references to our Lord's Passion, center of the liturgical life, heighten the contrast between the sinner's selfishness and God's infinite charity, place the contrite soul in immediate contact with the source of pardon and of life, fill it with an immense love and gratitude toward its Redeemer and urge it on to a real participation in the sufferings of Him who makes the soul a sharer of His infinite merits. Hence the soul feels the need of penance as a means of purification and of just participation in the sufferings of Christ.

Aside from this general effect which it has, the liturgy takes care to inculcate in practice the need for the Christian to purify himself and to do penance. Some of its sacraments and sacramentals have this immediate aim. In the most important acts of worship it is customary to begin with a humble petition for pardon, and the prayers often contain an acknowledgment of our moral wretchedness and our frailty and implore God's mercy and the grace of a total sanctification.

The parish Mass on Sundays is preceded by the purifying rite of the *Asperges.* The sinner's prayer, the *Confiteor,* with the corresponding absolution, usually precedes the sacramental rites; with this confession the priest and the faithful prepare for the celebration of Mass; and again it asks for the purification of all the day's acts at the Office of Compline. The rite of the Mass is full of expressions and formulas that keep the spirit of compunction constantly alive in the celebrant and the people. The psalm *Miserere* is one of those most frequently repeated in the Divine Office and in the administration of the sacramentals.

The great festivities are prepared for by a vigil of penance and purification. Four weeks of Advent precede Christmas. And the solemnity of solemnities, the Pasch of the Lord, is reached only after we have gone through Lent, the time dedicated in a particular way to penance.

He who lives by the spirit of the liturgy must feel perforce a profound need of penance, and must practice it in his life as a Christian. His model will be the Church, and his guide will be that which she gives him officially, especially during the Lenten period.

The Christian learns from the Church that the spirit of compunction, that is, interior penance, constitutes the essential basis of our conversion and that he must therefore make every effort to procure it, knowing that it is much more important than bodily penance. On the other hand, just as our wickedness has been exteriorized in the works of sin, so our interior compunction will have to show itself in the works of true conversion.

Metanoia, the change of mind, has always been the ideal of penance proposed by the Church, as following from the humble recognition of our own sins and from sincere compunction. The fruit and the demonstration of interior conversion must be the works of justice and of sanctity.

We need only take the missal and run through the many collects of the rich and varied Lenten liturgy, and we shall find in almost all of them the expression of concepts like these: "May Your family, Lord, while fasting from food to mortify the flesh, pursue justice by abstaining from sin;"[1] "as we abstain from meat, so also may we restrain our senses from all harmful excess;"[2] "as we deprive ourselves of bodily food, so also may we fast from sin in our mind;"[3] "the abstinence which we observe in the body may we also practice with a sincere heart."[4]

The effort to change our life and to practice what we profess by our acts of worship—such is the great fruit of penance which the liturgy inculcates in these texts. To obtain this fruit the Christian must labor constantly with humility, with patience and with a spirit of compunction.

The liturgy also teaches us to use various means of penance to obtain this sincere interior conversion.

Among all these means, the best and most efficacious, incomparably superior to the rest, is that which Jesus Christ was pleased to raise to the dignity of a sacrament and which by antonomasia is called penance. The

[1] Collect of Monday of the second week in Lent.
[2] Collect of Monday of the third week in Lent.
[3] Collect of Friday of the third week in Lent.
[4] Collect of Friday after Ash Wednesday.

sincere and thoughtful reception of this sacrament is beyond doubt the Christian's greatest penitential work. When he goes to confession, he is aware that the judgment with which the Father judged Christ on the cross is being renewed right then over his sins, and that by the sentence of justice which the Lord took upon Himself, a judgment of mercy is now being applied efficaciously to him.

After the sacrament of penance, the best work in expiation of sin is that which God Himself imposes on us and which Christ accepted in His person: death. The patient acceptance of death and of suffering—which is but a prelude of death—as expiation for sin and as a means of sharing personally in the Lord's Passion, is certainly a penance very efficacious and acceptable to God.

And after death and suffering there is work, another means of expiation imposed by God on all men. Work is also redemption, means of human perfection and of personal ennoblement, abundant source of enjoyment and happiness. Still, it always has aspects that make it unlikable and give it a penitential character: the intensity required to make it effective, the effort it demands, the perseverance that makes it fruitful, its monotony, and all the other circumstances that turn it into something painful and unpleasant. Not to run away from these qualities of work but rather to accept them and offer them to God with a contrite heart is a continual occasion of doing penance and making expiation for sins.

Besides these essential and necessary means, there are still other means that are secondary and are matters of free choice. Liturgical spirituality does not despise them; on the contrary, it receives them from the liturgy itself, and learns from the liturgy how to use them and give them the value they deserve in Christian asceticism. This value is always relative; that is, ordained to interior penance and subordinated to the other means we have set forth.

The Lenten liturgy gathers together the principal means of penance by which the Christian may spontaneously add something to the expiatory and redemptive work of Jesus Christ and of the Church; and it inculcates in us the spirit with which we should put these means into practice, that is, that "by the Lenten fast we may so purify ourselves that we may be able to celebrate the solemnities of the Pasch with a pure, sincere heart."[5] Thus the Lenten liturgy must be a basis for reaching interior purity, and this in turn must enable us to celebrate sincerely the sacramental participation in the Pasch of the Lord. Always that which is exterior must be ordained to that which is interior, and we must use material things in so far as they help us attain to spiritual realities.

If it were not so, the bodily penances would become almost useless, if not downright harmful by being the occasion of pride and of a false sense of security. The Church is very careful to inculcate this point in choosing

[5] Collect of Friday of the second week in Lent.

the Old Testament excerpts to be read in the Masses of the first days of Lent; for example, the text of Isaias which is read to us on the Friday after Ash Wednesday:

"Why, Lord, have we fasted, and You have not taken account of it? Why have we humbled our souls, and You have appeared not to know it?" "It is because in your fasts you do your own will. . . . Does the fast that I have chosen consist in a man's afflicting his soul for a day, or bending himself over double and making his bed on sackcloth and ashes? Is this what you call fasting and spending a day acceptable to the Lord? Do you know what is the fast that I want? To loose the bonds of iniquity, to undo the bundles that oppress, to set free those who are oppressed and break every yoke; to divide your bread with the hungry and bring the poor and the homeless into your house . . . ."

With this spirit the Church shows us the penitential means we should use as works of supererogation; and in part she imposes them on us herself, starting us safely on the road. We find the most important of them described in a stanza of the hymn for Matins during Lent, which was probably composed at the time of St. Gregory the Great:

Utamur ergo parcius	More sparing therefore let us make
Verbis, cibis et potibus,	The words we speak, the food we take,
Somno, iocis, et arctius	Our sleep and mirth; and closer barred
Perstemus in custodia.	Be every sense in holy guard.

It should be noted that the penitential practices described in this stanza, like all the others the Church teaches us to practice, usually have a negative character, the privation of something useful or pleasant; and, if the practice in question is something which in itself is irksome, it must always be ordained immediately to a more efficacious attainment of a supernatural end: "for the amendment of vices or the preservation of charity," according to St. Benedict's expression.[6]

The Church in her liturgy does not know of any penitential means that have a positively afflictive end, and limits herself to the traditional practices recommended by the sacred Scripture. We could say that penances, as the liturgy teaches us to practice them, do not have a vengeful character but rather a medicinal one. On this point also, as on all the other aspects, the liturgy knows how to maintain an intelligent balance, which is the index of a sane normality.

In the light of the liturgy the Christian understands very well that creatures are not bad, but good, as works of God and traces of His infinite goodness, which has given them their being. God Himself approved of them because He found them good. The goodness of creatures is more clearly

---

[6] St. Benedict, *Regula Monachorum*, prologue.

perceived if we consider that God has created them for our good, and that together with the whole universe they have been consecrated by the coming of Jesus Christ, who has introduced them into His kingdom to be a revelation of the heavenly Father's goodness, the instrument of His providence and the means of our return to Him. The liturgy does not despise any creature, but brings them all into the Church's universal worship of God through Jesus Christ, and for all of them she has appropriate blessings.

If sin has introduced disorder into the world, it is not creatures that have done evil to us, but we who by our sins make them sharers in our disorder. Hence "all creation groans and travails in pain until now: it is the eager longing of creation awaiting the revelation of the sons of God. For creation was made subject to vanity—not by its own will but by reason of him who made it subject—in hope, because creation itself also will be delivered from its slavery to corruption into the freedom of the glory of the sons of God" (Rom. 8:22, 19-21).

Meanwhile our penance accelerates this redemption of the universe; not indeed by destroying creatures or damaging them or involving them with us in an atmosphere of disorder and sordidness, but by making use of them to do good, treating them with delicacy and even with respect and reverence because they are traces of the divine perfection, sanctifying them by our contact as sons of God and members of Christ, and making them participate in our tribute of glory to the Most Holy Trinity.

This affectionate and reverent use of creatures demands of us a constant foregoing of our inclination to comfort and carelessness. It is therefore a penance that attacks the root of the evil where it is found, namely in our interior. In exchange, it procures for us an habitual elevation of spirit, a delicacy that is the fruit of faith and of charity, and it is a source of repeated occasions for reviving the awareness of the presence of God. It obliges us in practice to maintain a dignified and decorous bearing, even when we are alone, to keep the objects of our personal use in order, to observe propriety and cleanliness in our person and in our belongings.

The permeation with the spirit of the liturgy leads us to the conviction that the Christian's life is lived constantly in the presence of God, as in an uninterrupted act of worship, and that all the objects we use must be considered as sacred vessels of the altar.[7]

We certainly cannot close our eyes before the fact of sin and of its consequences. And since through our fault we have abused the goodness of creatures by letting ourselves feel an exaggerated attraction toward them which has alienated us from God, it is only just that, to return to God, we should deprive ourselves, even with sacrifice on our part, of the natural good which these creatures can place at our disposal; so much the more if we take

---

[7] St. Benedict, *Regula Monachorum*, ch. 31: *Omnia vasa monasterii cunctamque substantiam ac si altaris vasa sacrata conspiciat.*

into consideration our need to watch over the senses and keep the heart free so as to make the practice of virtue possible. This is the theological reason and the measure of penance. It is the norm proposed to us by the Church in St. Gregory's homily on the gospel of the fourth Sunday in Advent: "Bring forth fruits befitting repentance. If anyone has never committed unlawful actions, he may be granted the free use of all lawful things. But if someone has fallen into sin, he should abstain from lawful things so much the more as he recalls having committed unlawful actions."[8]

The most traditional form of penance is deprivation of the pleasures of the table and of bed, which are the ones most representative of the predominance of the flesh over the spirit. And as the predominance may take the form of an excess in quantity or of an over-refinement in quality, this gives rise to four kinds of bodily penance: on the one hand, fasting, which diminishes the quantity of food, and abstinence, which moderates "choosiness" about the menu; on the other hand, vigils which shorten the time taken for rest, and sleeping on a hard bed,[9] which involves abstinence from all the kinds of softness that may be found in the bed.

Although these penances are so simple, it seems to the liturgy that they might turn out to be dangerous because of their negative character. Hence the liturgy endows them with a positive purpose to make them more acceptable to God and more effective in purifying, by assuring a principle of charity for them.

What the Christian saves by his fasting and abstinence he should spend in alms to feed the hungry. There are many texts of the Lenten liturgy that invite us to act in this way. In the Office of the third Sunday of Advent

[8] St. Gregory, *Hom.* 20 *in Evang.*, 8; PL 76, 1163.

[9] The sacred Scripture and the ancient ecclesiastical authors mention the custom of sleeping *in cinere et cilicio* or *in cinere et sacco* and also of wearing haircloth or sackcloth as a means of doing penance. It is known that haircloth was nothing but a coarse cloth woven of goat's or camel's hair. It was used to make clothes for the lower class of people, and also for blankets, sacks and tents, because of its impermeability. The use of this coarse cloth was a mark of poverty, of austerity or of mourning. It was uncomfortable to wear next to the skin because of its roughness.

The ascetics of the East almost always used it, as a penitential measure, for clothing and bed-covering. In the West it was introduced later; some accepted it, while others rejected it. Thus Cassian, for example, did not allow its use. According to him, "it was not used by the saints of old who established the monastic life, nor has it yet found acceptance with the present Fathers who have our institutes in their keeping." He gives as a reason that "it is too ostentatious a garment, more apt to lead to vanity than to be of spiritual profit; besides, it is inconvenient for work, from which a monk may never be dispensed." Cassian, *Institutiones*, 1, 2; CSEL 17, p. 10.

When at times of penance it was customary to leave the bed and sleep on the ground, the hardness used to be alleviated a little by spreading out a layer of ashes of a certain thickness, which was covered with a sack or with haircloth. Later on, a monastic custom prescribed that when a monk was dying he should lie on the ground on a mat of haircloth over which a cross had been made with blessed ashes; thus he would die as a penitent. —Cf. the articles "Cilice" and "Cendre," *Dictionnaire d'Archéologie Chrétienne et de Liturgie*, vol. III, part 2, cols. 1623-1625, and *Dictionnaire de Spiritualité*, II, 899-902 and 403-404.

also, we are exhorted by the words of St. Leo: "Since the salvation of our souls is not acquired only by fasting, let us supplement our fasting by works of mercy towards the poor. Let us make that which we have taken away from pleasure serve for virtue. Let the abstinence of the one who fasts become the food of the poor."[10] And on the third Sunday of September, as preparation for the autumn Ember Days, the liturgy advises us again with St. Leo's words in the second nocturn of Matins, "Let the sin contracted by the frailty of the flesh and our base desires be wiped out by fasting and almsgiving. Let us suffer a little hunger, dearly beloved, and take away from our usual meals something that may help feed the poor."[11]

Similarly, the time taken away from rest is consecrated to God, being occupied in more prolonged prayer or in spiritual reading. That was what the Church used to do with the fruit of the Lenten fasts, which she distributed to the poor in the deaconries. It is also what she practiced and is again practicing in the nocturnal vigils dedicated to prayer in the great liturgical solemnities.

What we have said with regard to the reduction of food and of sleep, the Church teaches us to practice also under other forms of bodily penance, which she herself establishes in the liturgy and which pertain to the suppression of luxury, especially in dress (in sacco et cilicio, and also in the use of violet vestments and of simple prelatic clothes), in bodily adornment, symbolized by the hair (imposition of ashes), and in denial of satisfaction to the senses (absence of flowers on the altar, silence of the organ, etc.).

We might add further the prostrations and kneeling for prayer, as the Church does in the penitential seasons, as a sign of the humble attitude of our prayer as sinners; and also the pilgrimages to places particularly sanctified by the presence and the intercession of the saints, to implore their favor before God: let us recall the daily Lenten stations at the basilicas and the titular churches of Rome.

Conforming to these practical norms and letting himself be guided by these criteria, the Christian can and must practice the measure of penance that corresponds to his spirit of compunction. He will thus attain to a purity of heart that renders him fit for prayer: the subjection of the passions and of the external and internal senses will help him practice the other penance, consisting of recollection and interior silence, which creates an environment propitious to contacts with God; the habitual discipline of his mind will enable him to make the effort of attention necessary to adapt himself consciously to the Church's prayer and penetrate its content.

Herewith, he will attain to the maximum renunciation demanded by liturgical spirituality: the renunciation of his own personality and his own inclinations, even the noblest, in so far as they are subjective, to be fused

---

[10] St. Leo, Sermo 13, de ieiunio decimi mensis II; PL 54, 172.

[11] St. Leo, Sermo 94, de ieiunio septimi mensis IX; PL 54, 460.

into the ecclesiastical community, thinking as it thinks, feeling as its feels, living as it lives. This is the greatest blessing of penance. From the renunciation of the pleasures of our own body it brings us to the point of effective insertion into the praying body of the Church.

Proximate preparation: spiritual reading

Liturgical spirituality gives importance to another activity of the spiritual life of the Christian, which takes its place as a sort of proximate preparation of the individual for sacramental participation in public worship. This activity is spiritual reading, *lectio divina* as the ancients called it.

Being a school of supernatural doctrine, the liturgy supposes in the disciples who are forming themselves by it a personal effort of study, of penetration and of assimilation of the teachings received. Being a renewal and communication of the mystery of Christ, it arouses in the souls of the faithful the desire expressed by St. Paul of investigating the unfathomable riches of Christ, and of receiving light on the dispensation of the mystery hidden from eternity in God, and of comprehending with all the saints what is the breadth and the length and the height and the depth of Christ's love, which surpasses all knowledge (Eph. 3:8-9, 18-19).

The liturgy teaches us in practice that, by the Lord's kindness, we are privileged to know the mysteries of God's kingdom; and the soul formed in the school of the Church desires nothing so much as to be enlightened on these mysteries. This is the greatest gift that can be desired in this world, and the Church often reminds us of it to enkindle our desire, and makes us ask for it insistently in her public prayer, in many psalms and collects, particularly in those that follow the communion of the Mass.

The sincerity of our desire should be shown by our putting to use the means that are within our reach. And there is surely no lack of means; for God has given us the sacred Scriptures and has lighted in us the lamp of intelligence illuminated by faith, that we might study the word of God and seek in the sources of revelation the knowledge of the divine mysteries. Whoever shows this interest by doing as much as lies within his power will be able to receive from God an interior light to reveal the sense of the Scriptures to him.

At the beginning of Lent, the season particularly dedicated to reading and prayer, the Church in the communion antiphon of Ash Wednesday reminds us of a saying of the Lord which serves as a stimulus and guarantee of our faithful study, and which at the same time is a forecast of the resplendent light of Easter: "He who meditates upon the law of the Lord day and night shall bring forth his fruit in due season."

The *book* of all Christians, and in a special way of the ministers of the word of God, is the sacred Scripture, which brings us God's message. It is our duty and our incomparable dignity to welcome it and to investigate its contents, making it the habitual food of our spirit.

It seems, however, that this is not ordinarily the spiritual reading preferred by our Christians. God has deigned to speak to us to reveal the intimacies of His life and of His economy in relation to men, and we do not deign to interest ourselves enough to listen to His words and become acquainted with His revelation. There are data and statistics which ought to give us pause, for they show us the true state of the Christian life in our times.

We might find one of these indications by answering the question: How many Christians take the sacred Scripture as the habitual matter of their reading? Or, at least: How many have read it in its entirety even once in their life? And again, seeking to restrict the requirement as much as possible: How many have been interested enough to read the whole New Testament?

Every year the liturgy makes its own the complaints voiced by St. John Chrysostom when he considered that "not all Christians know St. Paul as they should; and some are so ignorant of him that they do not even know with certainty the number of his letters." Continuing with the words of the same Doctor, the liturgy reminds us that he who loves truly is wholly pre-occupied with learning all about the person he loves; and on this basis it urges us to devote ourselves to the reading of the sacred Scriptures if we truly love God and desire to know Him. And it gives us this norm: "Put into it at least the same interest you put into procuring material goods. For, even if it is true that the measure I propose to you is very stingy, it would be well that you give at least that much."[12]

In the school of the liturgy we learn to love the word of God, which is given us as the food of our spirit. Every day in the Mass and the Office the Church has us listen to or read some passages of the Old Testament and others of the New, in keeping with the solemnity being celebrated or according to the cyclical plan established for our spiritual instruction. If she offers us any other reading, it consists in a patristic commentary or homily to explain and illuminate the sacred text for us.

In so doing, the Church lets us know in practice what should be the basic matter of our spiritual reading: first of all and predominantly the sacred Scripture; and alongside of this but subordinate to it, the writings of the Fathers, the doctors and the authors who can comment on the doctrine contained in the holy books and apply it to us. With a broadening of the exegetical field according to the mind of the Church, the treatises that can help us probe the revealed doctrine have their place also in our spiritual reading: theology, the documents of the Church's *magisterium* and in general whatever constitutes ecclesiastical science, in so far as it acquaints us with some aspect of the mystery of God, of Christ and of the Church.

As to the distribution of the matter, especially with regard to the sacred

[12] Second Sunday after Epiphany: St. John Chrysostom, *Praefatio in Epistolam ad Romanos;* PG 60, 391.

Scriptures, the liturgy offers us two plans, one following a cycle and one based on circumstance.

Every year in the Divine Office and to some extent also in the Mass, the Church has us go over all the books of the Bible. She does not read them in their entirety, but usually gives the beginnings and some excerpts from each book, as if to indicate that we should complete the reading in private, following the order and the distribution she proposes to us. This order and the actual proportion of the biblical readings in the Divine Office and in the Mass may vary, and will probably be modified in future liturgical reforms. That does not matter. The point is to follow with the Church, in so far as possible, the ordered reading of the sacred books, or to devise a plan of reading in imitation of the Church's plan, taking whatever time we need to go through the whole of sacred Scripture.

It is the Church's practice to apply the other plan, based on circumstance, on the great solemnities and at certain seasons or on certain typical days of the liturgical year. On these occasions the liturgy suspends the cyclical reading and has us read selected passages better adapted to the mystery celebrated on that day, which will help us understand it better and live it more intensely. Sometimes these scriptural texts give the liturgical celebration its tone and constitute a most precious sacramental, which, while preparing us for the Eucharist, is at the same time a mystical extension of the mystery contained in it.

With this adaptation of the biblical texts to the principal object of the feast, the liturgy shows us another aim and opens up new fields for our spiritual reading: the preparation for the feasts and the study of the liturgical texts.

Our participation in liturgical worship is at the same time a social act and a personal assimilation of the mystery of Christ.

As a social act it requires an intelligent and ordered actuation on the part of all those who are to take part in it. If each one of the participants is not well posted on the role that falls to him, it will be hard for the common work to attain total perfection. It need hardly be said that this dispositive perfection is to be sought with so much the more diligence as the active part to be taken in the collective action is more important. In a purely human order, no one who is conscious of his own duty and responsibility will presume to exercise an important function without having a firm grasp of the knowledge necessary for it, in so far as possible. Here the concern is with a social act which, aside from the external actuation, which involves a knowledge of the ceremonies, depends above all on the spirit that must inform the outward rite perceptible to the senses.[13] Thus the spiritual preparation

[13] "One Holy Thursday morning the comedy company of Gaston Bary had been invited to our church of Faubourg Saint-Honoré. As they came out from the ceremony, one of the actors said to the Father Porter, 'You should not have invited us. This has been bad for us.

is the one that matters most for the integral perfection of the liturgical act; and this preparation consists not only in interior purity but also in the understanding of the mystery being celebrated and renewed in the Church.

On the other hand, as far as the personal assimilation of the mystery of Christ is concerned, we know that it can be achieved only through faith and charity, that is, the supernatural actuation of the intellect and of the will. The personal contact with the mystery will be so much the more vivid and effective as the adaptation of the intellect to the object of faith is more perfect and as the capacity for attachment in the will aroused by desire is greater.

Both reasons demand an intelligent preparation for celebrating the liturgical feasts. The theological depth of the mysteries, the difficulty of interpretation of some texts, the symbolism and the new meaning introduced into them by the liturgy, the historical motives and events which have given rise to certain rites and can explain the extrinsic reason for certain celebrations—all this must be an object of study if we want to penetrate the spiritual sense of the liturgy and receive from it the maximum communication of supernatural light and of divine life. Here is an immense field to be worked by spiritual reading.

For spiritual reading, *lectio divina,* is primarily a study; a study and therefore a labor of the intellect, though moved by charity, and for that reason an exercise of piety also. Its immediate aim is to acquire and to increase the knowledge of truths of a divine order, through the effort and the capacities of the intellect raised by faith, as the first natural step for reaching the desired goal, which is contemplation.

In liturgical spirituality, which does not have the systematic rigor of the "methods," this process takes place with the simplicity that belongs to life itself, with progressive continuity, without pre-established divisions. It begins with the attentive reading of the holy books, and goes on to a scrutiny of their meaning to arrive at a profound natural and supernatural knowledge of the truth. The object of truth is made present sacramentally in the liturgical celebration and is communicated to us in a living way in the Eucharist. By its sacramental contact and its divine efficacy the Eucharist increases the light, enlarges the capacity of the soul and leads it easily toward the simple, loving intuition of supernatural truth, in which contemplation consists.

The *lectio divina* is the first stage of this process. Precisely because it is the first, it involves a greater personal effort: the effort of the intellect seeking the truth. Its object consists in investigating the sacred Scriptures, the writings of the Fathers, theological doctrine and the liturgical formulas, in the presence of God, with the loving desire to know Him and to become capable of receiving His sacramental communications. The immediate goal of spirit-

How can you treat such grand ceremonies in this way, when we go through so much preparation just to present insignificant, stupid comedies?' " M. M. Couturier, O.P., *L'Art Sacré,* Sept.-Oct. 1952, "Théatres," p. 13.

ual reading is that knowledge of the mysteries of God and the doctrines of the Church which will increase our faith and enlarge our charity.

In the *lectio divina* we pass easily, and almost imperceptibly, from reading to meditation and to prayer, because the knowledge of the divine mysteries, acquired with light from God, fills the soul with spiritual sweetness, and from time to time a more vivid light testifies to the presence and action of the Lord, who is preparing the soul for a more intimate union with Him in His sacramental communications. The *lectio divina,* then, is the kind of study which, informed by charity, begets prayer, nurtures it and often goes so far as to merge with it.

2. Private Spiritual Activity as Vital Assimilation of the Liturgy

Prayer

Participation in worship and in liturgical prayer, as we have shown in the preceding chapter, is true prayer. It is public prayer and individual prayer at the same time. It is public because it includes officially the representation of the Church, in whose name and under whose inspiration it rises up to God. But it can also be called individual, in as much as it is recited by individuals who give it form and perfection by their personal spiritual activity.

When, for example, a priest recites his breviary, it is the whole Church that prays through her minister. Hence his action has a public character. But if, besides reciting it, he gives it all the attention it deserves and conforms his spirit to the formulas he is pronouncing, then he too as an individual is truly praying with the words of the Church. And what prayer can be more excellent than that which raises man's spirit to the same heights attained by the prayer of Christ's Spouse? If prayer is the raising up of the mind to God, we may well say that when a person's mind submits to guidance through the channels opened up by the Holy Spirit and makes contact with God by personifying the mind of the Church, that person is praying.

It does not matter that the way of his ascent has been marked out beforehand. Nor is the personal value of this operation of his mind diminished by the fact that he has been raised to the dignity of representing the whole Christian people before God. His role as a member does not disappear because he incarnates in himself the whole Body, nor does his mind fly up to God any less impulsively because it is borne along in the ascensional movement with which the Spirit of Jesus carries His Church.

To exclude individual prayer from the concept of liturgical prayer would mean that we did not know what liturgical prayer was. On the other hand, to want to limit individual prayer to the spiritual activity of the individual on the occasion of the Church's public prayer would show that we had never intensely practiced liturgical prayer. For if anyone has prayed with the

Church, letting himself be permeated with the light of her doctrine and the warmth of her emotions, it is no longer so easy for him to interrupt this intensity of spiritual life that has been communicated to him. He will need time to assimilate the abundant spiritual food he has received, and during the day he will feel the urge to savor again the sweetness of which that substantial food has given him a taste. And it is precisely in this that private prayer consists.

The first and most spontaneous manifestation of private prayer proceeds from a pressing need to continue in silence the contact with God established during the liturgical prayer. After the Mass, after the Divine Office or the administration or reception of a sacrament, the soul that has truly prayed remains as if submerged in a supernatural atmosphere, from which it cannot free itself abruptly. Rather, it must let the spiritual vibration caused by the contact with God die away softly; and meanwhile the labor of assimilation is proceeding in a normal way.

The liturgical texts are so full of doctrine and mystery that, despite every effort at adapting our mind, we cannot succeed in grasping them completely during the liturgical prayer. The soul must review them quietly, to absorb as much as it can retain, according to the gift of God and its own present capacity, out of the great amount of food that is given it. Our slow rate of assimilation does not permit us to convert into our own substance the abundance of thoughts and emotions expressed in the liturgical prayer. We need a time of repose and silence for pondering and savoring what has enlightened us best or moved us most. This is the personal labor of assimilation. It is the private prayer which completes and renders fruitful our personal contribution to the Church's public prayer.

Pius XII recommends it explicitly, referring to participation in the Mass: "When the Mass, which is subject to special rules of the liturgy, is over, the person who has received holy communion is not thereby freed from his duty of thanksgiving. . . . Admittedly the congregation has been officially dismissed, but each individual, since he is united with Christ, should not interrupt the hymn of praise in his own soul."[14]

When the time dedicated to prayer has passed and the ordinary occupations of life must be taken up again, the soul, prepared by spiritual reading and permeated with the light of the grace received in liturgical prayer, remains as if pervaded with a supernatural atmosphere, which maintains it in an interior recollection highly propitious for frequent contacts with God through faith and charity. There is a continuation or a repercussion in the soul of the sacred silence of the church, saturated with the perfume of the incense, in which everything takes on the quality of worship and beckons to prayer.

This sense of the presence of God and an almost worshipful reverence for

[14] *Mediator Dei*, nn. 123-124.

all creatures, which have become a sort of sensible manifestation of this divine presence and of its action, constitute a characteristic fruit of liturgical spirituality. They are the means used by this spirituality to attain the perfection of the Christian life in the perfection of charity.

The Christian who has become accustomed to participating in the Church's public worship and making it the center of his spiritual activity will readily model his own life on it. Then, imperceptibly, he will be assimilating everything that constitutes liturgical action: its doctrine, its practical norms of Christian life, its procedures. Even the very atmosphere in which the liturgy is performed will come to be a part of the habitual atmosphere of his soul. Hence arises the inclination to an interior recollection, an habitual sense of religious reverence, and a refined spiritual perception. Seeing material realities and sensible objects by this spiritual perception, the Christian makes use of them—as the liturgy does—to put himself in contact with God and offer Him the inner worship of his soul as an echo of the Church's public worship.

The Christian educated in the school of the liturgy has learned the positive value of his life in Christ, begun in baptism, nourished and strengthened by the other sacraments. He knows the transcendental value of his vocation and of his personal holiness, directed to the total perfection of the Church and to the supernatural embellishment of the mystical Body. He takes account of the actual presence of the mystery of Christ within the Christian family and in his own life. He is aware of the value as worship of all his acts as a Christian, in union with the priestly action of the Church and of Jesus Christ. Such a Christian cannot help finding in his ordinary life an infinity of occasions which will intensify the awareness of these sublime realities, reanimate in his spirit the joy of the presence of God, and be constant sources of true prayer.

This entrance of the soul into its own sanctuary to prostrate itself humbly before the Lord and take joy in Him usually takes place in brief moments. It is simply a conscious renewal of the mind's contact with God, a sort of resonance which from time to time makes the soul vibrate in unison with that which had been its intense prayer during the Mass and the Divine Office.

Usually these brief but profound resonances are limited in the beginning to the times immediately following the liturgical offices and to certain occasions most favorable to recollection and spiritual reflection. But later on they increase in frequency and intensity, and fill the day with their beneficent influence, like a widespread vibration which maintains the spirit in the sweetness of the presence of God. Purity of life and of heart are at the same time the necessary environment and the positive fruit of these communications of light and grace.

External occupations, of course, make it harder for the soul to keep its attention fixed on the presence of God. It needs some external help to recall its attention and put it in contact once more with the memory of what it has lived in the liturgy. Some short text of the psalms that have been recited or of the formulas expressing the content of the mystery, which were found rather striking during the time of the liturgical prayer, opportunely recalled and pronounced interiorly as ejaculations, will rekindle the fervor of the spirit and give unity to the life of the Christian.

To direct and nourish this life of prayer, the Church does not use a special method with a pre-established arrangement of acts and exercises, aimed at a practical moral end in harmony with a particular system of pedagogy. Liturgical spirituality leaves the soul full freedom of movement, that, following its own spontaneous interior inclination, it may open itself to the light of the divine mysteries, letting itself be gently permeated with that light, and may expand naturally and simply in intimate, reverent relationship with the Lord. Still it does not abandon the soul and leave it to itself, but, without forcing it, procures for it the means that will bring it to the desired goal, as if naturally.

During the liturgical celebration, while she is giving doctrine, the Church accompanies it with many material devices which may impress the senses and help the soul penetrate into the knowledge of the mystery. She attracts the eyes with the variety of the ceremonies, with the color and form of the vestments, with the flowers and the lights. She impresses the ears with the singing and the sound of the organ. She pleases the sense of smell with the perfume of the incense. She interests the whole body with the different positions, attitudes and reverences. She recalls to the memory the mysteries of the Lord, stimulates the imagination with the rich symbolism of the rites and the liturgical formulas, courts the esthetic sense with the style, order and combination of the different elements.

All this does not distract. Rather, it takes possession of the senses so that, instead of wandering about, to the detriment of the intellectual operation, they facilitate that operation by establishing unity in the whole being. He who knows how to take an active part in the liturgical action has nothing to do but to penetrate into the environment and let himself be penetrated by it: to observe, to listen, to breathe the atmosphere that has been formed around him, to live in harmony with what surrounds him, while his spirit is considering attentively the meaning of the words and the rites. During the liturgical celebration he does not pray better by keeping his eyes closed, but on the contrary by keeping them wide open, with his senses and his spirit attentive to the action that is going on.

Then, in the quiet atmosphere of private prayer, everything that has been lived during the Mass or the Divine Office will continue to exercise its impression, and the soul will be able to contemplate at its leisure the various aspects of the mystery, to dwell on those that affect it more, letting itself be illumined by them and taking pleasure in their contemplation.

Following the example of the liturgy, the activity of private prayer will fix itself more on the object than on the subject, will take more interest in the penetration of the mystery than in the consideration of the subject's own needs, will look more at God than at itself, will strive more to listen than to speak.

Liturgical spirituality, without in the least neglecting spiritual formation, seems to be forgetting it during prayer, intent as it is on seeking rather the knowledge of Jesus Christ and of His mysteries and on entering through Him into the marvelous realities of the supernatural world, which culminate in the mystery of the intimate, personal communications of the Most Holy Trinity, prolonged in the soul of Jesus Christ, in the bosom of the Church and in our life as Christians. The spiritual atmosphere created in the soul by the contemplation of these truths is the most solid guarantee that it will remain humble and charitable and that its interior life will develop normally.

It is not hard to see that for a soul educated in this environment of spontaneous, rich spiritual vitality, the rigidities of any method will soon be superfluous.

At first, by reason of ideology, formation or environment, a person is not yet accustomed to the freedom of spirit of liturgical piety, and this freedom may seem excessively broad, offering little protection against the dangers of distraction or of spiritual dilettantism. Then is the time to continue using the particular method of prayer practiced hitherto, while seeking to apply it to the consideration of the liturgical texts so as to find spiritual nourishment in them.[15] All this will be a mixture of *lectio divina* and prayer, which will serve to open the way to an appreciative understanding of the realities contained in the liturgy and will begin to establish unity between the Christian's public worship and his private life.

This is the most important point in liturgical spirituality: unity of life. It is important that there be no divorce between what the Church is doing over us and teaching us, and what we are living in our inmost selves; that it should not happen, for example, that while the Church is representing and contemplating the Ascension of our Lord, we in private, prescinding from that which constitutes the vital food of the mystical Body on that day, are isolating ourselves in a meditation on the flight into Egypt or on the scourging at the pillar, simply because this arouses more devotion in us or because it falls on this day according to the order followed in our book of meditations.

However slight may be the attention we pay to the texts and the meaning of the liturgical celebration, and however little we know of the place the liturgy occupies in the life of the Church and of souls, not only shall we be able to find abundant material for meditation and contemplation every day, but we shall feel the imperfection and the impropriety of ignoring what the

---

[15] We find an example of the application of the method of meditation to each day's liturgical texts in the works of Benedict Baur, O.S.B., *The Light of the World* and *Saints of the Missal* (St. Louis: B. Herder Book Co., 1958).

Church proposes and being guided instead by our own judgment or our own taste.

Moreover, the Church does have her own plan, carefully worked out according to a criterion which takes close account of the objective value of the supernatural realities and of the needs or expediencies of our human psychology. If we follow the program established by the Church, we find during the course of the year all the aspects of the mystery of God and of the Christian life that may be of interest to our spiritual formation. What is more, we find them presented in a form and a proportion more valuable for educating and for sanctifying, by reason of being more objectively adapted to reality.

The contemplation of the mysteries of Jesus Christ and of His redemptive actions occupies the central and most important place. Wonderfully articulated, they form the luminous outline of the yearly course. Around them, like gentle slopes that lead to the summit of each mystery or guide the descent from it, the various liturgical seasons—more or less extended in duration or intense in wealth of doctrine, according to the importance of that mystery in the general plan—serve to prepare us psychologically and morally for its celebration or to continue its enlightening and sanctifying action, centering everything in the annual celebration of the Paschal mystery, which gives unity to the whole. Meanwhile, every Sunday that does not have a special character takes the form of a weekly reflection of the Pasch; and the feasts of our Lady and of the saints occurring throughout the year are so many irradiations of the mystery of Jesus Christ, which is made more concrete and more accessible to us in the reproduction of it which the life of that saint constitutes.

While the mystery of the Lord forms the principal object of our prayer and contemplation, the soul gradually finds its own sanctification under the enlightenment of that mystery and in contact with it. The special grace derived from each mystery shapes the soul to the divine model, while the soul remains attentive to the contemplation of the mystery. Every redemptive action of Christ and every aspect of His life brings about in the one who contemplates them a spiritual reaction, which renews in the soul some aspect of the Christian life, and encourages and develops the practice of some virtue. Thus, without our being excessively preoccupied with it, our own spiritual perfection is growing in the gentle warmth of our contemplation of the Lord.

The liturgy's annual program is not lacking a consideration of the Last Things or of sin either; in fact, special attention is given them. But, like the virtues, they are always included in the unity of the mystery of Jesus Christ and contemplated in its light. This does not lessen their moral efficacy at all; rather, it increases it considerably by communicating a transcendental value to these realities and ordaining them directly to the work of the Lord.

The special attention the Church devotes to original sin and to its punishment in the time after Septuagesima, emphasized by the suppression of the *Alleluia,* a measure which makes us feel our well deserved exile more keenly; the reminder and the consideration of personal sin and of the fraternal solidarity of all men in the evil and the faults of each one, so insistently recalled during Lent—these things find their true value and their maximum efficacy when this whole accumulation of human miseries is related to the Lord's Passion and death in the celebration of the Paschal mystery.

During some weeks at the end of the time after Pentecost, the Church in the Sunday epistles and gospels stirs our mind with the thought of the judgment, at the end of a year of grace which will be closed with the sacramental commemoration of the last judgment. And again, this consideration, which brings us to the end of our life, obtains its deepest meaning by being placed in relation with the longed-for parousia, the second coming of the Lord which will definitively achieve the perfection of His work and of His kingdom, and which now, in time, is the announcement of a new liturgical year, of a new Advent, with the consequent renewal of the mystery of Christ.

The yearly renewal and contemplation of the same cyclical plan, adapted to human nature, moves us each time with an impression of newness, and leads us to probe ever more deeply into its theological content and to conform ourselves to its sanctifying power. The result is that every year the celebration of the liturgical mysteries is for us the best preparation for living them once more in the following cycle, which finds us better disposed and reveals to us new aspects of every mystery.

Moreover, as Pope Pius XII stated, the doctrinal plan proposed to us by the Church in the acts of public worship is so complete and perfect that "it would be difficult to find a truth of the Christian faith which is not somehow expressed in the liturgy, whether it is the readings from the Old and the New Testaments in the Mass and the Divine Office, or the riches which mind and heart discover in the psalms."[16]

From all these notions it is easy to deduce the spontaneous character of prayer in liturgical spirituality. It is at the same time life, the nourishment of that life and its manifestation. Hence that spontaneity proper to every healthy life is connatural to it. It will not refuse the disciplinary aid of a method when a method seems expedient to it, especially in the beginning. But, as it acquires its normal development, it will keep freeing itself of outward constraints so as to move with more breadth and liberty. Liturgical spirituality does not exclude any degree of prayer, but it does stop to examine the kinds proposed. It prays as its heart feels best and whither the Spirit of the Lord leads it.

In conclusion, adopting the present terminology, we might say that the

---

[16] *The Assisi Papers,* p. 225.

prayer inspired by the liturgy tends rather toward that which is called prayer of quiet, and, through this, toward contemplation.

The basis of this prayer is eminently doctrinal and therefore demands a laborious intellectual effort. As we have already indicated, this is the role that falls to the *lectio divina.* At the time of the prayer itself, on the other hand, it is not properly a discursive labor that should occupy the mind, but rather the mere act of looking at or contemplating the mystery scrutinized by the *lectio,* which has been lived sacramentally and tasted during the liturgical celebration and is now savored and assimilated in the supernatural warmth of prayer. The affective life has an important part in the prayer and is very helpful in the labor of assimilation. But it must always be guided by the light received, and thus it is not confined to a mere feeling; it uses the emotions to clothe the profound movements of charity in refinement, enthusiasm and human expression.

The practice of the virtues

The heightened spiritual vitality received in prayer must be manifested in fruits of Christian life, that is, in the acts of virtue which perfect our powers and direct them to the final attainment of their supernatural end.

Elsewhere we have said that the educational plan of liturgical spirituality consists in participating in the sacramental action, seeking to draw from it a double effect: the grace of sanctification derived from that action, and the spiritual understanding of it. Both effects, moreover, concur in a common result, the works of the Christian life. These reproduce morally the mystery of Christ, exemplary cause of our sanctification, and permit us to become finally included within His kingdom. We have also adduced some examples of prayers in which the Church proposes this plan and recommends it to God's blessing.

The intimate relation that exists between the life of prayer and the life of virtue has this effect, that in any spirituality the method applied to prayer determines the norms which are supposed to regulate the exercise of the virtues. So also in the spirituality derived from the liturgy the characteristics of its kind of prayer are reproduced in the practical ordering of the Christian life. Here again, liturgical spirituality is not too much concerned with methods or procedures; its prime interest is sincerity and profundity of life; and, as a means of attaining these more easily and with greater perfection, it insists on unity of action.

Liturgical spirituality is as simple on the topic of virtue as it is in its teaching about prayer. Because it is so true and so deep, its procedures can be reduced to a minimum: to fulfill what we live, to translate into action what grace realizes within us; in a word, to be consistent. Whoever is a Christian and knows what this means, should live as a Christian. If there is sincerity, nothing else is needed. If there is not, even the most carefully worked out requirements of the methods will be of no avail.

St. Paul used this very simple logic: We are dead to sin; hence it is not possible that we still live in it. Since through baptism we have been made one thing with Christ, who has risen, so it must be that we also live a new life (cf. Rom. 6:2, 4). The formula of liturgical spirituality could be expressed in this sentence which St. Paul gave as a guide to His Christians: "Now you are light in the Lord; walk, then, as children of light" (Eph. 5:8); or in this other sentence: "Be imitators of God, as very dear children; Christ has loved us: walk, therefore, in love" (Eph. 5:1-2).

This is the program the liturgy presents to the faithful: to know that we are children of God through love; to receive and contemplate the mystery of love personified in Christ—"who delivered Himself up for us as an offering and a sacrifice to God": God and us, the two termini of Christ's love—; then, to live this love and bring forth similar fruits of charity.

The summit of Christian perfection consists in *charity,* which establishes us in God and will remain with us in the possession of God. All the other virtues receive their maximum value from it; and, united under it as if forming its pedestal, concur with it for the integrity of the perfection which is found essentially in charity.

In the practice of charity we must distinguish between its *affective* side and its *effective* side, between the love and the works, between the pleasure we find in God and the practical demonstration of our love. Perfection has its roots more in the former than in the latter. The enjoyment of love which reposes in the loved one is the proper act of charity; the works are the fruit of other virtues commanded by charity, which range themselves under it so as to make visible the interior act of supernatural love.

The supernatural and perfective value of the acts of these other virtues is not in direct relation to the difficulty overcome or to the effort required to practice them, but is measured by the degree of charity with which they have been performed. A heroic act of virtue can have a minimum of meritorious value if it has been performed with a minimum of supernatural charity. On the other hand, the smallest act of virtue performed with perfect charity will be very meritorious. As far as perfection is concerned, then, the most important element is the affective quality of charity, while the effective manifestations of this virtue will be consequences of affective charity.

Still, placed as we are in our present condition, we cannot neglect the works of charity, not only because they concur objectively, as do the acts of the other virtues, in the material integrity of perfection, but also because our charity has need of external stimuli to purify it and strengthen it. Besides, one of the two termini of our charity—the neighbor—cannot be excluded from our works of charity while we are in this world; hence our affective charity towards him will not be sincere and true if we do not offer him, as far as lies within our competence, the works of charity of which he has need.

For all these reasons, the works of charity are simultaneously a stimulus of affective charity, because of our actual imperfect condition, and a proof of our love, prompted by the present conditions of our neighbor. It follows that our judgment on charity will revolve around the works of mercy, which will reveal at the same time that which is more external—that is, at what point the effect of our love has arrived: "whatever you will have done for one of these little ones"—and that which is more substantial, that is, the degree of affective purity which has been the motive of our charity—"you will have done it for Me."

In conclusion, Christian perfection is obtained in the measure in which affective charity increases and in which, under its influence, all the other virtues are being developed. Because of their connection with grace and with charity,[17] the other virtues increase in the same proportion as these.

It is not strange, therefore, that the Church's pedagogy should be more interested in the growth of affective charity than in anything else. The life of prayer, apex of the Christian's spiritual activity, tends directly to union with God through charity, as we have explained. The charity of Christ and the charity of the Christian, placed in vital contact by means of the sacraments and of prayer, establish in the soul a powerful center of attraction and of irradiation which, on the one hand, draws the virtuous acts to this center of charity, in other words orients them toward their supreme end, and on the other hand brightens and warms with its rays all the aspects of the Christian's individual and social life.

To orient all things to God, not only in so far as God is the object of worship but also in so far as this worship tends to unite us to Him, the liturgy reduces everything to the supreme motif of charity, and centers its worshipful and educational activity in the Eucharist, which is the sacrifice of Christ's charity, the sacrament of union with God and of brotherly communion. As a consequence, the liturgy is wholly impregnated with a sense of charity. It is impossible to understand the liturgy and its spirituality if it is not conceived under this formal aspect of supernatural love. Nor is it possible to enjoy it spiritually except in the measure in which, making our own egoism disappear, we really accept our personal inclusion in the community of the Church, with the idea of living in it with our brethren according to one spirit, one thought, one prayer: *cor unum et anima una.*

In his vigorous language St. Augustine explains how the Eucharist, center of the liturgy, is the sacrament of charity, because it realizes our union with Christ and our brotherly communion: "Since Christ suffered for us, He left us in this sacrament His body and His blood, and made us to be them too.

[17] Cf. St. Thomas, *Summa theol.*, I-II, 65.

For we also have become His body . . . ." "If you want to know what the body of Christ is, listen to the Apostle telling the faithful, 'You are the body of Christ and individually its members' (1 Cor. 12:27). If, therefore, you are the body and members of Christ, your mystery is placed upon the Lord's table: you are receiving your mystery." "You are there on the table, you are there in the chalice." "What you are receiving is what you are, the grace that has redeemed you; you subscribe to this when you answer 'Amen.' What you see is the sacrament of unity." "In this way Christ our Lord showed us to ourselves, willed that we belong to Him, consecrated at His table the mystery of our peace and of our unity. He who receives the mystery of unity and does not keep the bond of peace is not receiving the mystery to his advantage but a testimony against himself."[18]

There is nothing so opposed to the spirit of the liturgy as individualism, which is the predominance of the individual over the community and which is shown in practice by living and carrying on one's own activity in isolation. The worst individualism is spiritual individualism, because it affects that which in itself is the most unitive thing in the Christian community.

The liturgy, on the contrary, is essentially community: community of doctrine, community of worship, community of grace, community of means, in the common celebration of the mystery of Christ. It is community which is not limited to the substance of these realities, but which also comprises everything that is related to them or derived from them.

For this reason liturgical spirituality maintains a communitarian savor even in the personal acts of the spiritual life and of individual piety, which are thus more powerfully informed by charity: private prayer is nourished on the food that has been distributed in common at the family table; reading is preparation to enable us to bring better dispositions to the public action; the spirit of penance is broadened by joining our own compunction to the penance of the Church and augmenting the sorrow for our own sins with the consideration of the sins of others, in which we feel ourselves associated by our sincere brotherhood; the external works of penance are referred directly to charity by our destining for alms what we save by fasting and our devoting to prayer the time taken from our sleep.

He who informs his Christian life with charity does not have too much need of applying himself in detail to the practice of each one of the virtues. They will all be increasing and developing uniformly under the impulse of the habitual charity which is nourished constantly on liturgcal worship and on prayer. Every time during the day that the mind applies itself, even for a moment, to reviving the contact made with God in the liturgy and in prayer, charity is reanimated and extends a powerful influence over the

---

[18] St. Augustine, *Sermo in die Paschae* (PL 46, 835); *Sermo* 272 (PL 38, 1247); *Sermo Denis* 6, 2, and *Guelferbytanus* 7, 1 (*Mis-cellanea Agostiniana*, I, pp. 30 and 463); *Sermo* 272 (PL 38, 1248).

actions immediately following. The aim of liturgical spirituality is to make these contacts habitual, so that the effective stimulus of charity will come to be maintained without interruption.

It is true that everyone has his own failings which are an obstacle to perfection, and must oppose them wtih the contrary habit, that is, the corresponding virtue. But these virtues themselves are activated spontaneously in the warmth of the normal life of charity. In fact, when the sincere desire to please God by living a Christian life predominates, the very stimuli of the disordered passions excite charity by way of reaction; and charity comes to our aid at our weak point, either by commanding the corresponding virtue or by healing with a sincere compunction the wounds received. The frequency with which the predominant failing makes its goad felt will determine the frequency of occasions for repeated and intense practice of the corresponding virtue.

On the other hand, the liturgy does not fail to excite the other virtues in a particular way. We have indicated that every feast and every liturgical season throws a special light on things and thus produces a particular attitude of spirit very propitious for the development of certain particular virtues. If the liturgical year contemplates all the aspects of the mystery of Christ and of the Christian life, we may well say that he who is faithful about adapting himself to the practical demands that result from this contemplation will have occasion to practice the different Christian virtues in a degree and with a frequency proportionate to their objective importance and to their relation with the aim of the Christian life.

The liturgy insists in a special way on emphasizing the practice of some virtues, undoubtedly because it considers them basic in the Christian life and the best supports of charity.

Foremost among these stands the virtue of *faith*. Charity could not exist in this world without faith, being founded and nurtured on it. It is not possible to love God without knowing Him, and this knowledge is the object of faith. To love our neighbor with a supernatural love, we must recognize in him a child of God, a member of Christ, a fruit of the Redemption; and only through faith can we succeed in knowing and appreciating these realities.

The liturgy supposes and demands a constant exercise of faith, not only by the frequency with which it requires the explicit profession of the faith in the acts of worship, but even more because its worshipful and sanctifying action is performed by means of sensually perceptible elements, which signify, contain and cause the realities of the supernatural order. In the liturgy, outwardly everything is human, but in the depths of its reality everything is divine.

The measure of our compenetration with the liturgy and with its spirit corresponds to the degree of purity of our faith. Only by a sincere and living faith can we succeed in appreciating the supernatural content of every rite, of every ceremony, of every formula; the sacramental value of the praying community, of the hierarchical actions, of the liturgical institutions; the sacred sense acquired by persons, gestures, objects, places and times when they are introduced into the Church's worshipful action.

And then, in its extension to private life, this continual presence of God toward which liturgical spirituality tends; the exercise of this spiritual priesthood of the Christian, which can give all things a religious and worshipful meaning; the sincerity and depth of the Christian life as practical realization of that which is lived in the church—all this supposes a well grounded faith.

"The solemn liturgical ceremonies," said Pius XII, "are a profession of faith in action. They express the great truths of faith concerning the inscrutable designs of God's generosity and His inexhaustible goodness to men, concerning the love and mercy of the heavenly Father for the world, to save which He sent His Son and delivered Him to death."[19]

Joined to faith is *hope*. Hope is the smile of the liturgy. The liturgy is oriented toward the realities that are to come. It teaches us to live in mystery what we shall one day possess in a clear vision. It often repeats these thoughts in the Mass formularies: "that we may then receive in the fulness of its reality what we now celebrate in mystery;"[20] "let us possess in eternal joys what we now celebrate in time;"[21] "that, freed from earthly longings, we may pass on to heavenly desires;"[22] "amid the changing things of this world, our hearts may be set on that place where true joys are found;"[23] etc. What the Church asks in her prayer she signifies sacramentally in her rites, since, as St. Thomas teaches, all the sacraments, each in its own way, are signs prophetic of the glory to come.[24]

The liturgy possesses the greatest incitement to hope in the Eucharist, in which "a pledge of future glory is given us." In the Eucharist, which contains the whole mystery of Christ, and in the communion of saints, the liturgy has a perennial source of hope and consolation.

Because we possess the Eucharist and because we form a Church—Eucharist and Church which transcend eternity—we cannot be excessively sad if we evaluate these realities in the spirit of the liturgy. They give rise in the soul to an unchangeable peace and serenity which effectively dissipate any sadness and sorrow of spirit.

Lent, for example, with its austerities and its repeated consideration of sin, becomes a season actually to be looked forward to, because the liturgy

[19] *The Assisi Papers*, p. 225.
[20] Postcommunion of Ember Saturday in September.
[21] Postcommunion of Ember Wednesday of Pentecost Week.
[22] Secret of the twenty-fourth and last Sunday after Pentecost.
[23] Collect of the fourth Sunday after Easter.
[24] St. Thomas, *Summa theol.*, III, 60, 3.

illumines it with the splendor of the Pasch and orients it directly to the glories of the Resurrection.

The mystery of death is a mystery of life and of light: the thought of light and of repose in Christ predominates in the texts of the Mass of the dead, which so beautifully insists on the idea that through Jesus Christ "there has shone before our eyes the hope of a glorious resurrection, so that the promise of a future immortality is a consolation for those who are sad at knowing that they must certainly die; since for Your faithful, Lord, life is changed, not taken away; and when the dwelling-place which is their body in the exile of this world is destroyed, they enter into possession of an eternal dwelling in heaven."

Even the great purifications by which the Lord is accustomed to disposing certain souls to make them sharers in great supernatural graces, lose their note of profound obscurity in the school of the liturgy and take on a character that is more human and more in agreement with the normal process of the Chrisian life which these graces are crowning.

The final point on which the mysteries we celebrate during the liturgical year converge is a mystery of hope, the parousia, the second coming of the Lord. The thought of this second coming has given rise to some liturgical texts of a fine lyricism, which can be ranked among the most beautiful of the Church's repertory: *Quaesivi vultum tuum; vultum tuum, Domine, requiram; ostende faciem tuam.* These and similar expressions full of tranquil hope are found scattered through many different Offices throughout the year, and give the season of Advent in particular its character of sweet nostalgia.

Synthesis of the aspirations brimming with desire and hope which the liturgy prompted in the ancient Christians was the cry "Come, Lord Jesus!" with which St. John ended his Apocalypse and which still could sum up at the close of the yearly cycle the state of mind created by the liturgy in the Christian community.

Outstanding, of course, among the moral virtues particularly inculcated by the liturgy is the virtue of *religion,* since the liturgy is nothing but a constant actuation of this virtue, and liturgical spirituality proposes to give a religious and worshipful character to all the acts of the Christian's life. This concept coincides with the thinking of St. Thomas, for whom Christian life is synonymous with Christian religion.[25]

In especially close relation to the virtue of religion are the fundamental virtues of *humility* and *obedience.*

Worship is the relation between man and God, based on our recognition of God's infinite excellence in contrast to our insignificance. Nothing makes man so humble as the intelligent consideration of God's grandeur.

The liturgy constantly expresses the idea of simple humility in its relations

[25] St. Thomas, *Summa theol.,* III, 63, 1 and 2.

with the Lord. Its formulas can be pronounced and its rites celebrated with sincerity only by one who is humble of heart and who in the humble acknowledgment of his own nothingness shows himself still more humble, allowing himself to be joyously filled by the presence of the Lord's grandeur.

The humility which the liturgy teaches us to practice is that of St. Paul, according to the beautiful texts of the Apostle assembled by the Church to celebrate the Office of the day of his conversion. But there is an even more excellent model which the liturgy proposes to us every day, surrounding it with particular solemnity: the canticle of humility dictated by the Holy Spirit to the Mother of God, the *Magnificat*.

A splendid occasion for practicing true humility is offered us also by the liturgy when it urges us to fuse our personality with that of all the faithful, accepting what the community accepts, praying as the community prays, without being conspicuous in any way or making the prayer too personal; for individualism, even in petitions for virtue, obviously endangers the integrity of our humility.

On this point obedience comes into play, to manifest and to aid humility of intellect and of heart. Liturgical piety makes man humble because it makes him obedient to the Church; it teaches him to renounce his own taste and his personal judgment so as to accept what the Church does, teaches and prays; to accept it theoretically and practically, conforming his own life with all his convictions and all his acts to the thinking of the Church, which can never be more genuine than when she opens her spirit to send up to the Lord the perfume of her prayer.

3. Devotions

"There are, besides, other exercises of piety which although not strictly belonging to the sacred liturgy are, nevertheless, of special import and dignity . . . they have been approved and praised over and over again by the Apostolic See and by the bishops."[26] What place does liturgical spirituality find for these practices of piety to which the Pope refers?

Let us begin by specifying what these practices of piety are, since the expression is sometimes taken in a generic sense to signify any form whatsoever of private spiritual activity.

Let us recall that spiritual life and piety are not two synonymous terms. Piety is but one of the various activities that go to make up the spiritual life of the Christian.

In so far as it refers to God, piety is that virtue which moves us to render Him the honor and worship we owe Him by reason of our adoption as His children. Piety is therefore that good disposition of the spirit which impels us to make contact with God through acts of worship that express

[26] *Mediator Dei*, n. 182.

our filial love for Him. These manifestations are usually called acts of piety.

Because God is our Creator and our last end, we honor Him with the worship of religion. Because He is our Father, we render Him the worship of piety. But religion and piety are only two virtues, two activities among the many that constitute our spiritual life, the life, that is, which has its formal principle in grace, which involves our whole being, and which tends toward its fulness in the supernatural happiness of paradise.

The liturgy, if we want to speak precisely, is not the spiritual life of the Church; but it is the most important instrumental cause of that spiritual life, since the spiritual life is objectively and effectively communicated to us and increased in us through the sacramental action of the liturgy; moreover, it is the worship of religion and of piety which the Church officially offers to God. Thus it may be said that the liturgy is the Church's official piety.

Individuals also, among the various activities of the spiritual life of each one, offer God a worship of religion and of piety. Usually these two aspects of worship—that is, religion and piety—are not distinguished and are expressed in a single concept: what is called the life of piety, manifested through the acts of piety.

Now the acts of individual or private piety can be performed in two ways: by being joined to the acts of the Church's public worship so as to become a single worshipful act with that public worship, or by being practiced on one's own account as a spontaneous individual manifestation of filial affection for God.

In the sixth chapter we have treated of the acts of individual piety practiced in the first way. We have pointed out that there is a personal piety essential to every public act of worship, without which the ltiurgy would be nothing but a body without a soul. We have indicated also what this pious activity of individuals should be in order that it may be fused with the Church's public worship.

In the present chapter—taking into account that the liturgy, besides being the Church's public worship of religion and of piety, is also source and norm of the entire spiritual life of the Christians—we have examined up to now what a spiritual life should be if it is directed in a special way by the liturgy and oriented toward it. For if it is true that the liturgy has an objectively sanctifying character, it is also certain that this sanctification derived from the liturgy will not succeed in becoming a true spiritual life of the individual Christians if it is not vitally assimilated by each one of them. Hence we have hitherto referred to the private spiritual activity by which the faithful individually dispose themselves for receiving and assimilating the fruits they can attain during the liturgical celebration. But this activity is not only piety; it is also purificaton, it is practice of the virtues: precisely, spiritual life.

Alluding to this form of private spiritual activity, Pius XII wrote in the first part of the encyclical *Mediator Dei,* "Very truly, the sacraments and the sacrifice of the altar, being Christ's own actions, must be held to be capable in themselves of conveying and dispensing grace from the divine Head to the members of the mystical Body. . . . But observe that these members are alive, endowed and equipped with an intelligence and will of their own. It follows that they are strictly required to put their own lips to the fountain, imbibe and absorb for themselves the life-giving water, and rid themselves personally of anything that might hinder its nutritive effect in their souls."[27]

Among the various manifestations of this spiritual life inspired by the liturgy, we have encountered some, such as spiritual reading and prayer, which represent the part that belongs to piety in the spiritual life. But these we have treated rather as means for bringing ourselves into relation with God and for obtaining from Him the profound knowledge and the pleasant awareness of His fatherhood over us. Thus we have considered them rather as abundant *sources* of the purest piety. From them will issue those religious practices which are a sensible *expression* of this piety.

The two elements, inward consideration and outward practice, make up the whole of piety, according to the Pope's statement in the encyclical just quoted: "Genuine piety . . . needs meditation on the supernatural realities and supernatural exercises, if it is to be nurtured, stimulated and sustained, and if it is to prompt us to lead a more perfect life."[28]

Now we must treat of these practices of piety, that is, of the outward and spontaneous manifestations of individual piety. They are the concrete forms which private piety may take on. They are not the substance of piety, then, but rather the accidental forms under which piety may show itself in each Christian according to his preferences and his particular manner of thinking and feeling. These concrete manifestations of private piety are known by the name of *devotions*. The devotions are the acts of private piety to which we are referring in this section.

The better to clarify our presentation, we shall divide the devotions into three groups: 1) the devotions that imitate the liturgy in as much as their expression is collective in form, despite their individual character; 2) the devotions that correspond to the piety of which we have treated in the sixth chapter, that is, those that embody the spiritual activity by which the faithful participate in the celebration of liturgical worship; 3) the devotions that represent a simple, spontaneous expression of individual piety.

The devotions that imitate public worship

The concern, obviously, is with devotions that *imitate* public worship: we cannot say that they *are* public worship, that is, official worship, although

---

[27] *Mediator Dei,* n. 31.   [28] *Ibid.,* n. 32.

they are celebrated in public. Pope Pius XII specified this point: "they do not strictly belong to the sacred liturgy."

Still, some of them have a particular relation to the liturgy, both by reason of their outward form, which reproduces rites that form part of liturgical worship on other occasions, and by reason of having a public or collective character, which, however, is not official. The Pope mentions in particular "solemn processions, especially at the time of Eucharistic Congresses, which pass through cities and villages, and adoration of the Blessed Sacrament publicly exposed."[29] Referring to these rites, the supreme Pontiff says, "They spring from the inspiration of the liturgy and if they are performed with due decorum and with faith and piety, as the liturgical rules of the Church require, they are undoubtedly of the very greatest assistance in living the life of the liturgy."[30]

They may be considered, therefore, as an extension of the liturgy, from which they proceed, but without having a strictly official character. They do not represent the public prayer of the whole Church; but they are the collective and even official prayer of a particular church, and in their celebration they are governed by liturgical and canonical rules. They are very little removed, then, from the public and official prayer of the whole Church; and if they are practiced with due moderation, according to the dispositions specified in this regard, they promote the Christian life and even the liturgical life itself.

By extension we might include here, together with the various public forms of Eucharistic worship, those related devotions of a more private character which have also for their object the presence and the sacramental permanence of Jesus Christ in the Church. Pope Pius XII indicated them in his discourse to the Assisi Congress of Pastoral Liturgy: "visits to the Blessed Sacrament, . . . the prayer of the Forty Hours or 'perpetual adoration,' the holy hour, the solemn carrying of communion to the sick, the processions of the Blessed Sacrament. The most enthusiastic, the most convinced liturgist must be able to understand and to realize what Christ in the tabernacle means for the faithful who are deeply pious, be they simple or learned people. He is their adviser, their comforter, their strength, their refuge, their hope in life and in death."[31]

There are other devotions, likewise mentioned in the encyclical *Mediator Dei,* which, although they are forms of private vocal prayer, are often recited collectively also, and have been "approved and praised over and over again by the Apostolic See and by the bishops." The Pope enumerates some of these devotions: "the prayers usually said during the month of May in honor of the Blessed Virgin Mother of God, or during the month of June to the Most Sacred Heart of Jesus; also novenas and triduums, Stations of the

---

[29] *Mediator Dei,* n. 132.   [31] *The Assisi Papers,* pp. 234-235.
[30] *Ibid.,* n. 133.

Cross and other similar practices."[32] In another place the encyclical mentions the rosary, which may well be placed at the head of this whole group of devotions.

All these represent popular forms of piety, which may also be practiced privately, as in fact they are, but which have come to be ranked as collective forms of non-liturgical prayer.

Originally, many of them were inspired more or less by the liturgy, which in a certain way they sought to complement. The liturgical formulas, so doctrinal and concise, were becoming almost incomprehensible to the faithful in epochs of decadence or of little religious instruction. These devotions, on the other hand, expressed in a simple, popular manner, and with stronger accent on the affective side, the religious concepts and sentiments comprised in the liturgical year.

At other times they were pious developments which complemented or unfolded, with their more subjective character, the liturgy's severe life of piety. Propagated by some preacher or missionary, or spread by some religious institute, if they coincided in content or form with the sentiments of popular devotion, they received a ready welcome, put down roots and won the approval and even the recommendation of the Church.

In general it may be said that this class of devotions, which the Christian people practices collectively outside of the liturgy, had its origin as a devout or popular complement of the liturgy; but, in proportion as the knowledge and meaning of liturgical worship was being lost, these devotions kept growing until they became a substitute for the liturgy in the nourishment of popular piety. Satisfied with these practices, piety no longer felt the need of recourse to the liturgy.

The aim of these devotions should be to popularize certain aspects of Christian piety and make them more accessible, eventually channeling individual piety into collective forms of prayer which would prepare people to understand liturgical worship and make them want to take part in it. In fact, the Pope ties their purpose in with the liturgy when he declares that "these devotions make us partakers in a salutary manner of the liturgical cult, because they urge the faithful to go frequently to the sacrament of penance, to attend Mass and receive communion with devotion, and, as well, encourage them to meditate on the mysteries of our Redemption and imitate the example of the saints."[33]

Some of these devotions are so deeply rooted that, with the blessing and recommendation of the Church, they have come to form part of the usual repertory of collective, popular piety, so that they "may be considered in a certain way to be an addition to the liturgical cult."[34] This is the case, for

[32] *Mediator Dei*, n. 182.
[33] *Mediator Dei*, n. 183.
[34] *Ibid.*, n. 182.

example, with those devotions which have a time assigned to them in the Christian year.

It is clear that a person who lives the liturgy intensely feels no great need of these substitutes and knows how to evaluate them at their true worth, that is, as optional means for filling up with an easier devotion the measure of our divine service, already substantially satisfied through the liturgy and the piety derived therefrom. It is for the Church to determine the role that belongs to these exercises of collective piety alongside of its own official prayer and in relation to it; certainly as subsidiaries and never as supplanting the acts of public worship.

These, as an official document of the Church declares, "not only have a special dignity, but have also a special sacramental power and efficacy in nourishing the Christian life, and cannot be adequately replaced by those pious exercises of devotion usually called extraliturgical"; so that the liturgy always "far excels by its nature all the other customs and kinds of devotion, even the best."[35]

Even when we retain these devotions, we must seek to give them a character in agreement with the norm established by Pius XII in *Mediator Dei,* namely that "it is necessary that the spirit of the sacred liturgy and its directives should exercise a salutary influence on them." Consider, for example, the following case: The Church suppressed the octaves of the saints during Lent, that their festive commemoration might not obscure the liturgical meaning of Lent or distract our attention, which ought to be wholly centered on the Paschal mystery. The present rules for Holy Week insist on this point and the pastoral motives for it. But then we encounter the devotion of the month of St. Joseph, which coincides with the Lenten season every year. In many churches this devotion is, if not the only, certainly the most important collective exercise practiced daily throughout that whole month. The piety of the faithful is thereby directed to a particular, festive object very different from the character of the liturgy of that season.

The devotions that embody the personal contribution to liturgical worship

The necessity of bringing about active, personal assistance at the acts of public worship has given rise to certain other practices of piety. They have the function of giving definite form to the individual's contribution to the common action of the Christian family. Liturgical spirituality teaches us what this contribution must be in order to attain perfection. As things stand in reality, however, perfection is not always possible. "Many of the faithful are unable to use the Roman Missal even though it is written in the vernacular; nor are all capable of understanding correctly the liturgical rites and formulas. So varied and diverse are men's talents and characters that it is impossible for all to be moved and attracted to the same extent by

[35] *Ordo Hebdomadae Sanctae Instauratus:* decree, introduction; instruction, IV, 23.

community prayers, hymns, and liturgical services. Moreover, the needs and inclinations of all are not the same, nor are they always constant in the same individual."[36]

In this text the Pope makes known indirectly the causes that necessitate admission into the common prayer of the faithful of certain individual contributions which are not in perfect accord with the action the priest is performing in the name of all. As can be seen from the text, these causes indicated by the Pope are principally: insufficient preparation or religious instruction, diversity of capacities, defective or misguided formation, the deficiencies and psychological variatons of individuals.

Recognizing that there is almost always some defect at the basis of these causes, we must seek the principal remedy in the correction of that defect, even if the results may be quite remote. Suitable religious instruction, solid ecclesiastical formation, education to the sense of community and of Church, the overcoming of individualism through a strong personality, are the objectives to which we must tend if we aspire to a solid, effective Christian life.

But meanwhile "who would say that all these Christians cannot participate in the Mass nor share its fruits?"[37] The most indispensable requirement, if their material presence in the congregation is to be also a spiritual participation in the common prayer, is that they have the intention of praying with the Church, and that in one way or another they apply their mind to God, to whom the minds of all the assembled faithful are directed. The more they are identified with the letter and the spirit of the liturgical prayer, the more perfect will their participation be. This is the ideal to which they should aspire. If it is not possible of attainment, however, steps must be taken to see that the essential is not lacking: that they really pray, and that in so far as possible they unite themselves to the praying community.

In this sense, he who assists at Mass, for example, "lovingly meditating on the mysteries of Jesus Christ," is closer to the common prayer than he who is "performing other exercises of piety or reciting prayers which, though they differ from the sacred rites, are still essentially in harmony with them."[38] And we could say further that this latter one will be closer to the celebrant, if he really remains united to God by means of his simple prayers, than another who, while pronouncing with his lips all the formulas of the missal, is distracted and wandering in spirit far from the church.

By this we do not mean to propose as an ideal, and still less as a collective ideal, a participation in the divine worship based on devout exercises of individual piety. And we cannot emphasize too much how unbecoming it would be, and even irreverent, to use the celebration of the Mass as a pretext or an occasion for practicing certain devotions with greater solemnity or for being entertained by a liturgical spectacle or a concert of sacred music.

---

[36] *Mediator Dei,* n. 108. [38] *Ibid.*
[37] *Ibid.*

It is distressing to see, at times, a congregation, directed by a priest in the pulpit, busy with the collective performance of certain devotions, not always too solid or formative, without the least concern for the fact that there at the high altar another priest is celebrating the holy sacrifice, in which they participate only in as much as they stand at the time of the gospel and kneel during the elevation. These devotions, and especially the manner of practicing them, are not those of which the Pope writes that "they urge the people to participate worthily and devoutly in the Eucharistic sacrifice and make us participate in liturgical worship with great spiritual profit."

We have already described the ideal participation in the acts of public worship. Allow us to insist on it, so as to complete the presentation of the Pope's teaching on this point. This we shall do by using his own words: "The Mass can fulfill its appointed end" prescinding from external circumstances.[39] "Not all can be moved and attracted to the same extent by community prayers, hymns, and liturgical services. Moreover, the needs and inclinations of all are not the same, nor are they always constant in the same individual. Who then would say, on account of such a prejudice, that all these Christians cannot participate in the Mass nor share its fruits? On the contrary, they can adopt some other method which proves easier for certain people."[40]

Yet "they should not think it enough to participate in the Eucharistic sacrifice with that general intention which befits members of Christ and children of the Church, but let them further, in keeping with the spirit of the sacred liturgy, be most closely united with the High Priest and His earthly minister . . . ."[41] "Therefore they are to be praised who with the idea of getting the Christian people to take part more easily and more fruitfully in the Mass, strive to make them familiar with the Roman Missal, so that the faithful, united with the priest, may pray together in the very words and sentiments of the Church. They also are to be commended who strive to make the liturgy even in an external way a sacred act in which all who are present may share."[42]

Devotions as acts of mere personal piety

The liturgical life intensely lived still leaves a good margin for personal devotion. When participating in the liturgical acts, the individual must postpone all individualism, in order to identify his spirit with the praying Church. But later, even while the liturgy continues to be the norm and to give direction to the life of piety which it has nourished and fostered itself, the soul, unfolding in a personal way before God, can lay itself open spontaneously and let itself be moved by its own inclinations.

On this point liturgical spirituality differs notably from the other spiritual-

---

[39] *Mediator Dei*, n. 107.
[40] *Ibid.*, n. 108.
[41] *Ibid.*, n. 104.
[42] *Ibid.*, n. 105.

ities. These usually attribute great importance to the acts of personal devotion, establishing them and regulating them closely. Liturgical spirituality, on the other hand, gives them only a secondary and accessory value.

Moreover, for anyone who lives by the spirit of the liturgy, the spiritual education received in its school will have formed a sort of second nature, and even when he acts spontaneously under the impulse of his personal tastes, he will not go much beyond what the liturgy does and teaches. On the one hand, he will have no great need of devotions, since the liturgy itself and the intensity of spiritual life which it awakens in the soul will be enough to satisfy his own devotion and his own charity. On the other hand, if he does not need something more personal and concrete to nourish his own devotion, he will already have learned from the liturgy itself what is to be the order and the measure of the devotions, taking account of the order and the proportion with which the liturgy distributes in its calendar, in various categories, the feasts of the Lord, of the Mother of God and of the saints.

To clarify these concepts, we must distinguish between devotion and devotions. *Devotion* is the first and principal act of the virtue of religion, and is based, according to the teaching of St. Thomas, on the promptness of the will "to give oneself to those things which pertain to the service of God."[43] To give oneself to God in order to remain ever submissive and ever well disposed to whatever refers to His worship or His service—this is devotion.

A promptness of this kind cannot be explained without a great charity, a fervent love of God, which makes us forget ourselves and our own interests, to keep ourselves always at the disposal of anything that is an object of the divine good pleasure. And at the same time charity is increased by devotion. It is the same thing that happens between friends, writes St. Thomas:[44] for love prompts a person to serve his friend, and the services offered preserve and increase the friendship.

As interior acts of the will, devotion and charity can be aroused by the consideration of those things which move us to love and submission, and this consideration in turn can be helped by outward expressions and outward acts offered in service and homage to God, toward whom we feel devout. In as much as they proceed from the devotion of the will and tend to increase it, the pious considerations and the formulas and outward actions aimed at arousing them constitute precisely what we call *devotions*.

To be truly called devotions, they must proceed from devotion or charity and must have as their aim the increase of readiness to serve God. Thus we have:

devotion = promptness of will in the service of God; and

devotions = considerations which excite this disposition of the will, and

---

[43] St. Thomas, *Summa theol.*, II-II, 82, 1.   [44] *Ibid.*, 82, 2 ad 2.

more remotely the prayers and exercises of piety that arouse and stir up these considerations and this promptness.

From this it can be deduced how erroneous it is to call certain prayers and pious practices devotions when they are very far from being the fruit of charity and from leading to a greater faithfulness in the fulfilment of the divine will. Practiced routinely or out of sentimentality, they are of very little profit to the soul. On the contrary, they do it harm by deceptively bringing it a false security.

That which is more substantial, a living participation in the liturgy, is passed up because it is too lofty, cold and hard to understand; and the attempt is made to substitute for it in the individual life other practices more attainable and more affecting. But when a person lets himself be carried along in this way by the law of minimum effort, the result will be that he no longer seeks in these devotions that which is essential for arriving at devotion, that is, the consideration and contemplation of the Christian mysteries. A recitation of prayers which is often mechanical seems to satisfy the devout Christian that he has fulfilled his duties of religion, especially if the prayers have had a sentimental impression on him and have made him feel that tender emotion, perceptible to the senses, to which the name of devotion is given by equivocation.

The deceptive tranquillity of spirit produced by the many devout practices of this kind is responsible in large part for the religious ignorance and the superficiality of life which is unfortunately found in many practicing Christians. We are not even speaking of those whose Christianity consists in making some novenas or lighting candles before a certain statue or picture, without their being too much concerned about fulfilling the precept of Sunday Mass or adjusting their life to the practice of the virtues.[45]

Pius XII warns of this danger in the encyclical *Mediator Dei* when he says, "Any inspiration to follow and practice extraordinary exercises of piety must most certainly come from the Father of Lights, from whom every good and perfect gift descends; and of course the criterion of this will be the effectiveness of these exercises in making the divine cult loved and spread daily ever more widely, and in making the faithful approach the sacraments with more longing desire, and in obtaining for all things holy due respect and honor. If, on the contrary, they are an obstacle to the principles and norms of divine worship, or if they oppose or hinder them, one must surely conclude that they are not in keeping with prudence and enlightened zeal."[46]

---

[45] Cardinal Gomá writes: "Mr. Chipier refers to a parish priest who said to his bishop as he was leaving for his new parish, 'There are many devotions there; I shall have a lot of work to do to reestablish religion.' This sentence may not contain a rule for the apostolate, but its fine satire displays ample observation of the religious psychology of our times." *El valor educativo de la liturgia católica* (2nd ed.; Barcelona, 1940), II, 272.

[46] *Mediator Dei*, n. 181.

The promptness of will in which true devotion consists can have for its goal only God, not creatures. Only God has the right to take such absolute possession of our will. If we sometimes speak of devotion to a creature, such as the devotion to the Blessed Virgin or to the saints, we mean merely that we recognize in them perfect servants of God and that when we serve and honor those who are closer to us, the offering of our service to God becomes easier and more secure. In other words, we have devotion to them because of God; we serve God in them and through them.

The devotions too, like devotion itself, must in the last analysis be directed to God. The object of our devout considerations should always be the divinity in its nature, in its attributes, in the Trinity of its Persons. But, as St. Thomas writes,[47] the weakness of our mind makes it necessary that we have the aid of things perceptible to the senses and thus known to us, to reach the consideration of the divine realities; and for this reason the field of our devotions is broadened and we are placed in contact with sensible realities which make the contemplation of the divinity easier and more feasible for us, even though it is more remote.

From this point of view, we certainly shall not be able to find any medium which excites our love and our devotion towards God more than the humanity of Jesus Christ. Christ's humanity, writes St. Thomas,[48] arouses our devotion most powerfully, leading us to it as if by the hand. Jesus Christ, as God, is the proper object of our devotion; as Man, He is the most efficacious means for producing devotion. The person of Jesus Christ must therefore be the object of our first and principal devotion, by means of which we shall arrive with all certainty at the contemplation of the Trinity.

It is quite clear, then, that the greatest among all devotions, if we could classify it among the devotions, would be liturgical worship. For there is no pious practice or consideration of any kind that can refer more directly to God or move us more effectively to serve Him, since the liturgy is service and divine worship. Nor shall we find any practice or consideration that can infuse into us better than the liturgy a solid and fervent devotion to Jesus Christ, since the essence and the organic structure of the liturgy are formed precisely by Christ's priestly acts and His mysteries, renewed and contemplated.

But, aside from liturgical worship, if we take devotions as means taken on our own initiative to increase our devotion, the concrete forms and manifestations of devotion to Jesus Christ may vary according to each person's temperament and formation, but they must always occupy a preferred place in our spiritual life. The Christian who sincerely seeks the perfection of his own interior life and who has been formed in the school of the liturgy will turn into a passionate lover of Christ. He will long to fill up all the capacities

---

[47] St. Thomas, *Summa theol.*, II-II, 82, 3   [48] *Ibid.* ad 2.

of his own spirit with Christ's intimate presence, that he may identify his own life with that act of sublime devotion which summed up the Lord's human life from the very first moment: "Behold, I come to do Your will, O God! In this is My delight, and Your law is within My heart" (Ps. 39:8-9; Heb. 10:1-7).

With due proportion and with a character that is always relative, as it is in the liturgy, personal devotion can also be fostered by certain devotions to the saints, which are legitimate in so far as they help to preserve and increase true interior devotion to God. An objective measure of this legitimacy and of the importance that may be granted to the devotion to the saints can be deduced also from the degree and the quality of the relations obtaining between a certain saint and Jesus Christ and His Church.

For this reason, after devotion to Jesus Christ, the devotion to the Blessed Virgin must take first place; for she is the creature most intimately united to the physical Christ and the mystical Christ. St. Joseph, supposed father of the Lord and patron of the Church, merits special devotion. There follow in importance the devotion to the Apostles, intimate collaborators of Christ and pillars of His Church; the devotion to St. John the Baptist, the fore-runner; the devotion to the martyrs, because of the witness borne by their blood.

The devotion which the early Christians professed for the martyrs is well enough known, and yet St. Augustine wrote, "Churches and sacrifices are not offered to the martyrs, but only to God. The names of the martyrs are given a pre-eminent place at the altar. And yet, dearly beloved, in no way do we compare our martyrs to gods, or consider them as such, or venerate them as such. It is not to them that the priests sacrifice. By no means! The sacrifices are offered only to God. . . . And if you are asked, 'Do you worship Peter?' answer what Eulogius answered Fructuosus, 'I do not worship Peter, but I worship God, whom Peter also worships.' Then Peter will love you. For if you wanted to put Peter in God's place, you would offend Peter, in other words you would hit against the Rock. See to it that you do not break your foot by hitting it against the rock."[49]

After the martyrs we can have devotion to the other saints: bishops, confessors, virgins, etc. As objects of special devotion among the various saints we may single out those who bring us into contact with our Lord in a special way: the founders of religious orders, who are spiritual guides for their children; the patron saints who have been given us under one title or another as particular intercessors before God.

These devotions, legitimate as they are and even to be recommended, must be regulated intelligently and prudently. In other words, we must see to it that they do not take a place that does not belong to them in the

---

[49] St. Augustine, Sermo 273 habitus die 21 Ian. 396 in natali Fructuosi episcopi, Augurii et Eulogii diaconorum, 7; PL 38, 1251.

spiritual life, and we must always use them as mere optional means of obtaining true interior devotion.

The greatest danger in devotions is that they center the interior activity of the spirit on a concrete, partial point, which, however excellent it may be, has only a limited value, often a very relative value, in the whole of the Christian life and even in the whole of the life of piety. Moreover, since they exercise a strong attraction, being spontaneous and agreeable to the individual person's manner of thinking and feeling, the devotions satisfy the inner inclination to piety. Thus they limit piety in practice to that one concrete point, to the serious detriment of the subjective spiritual formation as well as the objective order of worship, which corresponds to a perfectly integrated Christian life.

Prudence must guide the choice of devotions and prescribe their proper measure, since they do have a powerful influence over our spiritual formation and the orientation of our piety. A certain number of solid devotions may complete the formation imparted to us by the Church in her liturgy, since they take over the more subjective and personal part of us, to bring about our sympathetic vibration with the divine rhythm, under the intelligent direction of liturgical piety. On the other hand, those devotions which are based on sentiment or which end up by saturating the religious capacity of our spirit so as to leave no room for the formation offered us by the liturgy, will necessarily mislead our spirituality and keep it superficial and inconstant.

That which is most spontaneous and easy to follow is not always best. When this quality of natural, easy spontaneity is derived, as it is in liturgical spirituality, from a wise, intelligent method which is well aware of our capacities and guides them through ways that are most apt to lead to the proposed end, this is an indication of worth and a guarantee of efficacy. But if we mean by "easy" and "spontaneous" that which is most to our taste, that which is best accommodated to our defective way of being, without any effort at education or any criterion for orientation, the ease will make us superficial and the spontaneity will leave us with our inborn defects.

A norm for all the devotions can be found in an official letter of the Vatican Secretariate of State addressed to the Italian National Liturgical Week held at Verona in July, 1954. In this letter the Holy See pointed out the proper direction for devotion to Mary: "May the devotion to the Blessed Virgin, recalled where necessary to purity of purpose, once again find its proper function as a way to Jesus Christ, through the most careful, complete and loving transformation of the old man into the man of justice and of Christian holiness. Any other form of devotion to Mary, not sufficiently oriented in this direction, would necessarily be defective and less pleasing to the heavenly Mother, who cannot have anything closer to her heart than our renewal in the life of her divine Son.

"Hence there is no telling what precious gains would accrue to each one and everyone in the Church if that mighty outpouring of love for Mary which gives to our troubled days their brightest ray of hope, were educated and disciplined according to the spirit of the liturgy. Then our relations with the Virgin, far from being confined to a shallow sentimentality or an anxious, self-interested plea for help in moments of need, would acquire the maturity and depth proper to a spiritual life that is persevering and fruitful."[50]

The spiritual life as we have described it in its various activities of penance, prayer, practice of the virtues and exercises of piety will perhaps seem too smooth and pleasant an affair for anyone who looks at it superficially. For an accurate understanding of it, we must bear in mind that anyone who wants to live by the spirit of the Church must take things seriously and not stop at a material performance, but push on to the ultimate consequences in such a way as to obtain the maximum spiritual effect, which is what we desire.

The practices of the Church, even those connected with a life of perfection, are usually very simple and within reach. But we must devote ourselves to them with the utmost sincerity and intensity: sincerely, that is, really seeking the end proposed; intensely, that is, applying to this end all the powers of intellect and will. Obviously, a careless and purely material application of the methods of liturgical spirituality would offer no guarantee of reaching Christian perfection, which has as its principle and foundation to love God with the whole heart, with the whole soul, with the whole mind, with the whole strength (Mark 12:30),[51] and which establishes as a practical norm that only those who do violence to themselves will seize the kingdom of God (Matt. 11:12).

The liturgy, official school of the Church, teaches us that this violence is rooted in continuous fidelity to Jesus Christ; in other words, that it consists in *living* in a Christian way. Life is lived in a natural way, without sensational contrasts, but also without interruption and with the due cooperation of the whole organism. Living in a Christian way involves a normality and a simple connaturality in the application of the vital principles of Christianity; but at the same time it demands that this activity be constant, whole-hearted and conscientious.

When these qualities are lacking, the organism is sick, and then living requires an exertion which may become intolerable. Then the normal, healthful food turns out to be tasteless and inadequate and perhaps even harmful; and recourse must be had to pills and medicines which condense into small doses the nutritive elements that would be found more widely distributed

---

[50] *L'Osservatore Romano*, July 23, 1954.   *spiritualis*, V, and *Summa theol.*, II-II, 44, 4
[51] Cf. St. Thomas, *De perfectione vitae*   and 5.

in the normal food. The Christian who does not live with intensity the normal life the Church offers him will soon grow faint, and will need stronger means of sustenance which from time to time arouse the reserves of his spirit and make him achieve in a short space of time that which he has not achieved with a smooth but intense continuity.

This procedure may produce good results in certain abnormal circumstances. But when it becomes habitual, it necessarily brings about a general lopsidedness of the spiritual organism. When a person has become accustomed to living by way of reaction, by being pushed, as it were, these extraordinary means themselves lose a great part of their effectiveness; and the original evil, the lack of sincerity and intensity, shows up again in a definitive way, giving rise to a superficiality that hinders the development of an authentic Christian life.

For superficiality in a Christian involves a crisis of doctrine, of piety and of morality. If there is no depth of doctrine, there can be no solid piety or correct morality. There remain only appearances without solid foundation, which hide and dissimulate the nature and the gravity of the evil. A piety based on sentiment is incapable of informing or nourishing the Christian life, which, for want of solid principles and deeply rooted convictions, cannot bear fruit in works that meet the steep requirements of gospel morality.

Here we might quote some words of Kurth which Cardinal Gomá makes his own: "In my judgment, one of the causes, if not the most important cause, of contemporary ignorance of religion, is ignorance of the liturgy."[52] We might also recall the sentence of Pius XI, that "people are instructed in the truths of faith and brought to appreciate the inner joys of religion far more effectually by the annual celebration of our sacred mysteries than by any official pronouncements of the teaching of the Church."[53] Or again there is the well known statement of St. Pius X that the active participation in the most sacred mysteries and in the public and solemn prayer of the Church is the primary and indispensable source from which the faithful can acquire the true Christian spirit.[54]

More recently, Monsignor Montini wrote from the Secretariate of State of the Holy See in a letter addressed to the Liturgical Week of Oropa, "Nothing is so urgent in this hour that is so grave and at the same time so rich in hope, as recalling the people of God, the great family of Jesus Christ, to the substantial nourishment of liturgical piety. . . . Thus the faithful will make contact once more with the values of the Christian life that are so often forgotten. In this way they will recognize more readily what is the substance of religion and piety for the Christian."[55]

---

[52] Cardinal Gomá, *El valor educativo de la liturgia católica*, II, 278.

[53] Encyclical *Quas primas; A.A.S.*, 1925, p. 603; see ch. 2, note 2, above.

[54] Motu Proprio *Tra le sollecitudine; A.S.S.*, 1903, p. 331; see ch. 2, note 1, above.

[55] See *Rivista liturgica*, 1953, p. 85.

This urgent need, which has made itself so keenly felt everywhere, met a kind response in the fatherly heart of Pius XII, to whom history will undoubtedly assign as one of the greatest glories of his pontificate the effective promotion of the restoration of the Church's liturgy and the renewal of the liturgical spirit among the faithful. He it was who wrote in the encyclical *Mediator Dei,* "Whatever pertains to the external worship has assuredly its importance; however, the most pressing duty of Christians is to live the liturgical life, and increase and cherish its supernatural spirit. . . . . But at that time especially when the faithful take part in the liturgical service with such piety and recollection that it can truly be said of them, 'whose faith and devotion is known to You,' it is then . . . that each one's faith ought to become more ready to work through charity, his piety more real and fervent, and each should consecrate himself to the furthering of the divine glory."[56]

[56] *Mediator Dei,* nn. 197, 99.

8 LITURGY AND PASTORAL ACTION

The liturgy presupposes a pastoral action, and pastoral action attains its full efficacy only in so far as it terminates in the liturgy.

The pastoral work of the care of souls includes all the activities in which the priest must engage to communicate the Christian life and make it increase in the individuals and the ecclesiastical community entrusted to him. In founding the Church on human supports, Christ willed that the institution and the spread of His kingdom should be subject to the effort and the personal exertion of men: "Go, therefore, and make disciples of all nations, baptizing them in the name of the Father and of the Son and of the Holy Spirit, teaching them to observe all that I have commanded you" (Matt. 28:19-20). Here is the pastoral mission of the Church's priesthood: to make disciples, to baptize and to teach observance; doctrine, sacraments and practice of the Christian life. The supernatural fruitfulness will all proceed from God. Normally, however, it will be communicated to individuals and to society only through a labor incumbent on the priesthood. The propagation of God's kingdom in extent and in depth is bound up with this labor.

The living expansion of the Church and the integral perfection of her worship are closely related, therefore, to her pastoral action. Through pastoral action the Church will acquire new members, and these will attain the necessary perfection to be adorers of the Father in spirit and in truth.

As subject of worship, the Christian must make use of his intellect and his will to bring about his union with God and his submission to God; without this, there will be no true act of worship. But this is not possible without a previous illumination of the intellect which will enable him to know the excellence of God, his relations with God, the necessity of offering Him reverence and submission, and the means by which he can and must perform his duty of religious worship. All this is contained in the "Teach!" of the apostolic mission. Only by the preaching of Christian doctrine will the next stage be attained, the "Baptize!"

Teaching is the normal medium for arriving at faith and bringing about those dispositions in the subject which are necessary for the fruitful reception of baptism and of the other sacraments after it. And then another task will be added to the pastoral duty: that of helping the recipient assimilate the effect of the sacramental action, to the point of translating it into the works of the Christian life, which in turn will be an excellent preparation for the further reception of the sacraments.

Ultimately, the objective of pastoral action according to Christ's command can be summed up in two words, teaching and worship: teaching, which prepares and perfects the individual; worship, which is summed up in the sacramental life, exemplified in baptism. And again, the teaching has the aim of putting into practice what is done in the sacramental action, and thus disposing the Christians for a more perfect participation in worship. And so the process continues, until they are introduced into the never-ending celebration of the heavenly liturgy. It is the same program we found when we analyzed the pedagogical method used by the Church in the liturgy; so that everything corroborates the wonderful unity we have seen in the Church's inner structure, under whatever aspect we look at it.

If the perfection of liturgical worship demands a preliminary labor of teaching, the pastoral action which sees to the teaching will attain its maximum efficacy only in so far as it terminates in the liturgy. For pastoral action, that is, the priestly action over the faithful, cannot lose sight of its twofold objective, sanctifying men and leading them to glorify God. Pastoral action will achieve its purpose in the measure in which it reaches these two objectives.

We know already that the necessary sanctification, the maximum sanctification—maximum in its efficacy and maximum in its objective reality—is that which comes to us from Jesus Christ through the sacramental liturgy. And the most perfect glorification of God is that which the Christian offers Him as a member of the Christian community, incorporated in it, forming a single worshiping subject with Jesus Christ by means of the Church's liturgy.

We could say, then, that the purpose of pastoral action consists in disposing men to form part of the Christian community, that in this community they may receive the sacramental life, by which they can glorify God through liturgical worship and the practice of the Christian life.

Liturgy and pastoral must be so united that neither one can be explained satisfactorily without the other. It is not strange, therefore, that in our age of liturgical restoration the need of a renewal in pastoral action should make itself very urgently felt also, and that pastoral action should seek its new life and fruitfulness precisely in a return to the liturgy.

We have indicated elsewhere that the decadence of the liturgy originated basically in the divorce between public worship and pastoral action. And let us add now that, despite the zeal of the shepherds of souls, despite the extraordinary apostolic activity displayed, pastoral action has suffered many failures and produced little fruit, precisely because it has deserted the school of the liturgy.

That is why the popes have shown such great interest in uniting once more these two elements so fundamental to the life of the Church. The measures taken by many bishops, the teaching of the recent supreme pontiffs, the liturgical regulations emanating from the Holy See, all display this constant preoccupation: the liturgy must again become something living, understood and assimilated by the Christian people.

Pastoral action must draw its inspiration from the liturgical action. It must tend to form Christians capable of acquiring an understanding, each according to his own capacity, of the sacramental life and liturgical worship. It must group them to form a community and a church, the parochial family, so that together they live the supernatural riches of the mystery of Christ communicated to men; and then it must be able to send them as so many messengers of Christ and of the Church, to inform with the Christian spirit their lives, the home, the villages and the cities, the fields and the factories, all human activities and all aspects of social and political life, and thus to restore the universal temple of God's glory on earth.

Since we are concerned with liturgy and with spirituality, we shall have to present at least the principal aspects of the relation that exists between the liturgical life and pastoral action.

1. Liturgy and Catechesis

It is a fact that the majority of the faithful do not understand the liturgical rites. Even among those who attend church often, there are very few who have any knowledge of the content and meaning of the rites at which they are assisting. For many of those who still practice their religious duties with a certain regularity, the knowledge of the liturgical acts is limited to a very general and not always sufficiently accurate notion of the effect that these rites produce. Aside from this, they are aware of the obligation to assist at certain acts of worship. All the rest is the affair of the priests.

The fact that they have usually seen the ceremonies performed in the same way has persuaded them that this is the way it should be done. At Mass, for example, they know that a gospel is recited and that all should stand and make the sign of the cross at that time; that the consecration and the elevation take place later and then all should kneel, etc. But the inner structure of the Mass, the content and the meaning of each rite, the reason for the different ceremonies, the part that belongs to the faithful in the liturgical celebration etc.—in other words, what constitutes the reality of Christian worship—of this they are almost completely ignorant. It is nothing that concerns them.

To verify these unhappy facts, one need only take a look at the various groups into which our Christians can be divided with regard to their assistance at Mass. It will readily be seen, right from the beginning, that numbers and quality are two factors which will be found in inverse proportion.

In the first place we shall find the great body of those, especially in the large cities of certain countries, who do not fulfill the precept of Sunday Mass. The official statistics for these countries show an appalling percentage in this group. To these who stay away we may add those who are willing to attend Mass a few times a year, on the occasion of an annual solemnity such as Christmas, or on their name day or the feast of a patron saint such as St. Anthony or St. Lucy; perhaps they also go to Mass on the feast of St. Joseph to make their Easter duty, and one or another day of the novena for the departed; they will not fail to make their appearance, either, when a social duty or a duty of friendship calls for it, as on the occasion of a funeral, a wedding or a first communion.

On these occasions, to be sure, they may experience a certain religious emotion. The surroundings, the circumstances, the motive behind their assistance at Mass, the ceremonies themselves if they are worthily carried out, their own good dispositions at the time, may stir up some good thoughts and desires in these Christians, which will perhaps be expressed in certain formulas of prayer more or less committed to memory. But probably that will be as far as it goes. What the priests have meanwhile been doing up there at the altar remains quite distant, because those gestures and those Latin formulas are the affair of priests.

Basically, for these people, the acts which the priests perform in church are as strange as the kind of life they lead or the clothes they wear in church and out of church. In the presence of the priests and their ceremonies, this lowest class of Christians—we are not even speaking of those who hate or despise the priest and any form of worship whatsoever—experience a mixture of admiration, sympathy and superstitious fear.

We could classify in another group the Christians who fulfill the precept of Sunday Mass more or less regularly out of a sense of religious duty, in which habit and social convention play a large part, along with a certain amount of fear, but who would not know how to give the reason why this duty is imposed on them. They are the greater part of the faithful at the late Mass, or of those who take up their stand near the door, where they can get out as soon as the celebrant has given the blessing. We could say of almost all of these what we have said of the previous group: they are ignorant of the value and the meaning of liturgy and worship.

Even in the relatively small group of Christians who fulfill their religious duties sincerely and conscientiously, we would find a good number whose notions about liturgical worship are very superficial or almost non-existent. Their answers would not be very satisfactory if we were to ask them what the Mass is, what mystery the Church is celebrating, how she teaches us to live it, why the celebrant performs this or that ceremony, etc.

They fulfill with sincerity and even with a certain devotion a religious duty imposed by the Church, but they do not succeed in grasping the intrinsic necessity of this obligation. Hence their attitude in relation to the liturgical rite is purely passive. If they pray, a little or a good deal, they do so on their own account, without any direct link with the action of the celebrant.

The liturgical action affects the spiritual conduct of these people only in so far as it determines the amount of time they must devote to the fulfilment of their Sunday obligation. At bottom, they are bored during Mass. It is no wonder that they like the Masses to be short. They pass this time in the best way possible, according to each one's degree of piety: reciting some prayers, reading a prayer book, listening to the music and the chant if there is any, or simply thinking about their own affairs.

Alongside of these groups of Christians who can hardly be called practicing or who are practicing in a form that is rather external and material, the number of the faithful who assist at the Sunday Mass, and perhaps the daily Mass, with true devotion, is almost insignificant.

Let us consider just this select group. We might still ask ourselves: are they all aware of the meaning of the various rites of the Mass? do they know the place that belongs to them in the liturgical action? do they unite themselves actively to the celebrant and adapt themselves to what the Church is doing and expressing in the name of all and for the spiritual formation of all? We know well enough that we could not give an affirmative reply to all these questions.

For some, more devout than well instructed, the Mass is simply the necessary rite for bringing about the real presence of Jesus Christ in the Eucharist. In practice, they value the Mass because of the consecration, which makes possible holy communion and the permanence of our Lord in the tabernacle. But the essential idea of sacrifice, with all its consequences for the life of worship and the life of the Church, passes almost unnoticed.

We thank God that the number of the faithful with a knowledge and a due appreciation of the value of the Mass keeps increasing as the liturgical apostolate bears fruit. Still we must bear in mind that this little group of Christians adequately instructed and formed in religious matters, capable of taking the place that belongs to them in the celebration of the liturgical rites, has to be compared with the rest of the baptized. The proportion is very small. Unfortunately, we cannot doubt the truth of the statement that the majority of the Christians do not understand the liturgical rites.

And yet, "this is the Church's official prayer, with these rites, with these formularies. We are well aware that the official prayer still has its value in the eyes of God, independently of the understanding the people may have of those rites and formularies. But even a superficial observation is enough to show that those rites were introduced for human beings. Well, then, were they introduced for the priests alone? That would be incongruous. Were they introduced for the intellectuals? The Church's worship is not designed just for intellectuals. Were they introduced for monks and nuns? The Church addresses herself to all her children."[1]

Then why do the ceremonies of public worship remain so distant from the faithful? Let us take the answer from a book written by Monsignor Ancel, auxiliary bishop of Lyon: "Because the Church's ceremonies are made for believers: for understanding a ceremony and profiting by it to enter into contact with God, what counts above all is faith. In the second place, because the ceremonies are made for the initiates; not for the intellectuals, but for the initiates. To understand a ceremony, it is not enough to have a vague religious sentiment or a more or less firm faith in God and in Christ; it is necessary to be penetrated by the Christian mystery and to live by it."[2]

To demand an initiation for the understanding of the rites does not contradict the statement that the liturgical rites are for all the Christians, since all the Christians are supposed to be initiates. Let us recall the ancient practice of the catechumenate, when baptism was ordinarily administered to adults. Before receiving the sacrament of Christian regeneration, they had to be instructed in the mysteries of the faith and of worship; and they were allowed to receive the sacrament only after they had given sufficient proof in the various scrutinies that they understood the creed and the Lord's prayer, as a compendium of all that they had learned. Meanwhile they were not permitted to assist at the celebration of the liturgy.

We can state that the cause, or the causes, of the great separation between

---

[1] Eusebio Vismara, Salesian, quoted in his biography: Eugenio Valentini, *D. Eusebio Vismara* (Turin, 1954), p. 433. — This testimony and some others cited in the present chapter are taken from the articles of Carlo Marcora, "Difficoltà e metodo di un'azione pastorale liturgica" and "La partecipazione alla santa messa nella teologia pastorale," *Ambrosius* (Milan, 1955), pp. 182-195, and (1956), pp. 99-112. We shall cite them by: Marcora, *Ambrosius.* — For the present quotation see Marcora, *Ambrosius,* 1956, pp. 103-104.

[2] Alfred Ancel, *Les Ouvriers et la Religion,* cited from the Italian version of G. Barra, *La Chiesa e gli Operai* (Pinerolo, 1951), p. 134.

the Christian people and the Church's liturgy are: lack of faith and lack of religous instruction; or, if you will, lack of faith through lack of religious instruction.

If we examine other points of the practical Christian life in our times, we arrive always at the same conclusion: our people are suffering from a very grave evil, religious ignorance. This is behind their lack of faith, their dechristianized mentality, the superficiality of their life. It accounts for their inability to understand the liturgy, as also for the existence of so many problems in the field of morality that are practically insoluble. The profound, positive principles of the Christian mystery, the value and meaning of the Church's public worship are unknown. There is no understanding of the eminently positive aspect of the gospel morality or of the extent of its practical requirements, which must shape the Christian's life from its very roots.

If, as we have seen, the liturgy involves doctrine, worship and the obligation of a deeply Christian life, there is no cause for wonder if the pernicious effects of religious ignorance are more conspicuous where the liturgy is concerned.

The liturgy is the great preoccupation which for some time has made itself felt in the Church, and which is exemplified in the pastoral-liturgical activity fostered by many bishops, apostles, organizations and publications, which concern themselves with it and nurture it, with very promising results.

In face of the undeniable fact of religious ignorance, and especially of the almost absolute ignorance of the liturgy, we may ask: who is going to bridge the enormous distance that exists between the liturgy and the people?

Various solutions have been proposed:

1) *Let things stand as they are.* This is a solution that may be presented under two aspects, convenience and haughty rigorism.

The solution of convenience follows this line of reasoning. Actually the liturgy cannot be understood and lived by the faithful. It must be recognized that in itself the liturgy is very beautiful, and that its celebration in the monasteries and the great basilicas can be magnificent, but it cannot be realized in the parish churches, especially the rural ones. The devotions to which they are already accustomed and which they practice with devotion and with spiritual fruit will be more within reach of the faithful and more efficacious for them. To impose participation in the liturgy on them now is to upset their spiritual life and make them abandon what they understand and like, in favor of reciting enigmatic formulas which will fill them with pride but leave them devoid of piety. It can easily be seen that this is the position of the "negligent and sluggish, the apathetic or half-hearted, with whom we do not agree," according to the words of Pope Pius XII in the encyclical *Mediator Dei*.[3]

---

[3] N. 10.

The other form of abstentionism is that of unbending pride. There are those who despise the uninstructed people. The artistic perfection of the liturgical services demands a rare formation and preparation which the people will never be capable of attaining. Leave them alone, then, with their simple devotions, while the group of the initiated offers God the perfect worship. Obviously, this would lead to a hateful pharisaical pride.

2) *Adapt the liturgy to the people.* Our rites are partly antiquated. They do not correspond to the spiritual needs and the social demands of the present way of life. The liturgy does not take account of the modern mentality, nor of important data such as the working world with its problems, its kind of life, etc. On the other hand, it is evident that the Christian regeneration of our present world must come from the return to the pure founts of Christianity, and above all from contact with Christ through the liturgy. It becomes imperative, therefore, that the liturgy be brought within reach of all. We must change the rites and the ceremonies, adapting them to the capacity and the understanding of our faithful.

"But this would be to destroy the liturgy. The liturgy cannot be adapted to a vague religious sentimentality or to a more or less firm belief. Then there would no longer be liturgy, but ceremony, the only purpose of which would be to arouse the religious sentiment. The secondary parts would be put at the center. . . . The essential would have disappeared. This the Church cannot accept."[4]

3) *"It is not a question of adapting the liturgy to those who assist at it, but of adapting them to the liturgy.* The thing to do is not to strip the ceremonies of their spiritual riches, but to help those who are assisting at them, in order that they may be able to enjoy some of these riches. The true solution must include two complementary elements: *a*) Above all, the first place must be given to religious instruction; *b*) Until a sufficient degree of faith has been attained, those who assist at the liturgical acts must be helped to participate truly in them."[5]

Here is the great mission of pastoral action: to prepare the people of God in such a way that they will be capable once more of taking part consciously and fruitfully in the liturgical action. Pastoral action must occupy a very important place in the movement of liturgical restoration. Without a pastoral action to bring about the proper religious formation of the faithful, the liturgy will continue to be something enigmatic and strange to their spiritual life.

It is important, however, to specify exactly the place that belongs to it. Pastoral action must be ordained to the liturgy, and not the liturgy to pastoral action. The liturgy is not a means of making pastoral action easier and more

[4] Alfred Ancel, *La Chiesa e gli Operai*, pp.   [5] *Ibid.*
134-135.

effective. The liturgy understood and lived by the faithful is the end which pastoral action must set itself. We are insisting on this point because there are those who mistakenly emphasize the pastoral aspect in such a way as to subject and subordinate to it even the liturgical celebration itself. In the last analysis, they would have to be classified among those who are trying to adapt the liturgy to the people.

Above all, religious instruction; but true religious instruction. The ignorance and superficiality which we decry have their origin not in the lack of activity and zeal of those who teach, but rather in the lack of solidity in the instruction they give.

Bishop Vicente Enrique Tarancón of Solsona, present secretary of the *Conferencias Episcopales* of Spain, in his celebrated pastoral letter "Total Renewal of the Christian Life," examines with the zeal of a pastor and the obvious sincerity of a father the disturbing paradox displayed in our people, traditionally Catholic and sincerely devout, but practically dechristianized. "This paradox," writes the illustrious prelate, "is truly disturbing, because it tells us that something is lacking in the formation of the faithful and that something is lacking in our priestly action and in our apostolate."[6]

Various causes, no doubt, can be assigned for this paradox. But at the bottom of all of them we shall have to place the lack of solidity in religious instruction. It is natural to tend to that which is easier, more concrete, more perceptible to the senses, more immediately useful. The feverish, absorbing pace at which the activities of life proceed in our times, hinders the reflection and the profundity necessary for assimilating the great principles of the supernatural life. Today we seek what is most useful, but this is not always what is best. This tendency also has had its influence on the religious instruction of the faithful.

Swayed by this necessity of turning toward the more practical, theology has too often taken a more apologetic than expositive character; in morality, preference has been given to casuistry; and two defective substitutes, rubricism and devotionism, have taken the place of worship.

The preoccupation of many shepherds of souls, unable to provide for all needs, is reduced also to that which is immediately most useful. They are concerned above all with seeing to it that their parishioners receive the sacraments when they are dying. If they can do something more, they try to get them to make their Easter duty. And an increase in the percentage of those who fulfill the Sunday precept is considered the greatest index of religious observance in a district.

In preaching, moral subjects have predominated over doctrinal subjects, because they are more immediately useful; and, for the same reason, among these themes the preference is usually given to those that are directed to re-

---

[6] Vicente Enrique Tarancón, *Renovación total de la vida cristiana*, pastoral letter of March 24, 1955 (Tárrega, 1955), p. 4.

pressing sin. Among the doctrinal subjects, the most frequent in missions, public devotions, novenas, etc., are usually those which refer to the Last Things, because they more readily affect the conscience of the hearers, and the immediate aim of these exercises is ordinarily to lead the parishioners to make a good confession.

All these zealous, very praiseworthy pastoral efforts have no doubt the highest of aims: to bring souls to heaven, almost forcing them in if necessary, or getting them through by a kind of subterfuge. But these efforts will not succeed in forming good Christians, conscious of their dignity, "strengthened with power through the Spirit for the development of the inner man, welcoming Christ through faith into their hearts, rooted and grounded in love, able to comprehend with all the saints what is the breadth and length and height and depth, and to know Christ's love, which surpasses knowing" (Eph. 3:16-19), as St. Paul wanted them to be. We know well what doctrine was preached to those Christians just converted from paganism and immorality and ignorant of every Christian concept, by the Apostle who gloried in having received the grace "to announce among the gentiles the good tidings of the unfathomable riches of Christ, and to enlighten all men as to what is the dispensation of the mystery hidden from eternity in God" (Eph. 3:8-9).

If we compare our Christians with those of whom we are given a glimpse through the lofty ideas expressed by St. Paul in various passages of his letters, we shall understand the conclusion at which Bishop Enrique y Tarancón arrives: "The Christian life needs to be renewed. For us it has been feeble and poor. We have not succeeded in giving it the strength and vitality that historical circumstances demand. In general, we are not living in a way that is adapted to our era. And for this reason the Christian life has lost part of its efficacy in the individual order and it has lost almost all its influence in the social order."[7]

His conclusion does not claim to be anything more than an application of the Pope's advice in insisting on the necessity of "a mighty awakening of *thought* and of *works,* an awakening which excuses no class, but involves all, clergy and people, authorities, families, groups, every individual soul, in the total renewal of the Christian life."[8] This "better world" desired by the Pope is the Christian world of the gospel, of the writings of the Apostles, of the doctrine of St. Paul, of the liturgy of the Church, which is founded on faith and love, nurtured on the tasteful understanding of the mystery of Christ, animated by the sacramental life, manifested by the sincerity and depth of a life as member of Christ within the ecclesiastical community.

And the solid foundation on which this world must be built is religious instruction, the first and most urgent mission of pastoral action. For "how

[7] *Ibid.,* p. 4.
[8] Exhortation of Pope Pius XII to the faith- ful of Rome; *L'Osservatore Romano,* Feb. 11-12, 1952.

are they to call upon Him in whom they have not believed? But how
are they to believe Him whom they have not heard?" (Rom. 10:14).

Actually there are many who have received no other doctrinal formation
than that which served them as preparation for first communion and which
was confined, therefore, to very elementary notions, often inadequate and
not gone into very deeply. Perhaps some of them will have continued their
catechetical instruction, almost always on the basis of concepts that are
elaborated and closely packed, reducing the Christian mystery to definitions
of the conceptual type without any relation to worship and to the Christian
life. Their lessons in religion were distinguished from lessons in geography
and in mathematics only by the subject matter. The preaching they may
have heard occasionally, not always sufficiently formative in character, has
not been able to fill up the great gap of religious ignorance.

What other means of formation aside from these have a positive influence
on the majority of Christians? Reading, perhaps? At times, yes, for some;
but ordinarily the reading matter of most of those who read anything of
a religious nature is small in quantity and inconsistent in quality. Usually
it does not include either sacred Scripture or the Fathers of the Church or
authors whose doctrine is very solid. A glance at any of the many magazines,
papers, pamphlets, etc., of a pious character which are published and are
most easily available to the faithful, will suffice to show how superficial and
lacking in formative power is the religious atmosphere which prevails today.

Referring to the religious associations, the bishop of Solsona writes, "None
of them has a truly formative effect on its members or exercises any notable
influence on their family and social life."[9]

If we wanted to mention certain religious functions, perhaps we should
cite the passage regarding them in the acts of the diocesan synod of Lodi:
"Preaching, which should be the quintessence of the 'functions,' is reduced
to a monotonous mouthing of platitudes, repeated for the 'enth' time always
to the same hearers. Such functions seem to be invented for giving oxygen
to the dying."[10]

Monsignor Fischer writes, "What end is served by the whole activity of
pastoral works, of the press, of visits to homes; what end is served by all
the pastoral expedients of preservation—gymnasiums, sports, music, motion
pictures—; what end is served by the methods of propaganda modeled on
the secular methods, if in the church, to which all these pastoral measures
should be directed, nothing is done that is capable of elevating man, im-
pelling him toward the good and enriching him spiritually; if, on the contrary, there is a perpetuation of the tedious system of an instruction imparted
in abstract forms and without any connection with the liturgical mystery

[9] Vicente Enrique Tarancón, *Renovación
total de la vida cristiana*, p. 3.
[10] Can. L. Salamina in *Synodus Dioec.*

Laudensis XI (Lodi, 1943), pp. 285-286. (See
Marcora, *Ambrosius*, 1955, p. 183, note 1.)

of the day, without a single allusion to the living, communitarian character of worship, so that the faithful have the impression of assisting at incomprehensible rites performed on the altar and hence go away just as they have come, satisfied with having fulfilled a duty, however serious a duty it may be?"[11]

Here is the conclusion deduced from what we have set forth: the most urgent task of pastoral action is the solid religious instruction of the faithful, aimed at an intelligent participation in the liturgical rites. This was the plan of the primitive Church. The long period of catechumenate was a time of doctrinal instruction and of preparation for receiving baptism and being able to participate with the faithful in the Eucharistic rite. After this basic instruction and with the grace of the faith and of baptism, the neophyte could gradually broaden his religious knowledge and go deeper into the mystery of Christ during the yearly course of the successive liturgical celebrations.

We must begin the Christian and liturgical renewal of our people, therefore, with a labor of doctrinal instruction and catechesis. Monsignor Ancel sets forth briefly the program of this preparatory course: "God—Jesus Christ —the Church. How we enter into the mystery of God by faith, hope and charity. Christ's sacrifice and the action of the sacraments. The way of love. — Then they will be prepared to understand the liturgy. Then they will have the sense of the mystery. Everything will become a sign of an invisible reality."[12]

Then, having been initiated to the liturgy, they can carry out Cardinal Lercaro's program, of which the objective is "slowly but persistently to form souls to experience through the course of the year the mysteries of redemption which the liturgy records and re-lives; to give the faithful a vital awareness and appreciation of their insertion into the Church, Christ's mystical Body, in virtue of which they can now worthily glorify God; and to have them relish the bond of fraternal solidarity which binds all the sons of God and forms them into His great family."[13]

This is also the directive given by Pope Pius XII: "Whatever pertains to the external worship has assuredly its importance; however, the most pressing duty of Christians is to live the liturgical life, and increase and cherish its supernatural spirit. Readily provide the young clerical student with facilities to understand the sacred ceremonies . . . especially to lead him into closest union with Christ the Priest so that he may become a holy minister of sanctity. Try in every way, with the means and helps that your prudence

[11] Mons. E. Fischer, "L'era liturgica nella vita della Chiesa," *Partecipazione attiva alla liturgia: Atti del III Convegno Internazionale di Studi Liturgici* (Lugano, 1953), pp. 64-65. (See Marcora, *Ambrosius*, 1955, pp. 184-185.)

[12] Alfred Ancel, *La Chiesa e gli Operai*, p. 136.

[13] Cardinal Giacomo Lercaro, *A messa, figlioli!* (2nd ed.; Bologna, 1955), p. 11; this passage translated in *Worship* (Collegeville, Minn.), XXX (1956), 599.

deems best, that the clergy and people become one in mind and heart, and that the Christian people take such an active part in the liturgy that it becomes a truly sacred action of due worship to the eternal Lord in which the priest, chiefly responsible for the souls of his parish, and the ordinary faithful are united together."[14]

As far as the pastoral duty of instructing the faithful is concerned, a practice to be avoided, of course, is that of taking advantage of the time when the Mass is being celebrated to perform this function of preaching. The primary sermon on the importance and value of the Mass should be of a practical order: to teach by example that nothing must have priority over the Mass; not even the preaching of the word of God may be preferred to it.

Much less, then, should the practice of pious exercises of devotion be preferred to the Mass! It is better not to practice them if they must disturb the active participation of the faithful in the holy sacrifice of the Mass. Whoever wants to have them may find another, more opportune time for them.

With regard to preaching, the Mass should be interrupted after the gospel and resumed after the homily, even if the preacher is a priest other than the celebrant; this praiseworthy regulation is already in force in various dioceses. It is not possible to give due attention simultaneously to the exposition of the word of God and to the liturgical action of the celebrant. Moreover, the faithful who are taking part in the celebration of the sacrifice should not be detained by acts that pertain to the Mass of the catechumens while the celebrant is already performing the great, solemn acts of the offertory and the anaphora.[15]

Some advice might still be in order about the catechetical instruction for the understanding of the liturgy.

From the very beginning of religious instruction, the catechism should not ignore the fact of liturgical worship. It is true that the catechism is not and need not be a doctrinal explanation of the liturgy; but it cannot be forgotten either that the catechism is directed to the liturgy, in as much as it prepares the subjects for it. "The catechism is one of the elements of the total initiation of the Christian: the initiation of the living faith, illustrated by the preaching of the Christian message." This initiation requires a sys-

---

[14] *Mediator Dei*, nn. 197-199.

[15] Cf. Marcora, *Ambrosius*, March-April, 1956, pp. 99-112. This article quotes also, in this connection, article 29 of the 43rd Synod of Milan: "We prohibit altogether the custom more than once condemned by the bishop of Insubria, of having the Mass continue at the altar while another priest explains the holy gospel to the people from the pulpit on festive days. For the two distinct precepts must not be confused: one requires that God be worshiped through the offering of the Eucharistic sacrifice, the other that knowledge of God be fostered through the explanation of the gospel. Each of these two very important precepts demands its own time. Therefore, while the gospel is explained to the people from the pulpit, let the celebration of the Mass at the altar be suspended."

tematic explanation of that which constitutes the object of the faith. This is the immediate object of the catechism.

The catechumen must recognize, however, that the knowledge of these truths which are explained to him in the catechism is not pure speculative knowledge or a means of increasing his religious culture. The concern is with a *living* faith, something that is to fill up and inform the Christian's whole life. He must recognize that the object of this living faith is found mysteriously present in the liturgy, precisely in order that it may be placed within his reach and may be communicated to him as the normal food of his supernatural life as a Christian within the ecclesiastical community.

When the Christian has arrived at the possession of this living faith, even if it be only an initial possession, his instruction may take on another character. Then the catechesis will proceed in a fully worshipful atmosphere. It is that catechesis which introduces one to worship and forms part of the worship. It does not solve problems, but initiates into the mystery. It initiates; that is, it is not so much concerned with giving conclusions as with procuring the rudiments and the light for a personal assimilation which will be achieved not during the course of the lesson but in the mystery of worship and of daily life. It is in the nature of this catechesis that it is renewed indefinitely, that it never ends, that it is never a source of boredom, bcause it is based on a present reality.

2. Liturgy, Paraliturgy and Participation of the Faithful

We have said that the true pastoral solution for the return of the faithful people to active participation in the liturgy must consist of two elements. We have spoken of the first: religious instruction.

In the second place, those who assist at the liturgical acts must be helped to participate really in them. Here is another field for pastoral labor. In this regard the Church has begun by her own example. With fervent zeal she has been concerned with that which is her exclusive privilege and cannot be left at all to private initiative: the renewal of the liturgical rites. She has sought to purify them, she has restored ancient rites, created or adapted new ones, all with the aim of making the divine worship dignified, more intelligible and more within reach of the faithful.

Moreover, in the restoration of the Holy Week, not only has she been concerned with the revision of the rites, but in the rubrics she has sought to take pastoral action explicitly into consideration. The Church has prepared the rites in such a way that they may be within reach of the Christians; the pastoral action must complete this work by disposing the faithful for a vital participation in the rites. This is the precise order.

When we examine the pastoral directives given by the Sacred Congregation of Rites in the Instruction for the application of the Holy Week reform, we find at once three general principles which should be the norm of all pastoral action directed to the liturgy: 1) "Let the priests, especially those who have the care of souls, be well instructed, not only on the ritual celebration of the new *Ordo* of Holy Week, but also on its liturgical meaning and its pastoral aim." 2) Let the faithful be instructed at the proper time and in the most suitable way, so that they are brought to a right understanding of the liturgical action, with regard to both its doctrinal content and the meaning of the rites and ceremonies. 3) Let the faithful take a devout and active part in the celebration of the liturgical rites, each according to his own condition, and always with sincere assent of mind and spirit.

We shall take these pontifical directives as the basis of our exposition.

We must note first of all that it is not within the competence of pastoral initiative to reform or adapt the rites but only to prepare or dispose the faithful. The Church and the faithful themselves have a right to demand that the priest carry out the liturgical rite and the ceremonies in full, according to the laws established by the Church herself. The Church's authority would be usurped by any of her ministers who did not fulfill duly what she has laid down for him but made some innovation on his own account, even if this were done by reason of pastoral zeal and with the aim of putting the rites within easier reach of the faithful.

Moreover, the faithful, like the Church, have a right to demand that the liturgical action be not deformed, being clothed with a kind of borrowed robe with the idea of making it more attractive to the faithful who are poorly instructed. That would be a cheapening of worship.

It is important to observe this principle: the liturgy is not chiefly a spectacle; it is an action, the joint action of the priest and the faithful. This principle has often been taken in reverse, undoubtedly by reason of pastoral zeal. To attract to the church those who are not used to going, or to arouse more devotion in those who do go, a pastor will celebrate or announce Masses and functions made pleasant with singing and music. In some churches of the large cities, funerals and weddings are celebrations which seem more like sacred concerts or secular gatherings, considering the profusion of decorations, lights and flowers and the attitude and clothes of those in attendance. Those Masses of the greater solemnities in which it would seem that the most interesting thing is the music with many voices and orchestra and the preaching with large, sweeping gestures, also have the character of a spectacle rather than that of a collective action of worship.

All this amounts to disrespect for the faithful, because it slights their dignity as a priestly people, and disrespect for the liturgy, which is relegated to a very secondary rank.

With the liturgical movement, this way of making the liturgy more pleasing and bringing it to the level of the faithful who are poorly instructed has taken on another, quite different form and a solemn name. It is called *paraliturgy*. Not all paraliturgy is to be condemned. Certain forms may well be employed to instil in the faithful a higher regard for the liturgy; but, though they may be acceptable, they must always be used very cautiously, since their effect may be the opposite: instead of being a pastoral aid in the service of the liturgy, they may turn into substitutes for true public worship.

The Assembly of Cardinals and Archbishops of France, in a "note on liturgical initiatives," published in 1954, to which we shall refer again, gives us this definition of paraliturgy: "ceremonies of a liturgical appearance, inspired by liturgical texts and gestures, but without official character."[16]

In attacking the problem of educating the faithful for the liturgy, it seemed as if the solution was found in organizing some ceremonies that were attractive and easy to understand which, drawing their inspiration from the liturgy, explained its gestures, clarified its texts, brought within reach of the ill-prepared faithful the ideas and the realities of the liturgy, bringing out its spiritual meaning and its influence on the Christian life. The attempt was to habituate the people gradually, by means of these ceremonies, to the style and the concepts of the liturgy, thus preparing them, step by step, eventually to take part in the liturgical celebrations.

The plan was tried with success. But serious difficulties arose very soon: first of all the danger of confusing the Church's official worship with the paraliturgies; then the inclination to prefer these more popular, easier forms to the liturgy itself, so that instead of being a preparation for the liturgy they would come to take its place in the popular esteem, in which case they would become new forms of devotion that might be another obstacle to the true participation in liturgical worship.

No less a danger is that which results from the improvisation and the private initiative involved in paraliturgies. Everyone could improvise to his own fancy and create new forms of worship, collective but not official, which might easily lack the purity and depth of doctrine proper to worship, with the possibility that the authors of these paraliturgies might come to suppose that they were better than the liturgy itself, as Cardinal Feltin observed, referring to the rules dictated on this matter: "We are most anxious that you conform to the rules and above all that you do not suppose that your little personal ideas are of greater value than that which the Church formally prescribes."

To avoid the disadvantages mentioned above, the assembly of French archbishops laid down some rules for the paraliturgies in the document cited. In summary they are: the paraliturgies must not lose sight of the superiority of the true liturgy; much less may they presume to substitute for it; paraliturgical ceremonies may not be mixed with liturgical rites; to compose ceremonies of this kind, one must have a careful technical, theological and historical preparation and a profound liturgical sense; they may be used

---

[16] "Note de l'Assemblée des Cardinaux et Archevêques," *La Maison-Dieu,* 42 (Paris, second quarter of 1955), p. 31.

only in moderation, and always under the immediate vigilance of the bishops.

We shall not deny that, under these conditions and in certain environments, the paraliturgies may be a subsidiary element in the liturgical preparation of the faithful. But, as a general rule, the method indicated by the Church in the documents establishing the new rite of Holy Week, which we have mentioned above, seems to us to be safer and more effective.

Turning to the three general principles regulating pastoral action with the aim of helping the faithful to take part intelligently in the liturgical rites, we find inculcated above all the necessity of having the priests, especially those in charge of souls, well instructed not only in the ritual arrangements but also in their liturgical meaning and pastoral aim.

Improvisations can never give good results. Preparation and competence are required in every undertaking, so much the more when the concern is with an action in which the Church is officially represented, which has as object the divine worship, and which constitutes the goal of pastoral effort. A liturgical action can be well performed only in the measure in which its meaning is grasped and its spirit is lived. The faithful have a keen sensibility for appreciating and distinguishing between ceremonies which are carried out to fulfill a need of the spirit and those which merely obey the directives of a ritual. And the spirit is not improvised: it has to be enlightened, it has to be cultivated slowly and painstakingly.

The pastoral aspect of our rites also requires effort and careful preparation. Before celebrating them, we must reflect, calculate, foresee circumstances, arrange everything in such a way as to make them as easy of access as they can be made. Only thus will they actually have the dignity and efficacy the Church has provided for them. The Jesuit Father de Coninck writes, "Let us ask ourselves in all sincerity whether we are as concerned to prepare, for example, the Christmas rites or the paschal triduum according to the liturgical rules, as we are to conduct an outdoor festival, a benefit fair, or a play. For these last, how many discussions there are, how many sessions far into the night, how many rehearsals, how much preparation and construction!" And he adds later, "And we must see in the liturgy not just a 'sacred theater' but that which the liturgy truly is: a magnificent exchange, through Christ living in His Church, between God and His children."[17]

Moreover, we must take into account that we are living in an age of transition. The majority of the apostles of the liturgical renewal have been spiritually formed and educated according to the standards of a spirituality very different from liturgical spirituality; and it is not easy for them to free themselves from concepts and habits deeply rooted, which, moreover, have borne and continue to bear excellent fruits. The spiritual formation received from childhood on, and favored by the religious mentality pre-

---

[17] L. de Coninck, *Problemi di adattamento nell'apostolato* (Brescia, 1950), p. 151. (See Marcora, *Ambrosius,* 1955, pp. 188-189.)

dominant on all sides, cannot help influencing the thoughts and actions of the present generation; so that those of our day, even without wanting to, and in fact while trying to give a liturgical direction to their own spiritual life, often do nothing more than to cover, with a garment borrowed from the liturgy, forms of piety which have nothing to do with the spirituality derived from the liturgy.

It is very hard for us to assimilate certain principles of liturgical spirituality which offer a notable contrast to the principles and the practice of those other, more individualistic methods which for many years have modeled our lives. The decadence of the liturgical life has been the result of many centuries; its renewal will also have to be gradual. A life is not made up at a moment's notice. It is a work of assimilation and of slow development.

That is why we are insisting on the need of beginning the liturgical renewal with a labor of intellectual formation. We must probe the theological concepts on which the liturgy is based and analyze the inner structure of public worship until we can grasp its doctrinal content and appreciate its regulative value for the spiritual life of every Christian. Then we must *live* intensely what the Church is doing in her liturgy, applying our own spiritual activity to it and letting ourselves be penetrated by its formative influence. External action on behalf of the liturgical renewal can be effective only in so far as it flows spontaneously from principles that have been successfully assimilated and applied in our own lives.

While we are on this point, it is worth noting that the labor of renewing the liturgical spirit in our own life and in that of others is to be a constructive work, not destructive.

As far as our own interior formation is concerned, it would be a mistake to abandon forthwith the methods and practices we have been using. Such an action would leave us without help and without stimulation in the exercise of the spiritual life. It is more important to live sincerely and intensely the acts of public worship in which we take part in the congregation or at the altar, and then to begin informing with their spirit the individual acts that we are used to practicing. In proportion as the mind and the spirit of the liturgy penetrate into our spirituality, a process of selection will begin to take place spontaneously. Some of these acts will take on a new aspect and new vigor. Others, which we may have considered indispensable hitherto, will definitely take a secondary rank. Still others will gradually disappear as our vision of the Christian life is broadened, yielding their place to measures directly inspired by the spirit of the liturgy.

When the acts in question are public acts which can and should influence the spiritual formation of others, we should look ahead and proceed in such a way as to educate and to guide. Acting prudently but decisively, we may well begin to adapt the organization of parochial worship, both the liturgical actions and the extraliturgical functions, to a criterion and a spirit inspired by the liturgy. Thus the faithful will become used to the liturgy and will acquire from it an orientation that will make them understand and love public worship, stimulate them to take an active part in it, and make them feel the need of conforming their own spiritual lives to it.

The second norm deduced from the document of the Sacred Congregation of Rites which we have mentioned above and to which we are referring, is the proper instruction of the faithful. We are not treating here of liturgical instruction of a general nature, which is presupposed, but of that which is aimed immediately at preparing for a particular solemnity and at explaining concretely what the celebrant is doing or saying at the altar.

This instruction includes a remote preparation and a clarification simultaneous with the celebration itself.

What we have indicated with regard to the celebrant's preparation can be said, if we observe due proportions, with regard to the faithful, since they also are to participate in the action. Precisely because they are lay people, not so fully instructed in ecclesiastical matters, we must give them a careful, thorough preparation if we want them to perform the part that belongs to them in worship worthily and intelligently.

None of them would presume to perform some public act in a society meeting on the spur of the moment, without being very sure of his own task. They must be properly instructed, then, on the various solemnities of the year that involve some special rite, and on everything connected with the administration of the sacraments and the sacramentals, whenever they have to take part in the administration. Let no liturgical act be celebrated without a preparation by way of suitable instructions for those who are to take part in it.

The directions for the new rite of Holy Week insist that the whole season of Lent be employed in the aim for which it was instituted, that is, as a time of instruction and preparation for Easter. In a similar way, Advent should prepare for Christmas and Epiphany.

In the parishes where a select group has adopted the praiseworthy custom of meeting every month for a day of recollection, it would be well to have this day coincide with the vigil of a liturgical feast or with one of the days immediately preceding it, in order that this group might be prepared by instruction and prayer for the celebration of the feast.

None of the better educated Christians in a parish should be ignorant of the date and the meaning of those very important liturgical celebrations which constitute the milestones of the liturgical year, the Ember Days.

A further necessary measure is the timely explanation or clarification given at the climactic and most deeply significant moments during the very celebration of the act of worship.

The missals in the vernacular, properly used, can give very effective service. But they are not enough. Not all the faithful have them, and not all those who do have them know how to use them properly.

There is an excellent means of guiding the faithful along the route taken by the liturgical celebration: the directions or interventions by the deacon, so frequent in the Eastern liturgies, as a means of liturgical instruction. Among us, they had been recommended by the Council of Trent, and Pope Pius XII again recommended them in his encyclical on sacred music. They consist in interjecting, during the celebration of the rites, brief explanatory remarks which illuminate quickly but profoundly the sacred action being performed, and thus keep the faithful closely united to the celebrant. The Pope says:

"It has pleased us to make our own the exhortation made by the Fathers of the Council of Trent. 'Pastors and all those who have care of souls' were especially urged that 'often, during the celebration of Mass, they or others whom they delegate explain something about what is read in the Mass and, among other things, tell something about the mystery of this most holy sacrifice. This is to be done particularly on Sundays and holy days.'

"This should be done especially at the time when catechetical instruction is being given to the Christian people. It may be done more easily and readily in this age of ours than was possible in times past, because translations of the liturgical texts into the vernacular tongues and explanations of these texts in books and pamphlets are available. These works, produced in almost every country by learned writers, can effectively help and enlighten the faithful to understand and share in what is said by the sacred ministers in the Latin language."[18]

Before the Mass is begun, before the offertory as preparation for the "prayer of the faithful," before the communion and at other times that seem opportune, a few brief words spoken by one of the clergy or read aloud by a layman can keep the faithful united to the celebrant and permeated with his prayer, can point out to them the place this prayer occupies in the Mass and the particular meaning it receives from the feast being celebrated. The reading of the epistle and the gospel in the vernacular, after they have been read or sung in Latin, may often be the best doctrinal instruction and the best homily.

If attention is given to careful preparation and clear pronunciation, consider what would be the spiritual fruits that might eventually be gathered by following this procedure on the occasion of baptisms, weddings, funerals, etc. We would not have to rely so heavily on music, and the functions would be more profitable for those in attendance, many of whom may not go to church very often. In the case of funerals, this more conscious union of the faithful to the Mass would be a more efficacious suffrage for the

---

[18] Encyclical *Musicae sacrae disciplina*, translation provided by the N.C.W.C. News Service (Washington: National Catholic Welfare Conference, 1956), nn. 48-49.

departed than many decades of the rosary recited mechanically and distractedly by those who are attending the funeral.

Let it be kept in mind that these didactic interventions must not excessively occupy the attention of the faithful, which is to be centered on the
sacred rite, nor must they reduce the faithful to mere listeners, to the
detriment of their active participation. They must direct them to the sacred
action and keep them united to it.

Hence long explanations and extensive commentaries must be avoided,
since in the end they would only distract the congregation and the celebrant.

Nor is it particularly advisable to read aloud in the vernacular everything
that the priest is saying quietly in Latin. To keep up with the priest, one
would have to speak hurriedly, leaving words or phrases half unsaid. Moreover, we are well aware that the liturgy is an action of the community and
that each one has his own part in it. It is not up to every individual to
say or do everything: he need only be spiritually united to the celebrant,
who presides over the assembly and performs the sacred action. It is enough,
therefore, if the people have read to them in their own tongue—in the form
that seems most suitable—those parts which have a didactic character, which
form part of the liturgy precisely in order that the people may understand
them and be instructed by them; and, on the other hand, if the spirit of the
faithful be kept united to the priest's prayer, by remarks that are brief and
well thought out, when this prayer turns to God.

There still remains a third principle of liturgical pastoral, and it is the
one that completes and gathers the fruits of the two preceding ones: that
the faithful take an active and devout part in the celebration of the liturgy.
We shall develop it in treating of the parochial life.

3. Liturgy and Parochial Life

The liturgy is essentially communitarian. It supposes a community as
subject of worship: a church; but a church of human proportions, in which
the various members that compose it can be related to one another reciprocally
and normally to form a body in reality, the body of the praying community.

The ideal liturgical community will be that which allows the faithful
who make it up to live the rite of the Christian religion with fulness of
individual and communitarian life. This community is the parish. It is like
a micro-organism of Christ's mystical Body, reproducing in miniature the
essential traits of the universal Church with an aim to the divine worship
and the practice of the Christian life.

True, the parish does not have a perfect autonomy in its juridical personality, because its head, the pastor, does not possess the fulness of the
hierarchical powers of sanctification and government, but has received them
as a limited participation of those powers by which the bishop rules and
sanctifies the community of the diocese, formed as a perfect body through

the collection of the parishes under his shepherd's crook. But the parish does have sufficient individuality to form a true organic body and to realize in itself all the normal activity of the Christian life.

Monsignor Montini, when he was pro-secretary of state for the Holy Father, thus described the parish in a letter of August 14, 1953, addressed to the Canadian "Social Week": "What is a parish, then? It is the smallest portion of the one universal flock entrusted by God to St. Peter. Under the authority of a responsible priest, who has received the care of souls from his bishop, the parish is the primary community of Christian life in Christ's Church, a community of human dimensions, so that the shepherd can truly know his sheep and the sheep can know their shepherd. Its boundaries are normally set around a defined territory within a diocese, and thus the parish is fixed to a locality, inserted in definite traditions and horizons. Finally, in the center of this territory is the parish church, surmounted by its belfry, with its baptistry, its confessional, its altar and its tabernacle; the church, symbol of unity, center of the common life."[19]

Thus the parish as principal nucleus of the Christian life is formed by five elements: a pastor, a community of the faithful, a territory or parochial demarcation, a church, common means of worship and of sanctification.

The parish is the normal center of the Church's liturgical life. There are those who think that the liturgy belongs to the monastic churches, and that it can be practiced in the parish churches only in a very limited and imperfect way, as far as the circumstances and the other demands of the parish life permit. This is not so. Quite to the contrary: the possibilities are limited; but, precisely because of the requirements of the care of souls, the parish is the normal center of the liturgical life.

The monastic churches, as such, accomplish only a part of the liturgical action: the liturgy of sacrifice and of praise, that is, the conventual Mass and, framing it, the Divine Office. Since they ordinarily have sufficient personnel and means, since their members by vocation profess the perfection of the Christian life, since they prefer the divine praise to all other activities and devote the better part of their life and of their time to it, the monasteries give solemnity to the liturgy of praise and celebrate it with a perfection that would be hard to find anywhere else.

There are also the cathedral churches. The cathedral church is the church of the diocese, the bishop's church. In it the liturgy should be celebrated in such a way as to partake of the solemnity of the monastic churches and the pastoral vitality of the parish churches. On the one hand, the Divine Office is celebrated there daily as a summing up and expression of the divine praise of the whole diocese; hence it has a chapter of canons, with the principal

[19] Letter of Monsignor G. B. Montini to Cardinal Léger, archbishop of Montreal. The portion quoted is from the Italian version as found in *La Scuola Cattolica*, 1953, pp. 555-556.

aim of "offering God a more solemn worship in the Church" (canon 391, 1). On the other hand, on the great liturgical solemnities and the most notable occasions in the religious life of the diocese, the cathedral church should gather the multitude of the faithful around the bishop, to pray with him, to receive from his hands the bread of the Eucharist and from his lips the bread of the divine word, and to form the church of the diocese, gathered under his shepherd's crook. These are not the usual liturgical assemblies, however; the cathedral church is the church of the great solemnities in the religious life of the Christian people.

The normal center of worship is always the parish church, the parish. Here are centered and reflected all the aspects of the individual and social life of the Christian. Here is the normal channel for all the graces of sanctification for the faithful, who by means of the parish come to form part of the people of God, in communion with the bishop of the diocese, with the Pope of Rome, with Jesus Christ, Head of the Church.

Parochial activity is as rich in human aspects and as full of supernatural meaning as the Christian life itself which revolves around it. We are interested here in only one of these aspects, the liturgical, which is the most profound because it reaches to the very roots and touches on the *raison d'être* of the parochial life; it is also the most extensive aspect because it comprises all the activities of the parish. We shall consider it according to the five elements we have found in the description of what a parish is.

The parochial demarcation

Ordinarily the parishes are territorial. That is to say, a territory circumscribed within well determined boundaries marks the extent of the pastor's jurisdiction. Those who have their domicile or their quasi-domicile there are his parishioners and constitute the parochial community. There is no juridical difference between a parochial territory containing a group of scattered farms, one containing a nucleus of people more or less grouped around the church, or one comprising a quarter or a section of a large city.

The problems presented by these different groups of people are quite varied, and pastoral action must take this fact into account if it is to be effective. With regard to the liturgy also, the possibilities offered by these different kinds of parishes are very diverse.

If we keep in mind that the liturgical life supposes principally a community, a parochial family, we can see that the ideal parish from the viewpoint of the liturgy will be that which offers greater prospects for the formation and the normal functioning of a community. In this sense, the parish established in a village, a town or a small city, or even in a well defined quarter of a larger city, can more easily rely on a parochial family. Traditions, history, environment, mutual family and social relationships, similar interests—all will help to form a compact nucleus with unity of spiritual life around one and the same church.

A rural parish, with a very small number of residents, scattered and separated from one another and from the church by considerable distances, will find it harder to gather together for the common celebration of the liturgical solemnities or for celebrating as a family the principal acts of the Christian and parochial life.

The problem of the country parishes is seen to be more serious if we take into account the scarcity of priests. Little settlements which formerly had a pastor cannot have one now. Moreover, the necessity of distributing many priests over villages of small population reduces the possibilities of adding to the parish clergy in the cities, where the needs are greater and every priest must take some thousands of souls under his pastoral care.

To be taken into consideration also is the personal situation created for these priests, who are often young, obliged as they are to live in isolation, far from any center of culture, with hardly any possibility of improving their own formation and without much intensity of pastoral action.

In a city parish, that is, in a section of a large city, the heterogeneous character of the population contained within the parish boundaries, the continual change in parishioners as families move about, the fact that few families have relatives in the parish, the lack of a common basis of tradition or of interests, the arbitrary character of the parish boundaries, the proximity to other churches, etc.—all contribute to making the constitution of a true parish family more difficult. And if one is finally formed, it is only a small minority in comparison to the totality of the parishioners.

This is a most important problem for the restoration of the Christian life in the great urban centers. Its solution is beyond the capacities of the parish priest, and must be found in a new parochial organization of the large cities, taking into account the situation created in fact by modern life.

And then again, there is the progessive growth of the cities with the formation of great suburbs which also present grave social, religious and moral problems; the increasing density of population in the urban centers; the appearance of new, urgent spiritual needs which demand a fatiguing and more complex activity on the part of the priests. Thus a difficult situation has arisen, which is aggravated by the simultaneous decrease in vocations. All this is reflected in a deplorable weakening of the relations between pastor and people, and in an almost complete disappearance of the sense of parochial family and community, which is a very grave threat to one of the most solid foundations of the Christian life.

In the largest cities of some countries the bishops have attacked this problem in a concrete way and have tried some tentative solutions, with relative success: new distribution of the parochial districts, better adapted to the various groupings of the population, with a certain basis of unity; extraterritorial parishes for the various national groups; formation of communities of priests, with the priests belonging to more than one parish for inter-parochial work and having specialized activities assigned to each one of them.

The dioceses have a twofold problem, that of the country parishes and that of the big city parishes: two problems that must be studied and solved as a basic prerequisite for the inauguration of a better world founded on the total renewal of the Christian life. For the parochial organization can change and perhaps must change according to the times and the needs of the times; but the parish, as ultimate ecclesiastical unit, as spiritual family, as community of the faithful, will always be the normal basis of the whole liturgical life and hence of the whole Christian life.

The parish church

The parish church is the center of the liturgical life of the parish. It is the place meant for the divine worship and the administration of the sacraments. It is the place where the parish family gathers to live in common the mystery of Christ. It is the center of irradiation of Christian life over all the individuals and all the homes that go to make up the parochial community.

There may be other places in the parish where other parochial activities take place in common, but they will always have a secondary value, definitely subordinate to the essential activity pursued by the parochial family in the church. That was what the Pope said in a speech addressed to one of the parishes of Rome on January 21, 1953: "The playing field, the theater, the parish motion pictures, the school itself if there is one—all very useful and often necessary institutions—are not the center of the parish. Its center is the church."[20]

In some parishes there are various churches. All will have a more or less solemn worship; but there is only one parish church. The other churches either depend directly on the parish church, as its branches—and then they are nothing but a prolongation of the parish church and form a single reality with it—or they are private churches, served ordinarily by religious communities. Every religious house forms a family, an ecclesiastical center, a community with its own life and its particular rules, often exempt from the bishop's jurisdiction. It has a right to its own church, its own place of worship; but this is not the parish church, the center of Christian life for the parishioners. The parishioners may attend a church of a religious community, but then they do not find themselves in their own church; they are guests of the church of the religious.

[20] Discourse of Pope Pius XII to the parish of St. Sabbas; L'Osservatore Romano, Jan. 21, 1953.

The churches of the religious can render an excellent service to the parish community when, in agreement with the pastor, they collaborate with him, combining the schedules and coordinating their own activity of worship to the spiritual needs of the parish, without prejudice, of course, to the needs and proprieties of the religious community itself. In the cities, this collaboration becomes almost indispensable. The priestly action of the religious in their churches is a precious element which must certainly be taken into account in the parochial reorganization of the large cities.

But the private churches can also be a great hindrance to the normal development of parish life. If in their activity of worship they prescind from the parish, they may take many constituents away from the parochial community. Greater proximity, certain facilities, personal sympathy, proselytism, etc., may attract a good number of parishioners who will constantly attend a certain church conducted by religious and thus lose all contact with their parish church and community. Moreover, the churches of the religious are not always centers of liturgical life. More often they are centers of propaganda for particular devotions which are not always compatible with a true liturgical spirit.

But if the faithful are leaving the parish church and frequenting other churches, the fault does not always lie with the religious. It is often due to the lack of facilities and the deplorable shortcomings in the worship of the parish church. The parish church should be attractive: as simple and modest as you will, but clean, orderly, arranged tastefully and artistically. The parishioners should be able to feel at home there. It is the house of God and of His children. In a well organized parish the task of cleaning and decorating the parish church should not be in the hands of paid employees; the parishioners themselves should deem it an honor to take care of the house of God, their parish church.

Inside the church everything should show forth order, beauty and dignity; everything should help the faithful to lift their hearts to God. The simplicity of the Christian life and of the liturgical life should be exemplified in the sobriety and simplicity of the decorations. Many churches, crowded with side altars, pictures, statues, votive stands, flowers, etc., are the image of souls full of devotion but devoid of liturgical spirit.

In the parish church everything should converge towards the altar. The altar is the most important element of the church, just as the sacrifice of Jesus Christ is the principal reality in the Christian life. Pope Pius XII went so far as to say that "the altar surpasses the tabernacle because on it is offered the sacrifice of the Lord."[21] All the parishioners should have a great reverence for the altar, and show that reverence outwardly when they pass before it. And it should never be used as a table to hold objects other than those prescribed by the liturgy.

[21] *The Assisi Papers*, p. 233.

Among the objects prescribed by the liturgy, the tabernacle has particular importance. Pius XII said more than once, renewing the decrees of the Council of Trent and of canon law, that the tabernacle must be placed at the center of the altar in an immovable way. But it must be noted at the same time that in saying this he was not insisting so much on the material placement of the tabernacle on the altar as on the idea that the person of our Lord must occupy the center of worship, since it is His person that establishes the relations between altar and tabernacle and gives each of them its own significance. But the Pope made it clear also that the tabernacle should be placed on the altar in such a way as not to hinder the celebration facing the people.[22]

In fact, the celebration of Mass facing the people, in accord with the constant tradition of the Roman basilicas, is one of the external means which can contribute most effectively to giving a sense of community to the liturgical action and establishing a current of unity between the celebrant and the faithful. In the churches where there is an altar of the Blessed Sacrament distinct from the main altar because "it seems more convenient or suitable for the veneration and worship of the Eucharist,"[23] the celebration of the Mass facing the people offers no difficulty from this point of view.

In other churches there may be solutions, some of which have already been in use for some time, while others have been introduced tentatively, in harmony with the structural requirements of the individual churches. The experts, however, to whom the Pope left this task, will have to be guided henceforth by the rules more recently given by the Sacred Congregation of Rites in a decree of June 1, 1957. Therein it is specified that the location of the tabernacle would be an impediment to the celebration facing the people in churches where there is only one altar.[24]

After the altar comes the baptismal font. The baptistry is a doubly sacred place, which should be a center of pilgrimage for the faithful when they visit their parish church. The people should be urged to combine with their visit to the Blessed Sacrament a visit to the main altar, where the sacrifice of the parochial community is celebrated, and a visit to the baptistry, where the faithful have been incorporated into Christ and into the Church.

The baptismal font, called the womb of the Church by the liturgy and by the Fathers, is to be held in great honor. The ritual prescribes the qualities the baptismal font and the baptistry must have, and the respect with which they are to be treated. Objects other than those necessary for the administration of baptism should never be put in the baptistry. It would be suitable that the baptistry enclose enough space for the dignified celebration of the ceremonies. It is ordinarily shut off by a grating, out of respect, but is visible,

[22] Ibid., p. 234.

[23] Instruction of the Holy Office De arte sacra of June 30, 1952; A.A.S., 1952, p. 544.

[24] Decretum de forma et usu tabernaculi, June 1, 1957; A.A.S., 1957, pp. 425-426.

that the faithful may contemplate and venerate the place of their spiritual rebirth.

The sacristy not only has the function of holding the objects destined for worship, but it is also the place of immediate preparation for the celebration of the holy sacrifice and of the other liturgical acts. The atmosphere of the sacristy should therefore be one of silence, of recollection, of dignity, of inspiration, in which the sacred ministers can feel themselves surrounded and penetrated with the supernatural, even in the material arrangement and decoration, as they approach the divine mysteries which they are about to celebrate. Hence was derived the importance attached in more spiritual times to the decoration of the sacristies in the great basilicas. Though with greater simplicity of ornament, the sacristy of a parish church need not lack this note of sacred dignity.

We could say the same of the other objects that form the furniture and vestments of the liturgy. The wealth or poverty of the vestments and sacred vessels is of little importance. What is of interest is only their dignity, beauty and good taste. Let it be considered, again, that they have not a solely utilitarian end; they are also a means for conferring dignity, even in a human way, on the divine worship, and for helping the faithful understand the liturgical mysteries. Their form, their style, their decoration are not very important, as long as they possess the required qualities and are dignified, clean and in good taste. Still, even these external things can influence the spirit of the faithful.

If the parish church ought to be dignified in its structure and in its various elements, it should not lack that which is its greatest ornament and its most highly prized title of nobility: consecration. Before it is opened to worship, every church must receive a blessing which purifies it, separates it from profane uses and dedicates it to God. But beyond this the Church has a rite of profound significance and extraordinary beauty by which she dedicates churches and altars to God in a definitive and solemn manner: the rite of consecration. A church, an altar consecrated to God are of themselves witnesses to the presence of God in the midst of His people, source of grace and of perennial prayer. The long, solemn rite of consecration is like a baptism of the altar and of the church, which is commemorated every year with one of the most beautiful offices of the liturgy.

It would be well that all parish churches be consecrated. Cardinal Schuster wanted all the parish churches of his archdiocese of Milan to possess the grace of this consecration. He himself consecrated all the new parish churches being built, as well as the already existing churches which had not yet been consecrated, and renewed the rite in those concerning whose consecration there was some doubt. Thus in 25 years of his episcopate he personally consecrated 275 churches, besides 154 altars which he enriched with precious relics.

The parish church should be constructed, whenever possible, in the most central location within the parish boundaries, so as to make it of easy access to the faithful. This is to be kept in mind above all in the creation of urban parishes.

At Milan, Cardinal Schuster kept careful watch over the suburbs of his archiepiscopal city, to see in what direction the new construction was spreading and be able to acquire land at once where a parish church could be built in due time. "Because I did not do this at the right time," he said, "I now find that I have parishes of 50,000 souls in which it is no longer possible to find suitable land for sale on which to build the parish church."

The scarcity of parish churches is one of the most pressing problems of our day, and one which causes great difficulty for the renewal of the Christian life in the large cities.

The pastor

"The pastor," wrote Monsignor Montini in the letter to the Canadian Social Week already quoted, "is not the head of the community in the profane sense of the term. He is rather the minister of the people of God, having received spiritual authority over his flock only that he may be the dispenser of the mysteries of God among them, 'that they may have life and have it more abundantly.' "[25]

The pastor, father, shepherd and head of the parochial community, can never forget that he is a priest and that the priesthood is ordained principally to the Eucharist. All his priestly powers find their application and their reason for being in the Eucharist. Only by reason of the Eucharistic Body of Christ has he received power over the mystical Body, over souls. His pastoral action has as its ultimate end to bring souls to the Eucharist. The pastor's activity is therefore eminently liturgical.

The most important action the pastor can perform, taking his pastoral aim into account too, is the celebration of holy Mass, and in particular the celebration of the parish Mass. The pastor is never so much a priest or so much a pastor as when he stands at the altar, surrounded by his parishioners, offering the holy sacrifice with them and for them.

And throughout the day the pastor offers his sacrifice of praise as a continuation of his priestly offering for the whole Church, but especially for his own flock. The pastor's Divine Office maintains his spiritual, fruitful union with his parishioners. While they are laboring and struggling to make a living and enjoying the intimacies of the family, while they are suffering and amusing themselves and living as good Christians or else offending God, the pastor has them all in mind when he recites the Hours of his Office, and he prays for them, and draws down God's blessings on them, renewing the priestly action of his parish Mass.

[25] Cf. *La Scuola Cattolica*, 1953, p. 556.

Baptism, penance, the blessing of the newly married, the service to the sick and the dying; the blessing of mothers, of fields, of the fruits of the earth and of everything that can be an object of God's blessing; funerals, the preaching of the word of God; in short, everything that has a sacramental value, everything that is ordained to the Eucharist or derives from it in one way or another, is the principal object of the pastor's liturgical-pastoral action. The rest, however important and urgent it may seem, will always have a value relative and definitely subordinate to the principal object.

The pastor must be fully convinced of this truth: his mission is primarily liturgical. The effectiveness of his pastoral action will be proportionate to the liturgical orientation which he knows how to give it. If the pastor gives the worthy, devout celebration of the Mass and the Office priority over all other activities and all other interests; if he knows how to form a parochial community with his parishioners, so as to live together with them the sacramental renewal of the mystery of Christ; if he succeeds in making them understand and savor the Christian mystery so that they will seek to make it something real in their own lives—then he will have attained the supreme ideal of the shepherd of souls. The other moral and social problems of the parish will find an opportune solution in the healthy development of the parochial community's Christian life under the warmth of the sacraments and the liturgy.

In these times of such great material needs and miseries, the pastor may find a danger in his priestly zeal if he himself does not have a solid formation according to the theological principles of the liturgy and does not live the liturgy completely, to the point where it becomes a demand of his conscience and of his spirit. Social problems in their various forms, methods of propaganda and of persuasion which invade the field of pastoral action from the secular world, the idea of democracy and the pragmatism which saturate our environment, can exercise a powerful attraction on the pastor's zeal and carry him into other paths, which, humanly considered, will be more logical and effective, but which in the end will draw him away from the supernatural realities on which Jesus Christ chose to build His Church and the whole edifice of the Christian life.

Of recent occurrence is the experiment of the priest-workers in France. Faced with a real and inescapable problem, and motivated by a laudable priestly zeal, full of charity and of self-giving, they went to lamentable extremes by relegating to second place the primary aspect of pastoral action which we have just pointed out. Hence in the joint declaration of the French hierarchy on this subject, published January 19, 1953, it was stated, "The Church desires, before all, to safeguard that which constitutes the proper mission of the priest. She wants to give priests to the working world, priests who live, within this world and on its behalf, a fully sacerdotal life. Now the priest is ordained to offer to God the adoration of the whole people, in the first place for the celebration of holy Mass and the public prayer of the breviary. He is also the dispenser of the divine benefits to men, through the preaching of the word of God and through the administration of the sacraments."

Another obstacle which may impede a full liturgical-pastoral action is the present economic and bureaucratic organization of the parochial clergy. The stipends tend to spoil for our parishioners the liturgical services which it is the pastor's duty to offer them, and the parochial office work absorbs many hours that could be dedicated to the priestly ministry. There is pressing need of a radical revision of the present organizational scheme for assuring the economic maintenance of the parochial clergy. There are solutions that have been applied with success in some countries and might well be considered in others. The organization of the parish business also deserves a revision.

In the face of these two problems, as well as others which may arise out of the needs of the faithful, it would perhaps be worth while to reflect on these words of the Acts of the Apostles: "It is not desirable that we should forsake the word of God and serve at tables. Therefore, brethren, select from among you seven men of good reputation, full of the Spirit and of wisdom, that we may put them in charge of this work. But we will devote ourselves to prayer and to the ministry of the word" (Acts 6:2-4).

Perhaps Catholic Action could offer a principle of solution. Besides, seculars understand questions of economic organization better than clerics. In saying this we are not forgetting that what is given voluntarily is given gladly, that the faithful know well enough that their priests have a right to an adequate living, that their generosity increases when they know personally the material needs of the pastor and know that he is neglecting those needs to take care of the spiritual needs of the parish.

In some parishes the pastor has one or more priests assisting him in his pastoral mission. For many important reasons, but above all for the sake of the liturgical apostolate, it is advisable that these priests live together close to the pastor or with him. If the faithful ought to form a community so as to be able to live the Christian and sacramental life intensively, so much the more ought the priests to gather around the pastor, to form together with him the principle of unity in the parish family.

And this holds not only in every parish where the clergy are numerous, but also, when circumstances make it possible and advisable, for the priests of various parishes in the same city: they can form little priestly communities, with great profit for the priests themselves and for the respective parishes. Great spiritual benefits have accrued in fact wherever this experiment has been tried.

Parochial community and common means

It is supremely necessary for the development of the liturgical spirit that the faithful of a parish be brought to the conviction that they all form one family, a parochial community. And a theoretical conviction is not enough; it must be translated into a practical rule of Christian life, as it was for the ancient Christians, who had but one heart, one soul and even a community of material goods. This last is not demanded today, but it is imperative at least that to the unity of spirit and of heart there be added a unity of moral interests, of preoccupations and of desires, which unity will be exemplified in deeds.

In the parish church the faithful ought not to look at one another as strangers, each one shutting himself up in his own prayer, preoccupied with his own interests, or at most with the needs of those who are personally related to him. "Let common prayer accompany the common desire" is the bishop's exhortation to the faithful in attendance at the ordination of deacons. We might say also, "To the common prayer—to the prayer which the priest offers in communion with all the faithful and in their name—a common desire should correspond." Every member of the community ought to associate himself with whatever lies close to the heart of his brother, whether it be something favorable or something adverse, so as to present everything before God in his prayer with the same interest as if he were treating of his own affairs.

God's plan was to save all men by forming a Body, a Church in Jesus Christ. His Redemption is to be applied in a communitarian way also; not that it is to be applied to all simultaneously and in the same way, but that it is to be applied to each one in particular as a member of the Christian community. The liturgy, which carries this application of the Redemption to the highest degree, also strongly emphasizes the sense of community.

The sacrament of Christian regeneration is the sacrament of incorporation into the Christian community. Every sacrament received establishes a new bond with the community or strengthens the relations already existing. And the sacrament which is at the center of the liturgy and communicates its particular character to the liturgy, the Eucharist, is also the sacrament of unity, as St. Augustine says.

The pastor must promote everything that tends to manifest and to strengthen this unity among his parishioners and to make them feel like a church, a community. Thus, in so far as the circumstances of the parish make it possible, it is desirable that the administration of the sacraments have a communitarian character.

The baptism of an infant, that is, the entrance of a new member into the parish community, is an event that should interest all the parishioners. The time, the outward solemnity, the circumstances of its administration should be arranged in such a way as to make it a community act.

We know of a rural parish where every baptism was awaited and prepared for by all with true enthusiasm. Every family in the parish took charge of a definite function for the day of its celebration: one procured the candles, another had the honor of sweeping the church; some brought the flowers, others decorated the baptismal font; to the mother of the infant was reserved the honor of making the baptismal robe for her little one. In the catechism lessons preceding the baptismal day the ritual of the baptism was explained. Representatives of all the families of the parish assisted at the baptism, taking active part in it by their responses; and at the time of the triple renunciation they publicly renewed the promises of their own baptism. Afterwards they gathered for a real family festival in the home of the newly baptized, and meanwhile there was always someone who quickly gathered the flowers from the baptismal font and decorated the family table with them.

The pastor's zeal and liturgical spirit can easily find numberless occasions and methods for infusing into his parishioners this warm family feeling, based on the celebration of the liturgical worship.

The liturgy of the restored Easter vigil offers an excellent opportunity for giving the whole of Lent a communitarian sense, not only under its aspect of a time of public and collective penance but also as common preparation for the common renewal of baptismal promises in the night of Easter.

The administration of the sacrament of confirmation, which involves the presence of the bishop in the parish, is a very timely occasion for explaining to the faithful the concept of hierarchy and for reviving the sense of community in the presence of the bishop, formal principle of the ecclesiastical unity of the diocese. It is also suitable to relate the liturgy of Pentecost to this sacrament. If the night of Easter brings with it the collective renewal of the baptismal promises, Pentecost should see the celebration of the public renewal of that consecration to God which establishes us in a perfect Christian life. It is the day of the Church, of the hierarchy, hence the day of the parish, the most opportune occasion for giving new life to the activities of the parish apostolate, entrusted to the parishioners themselves.

The First Communion day, the spiritual assistance to the sick, the viaticum and extreme unction, the burial of the dead are so many acts of liturgical-parochial life which should be of interest to the community and which offer a very propitious occasion for instructing the community and stimulating it to an active participation in worship. The rubrics of the Ritual themselves suppose, and even recommend, that representatives of the parochial community take part in the celebration of these sacred rites.

As for the spiritual assistance to the sick, let us recall that in the Roman Ritual, besides the various blessings for sick children and adults, for the medicines, clothes and linens they are to use, there is a special rite, generally forgotten and almost unknown, which is entitled *De visitatione et cura infirmorum*, "On the visiting and care of the sick." It is a very beautiful rite composed of psalms, prayers, recitation of excerpts from the gospels, laying-on of hands, etc., which as a whole contain the efficacy of the Church's prayer and action over the sick person. With this rite the pastor's visit to his sick parishioners acquires a sacramental value, and the words of consolation which his pastoral zeal may suggest if he is inspired by this rite, attain a loftiness of concept and an ecclesiastical value such as only a liturgical action of the Church can give them.

It would be conducive to an intense liturgical life to inculcate and cultivate in the faithful the devout celebration of the anniversary of baptism, and in general to carry over into family and social life the principal parochial celebrations marking the solemnities of the liturgical year.

Advent and Lent are particularly adapted for living the expectation of Christmas and of Easter in community, even outside the walls of the church. Only a little initiative and liturgical-pastoral spirit is needed to find the practical way of carrying out this idea suitably in every place.

The celebration of processions as an overflowing of the life of worship outside of the church, the participation in the Rogation days suitably explained, the annual blessing of the parish territory and of the fields, the blessing of houses at Easter—all are liturgical rites of collective interest which, well prepared for, can nourish the liturgical life and strengthen the communitarian relations among the parishioners.

What is most important in each of these cases is that the faithful be instructed in the wealth of spiritual content in these rites of the Church, and that a way be sought of having the parishioners take the active part in them which is their function.

Very important for the formation of new Christian homes in the parish is the timely instruction of the young men and women who are preparing for marriage. It is essential that they understand the sacramental value of the Church's rite which will unite them for life. Let them be taught the theological and positive meaning of the married state and the mystical significance attached to the most intimate relations between Christian husband and wife.

In the celebration of matrimony a commentary on the liturgical texts of the nuptial Mass could be very profitable.

If necessary, the couple should be instructed on the Church's motive for prohibiting the solemn celebration of nuptials during the penitential seasons, and they should be urged to abide by this ecclesiastical precept. Too often a dispensation from this precept is requested and granted. Even if this is permitted by canon law, the ecclesiastical sense and the liturgical spirit counsel a greater austerity and a greater respect for the spirit of the law.

If the administration of all the sacraments and sacramentals is to take on a communitarian character, in keeping with the social value given them by Christ and the Church, this character must be most outstanding in the celebration of the Mass. It is the act of ecclesiastical unity, of the union of the members with one another, with the hierarchy and with Jesus Christ.

For this reason Pope Pius XII specified that, even if it is true that the essential element of the Eucharistic sacrifice is the consecration, which is exclusive to the celebrating priest because he alone acts as a representative of the person of Christ, "when the consecration is completed, the 'oblation of the Victim placed upon the altar' may be done and is done by the celebrating priest, by the Church, by the other priests and by each of the faithful"[26] in the measure that belongs to them.

The various rites in the celebration of the Mass can be summed up in three actions: to pray, to offer, to communicate. To pray is to speak to God and listen to His word. To offer is to present to the Father the oblation of Jesus Christ and with it that of His members. To communicate is to receive the Body of Christ sacramentally and tighten the bonds of charity that unite us with Him and with His members. Praying, offering, communicating, the three acts of the Mass, are three acts eminently communitarian. The faithful are to take part in them, not only as individuals, but as a community.

The prayers of the Mass present to God the needs of the Church, of the community; and, if they sometimes refer to a concrete need or pray for one person in particular, it is the whole community that makes this intention its own. No member of the mystical Body is excluded from the prayers of the community. Just as she does in an explicit way on Good Friday, the Church presents to God every day in the Mass the most varied needs of all the faithful, and at the same time interests herself on behalf of sinners, heretics, schismatics, Jews and pagans.

A prayer so catholic in its object must also be such on the part of the praying subject. The faithful who gather in church to assist at Mass do not come together like travelers in a railway car, but rather as forming a single family, the parochial community which is going to celebrate collectively the Lord's Supper. Here no one must be indifferent to another, no one must remain isolated from the rest of the community.

The timely clarifications or interventions for didactic purposes, of which we have spoken elsewhere, will make the community of prayer possible, will make it a conscious thing and keep it alive.

In some churches the following custom has been established to make the community of prayer of the faithful of the parish more living and more real: on a table in the vestibule of the Church a record book is placed in which the parishioners write down their particular needs, which are then read out publicly at the time of the *oratio fidelium* of the parish Mass, so as to make them the object of the community's prayer.

If we want to take part properly in the celebration of the Mass, it is not enough to be united individually to the celebrant; we must be united to him as forming a community with all the rest of the faithful. For this reason, the use of the missal in the vernacular, so profitable for the understanding

---

[26] *The Assisi Papers*, p. 229.

of the Mass texts, can turn into a real danger if the individual with his missal becomes shut up in himself, abstracting himself from everything around him; in this attitude there could be hidden, behind a liturgical front, a form of individualistic devotion.

Referring to this, Cardinal Lercaro writes, "Entering some churches, even those in which many of the faithful diligently use their missals, I have had the impression of entering a restaurant. A hundred or more persons may be eating their meals at the same time, perhaps the same choice of food, but each one ignores the other, each one is for himself, cut off from the joys as well as the sorrows of his neighbor. The house of the Lord is not a restaurant: His table is a family meal table!"[27]

It is important, therefore, to make use of all the means that may be effective in promoting the community of prayer: communal responses to the celebrant's prayers and salutations, brief explanations which keep the minds of the faithful in agreement with the voice of the celebrant, and, in a very special way, singing. Liturgical chant and religious song, properly combined, are a most effective means of common participation in prayer. Song is the most beautiful form of public and collective prayer, and by its modulations lends itself to reflection and to contemplation of the text.

Pius XII writes in his encyclical on sacred music, "The dignity and lofty purpose of sacred music consist in the fact that its lovely melodies and splendor beautify and embellish the voices of the priest who offers Mass and of the Christian people who praise the sovereign God. Its special power and excellence should lift up to God the minds of the faithful who are present. It should make the liturgical prayers of the Christian community more alive and fervent, so that everyone can praise and beseech the triune God more powerfully, more intently and more effectively. . . .

"It is easy to infer from what has just been said that the dignity and force of sacred music are greater, the closer sacred music itself approaches to the supreme act of Christian worship, the Eucharistic sacrifice of the altar. There can be nothing more exalted or sublime than its function of accompanying with beautiful sound the voice of the priest offering up the divine Victim, answering him joyfully with the people who are present and enhancing the whole liturgical ceremony with its noble art."[28]

The uniform external attitude of the faithful assisting at Mass contributes a great deal to giving the assembly a sense of unity, which is sacramentally reaffirmed and strengthened by the kiss of peace.

We know by experience how effectively the spiritual formation of Christians and the re-establishment of a solid piety is influenced by the persevering and insistent employment of these external means which give parochial worship a truly collective character. Their educative value penetrates

[27] Cardinal Giacomo Lercaro, *A messa, figlioli!*, p. 14; cf. *Worship*, XXX, 600.

[28] Encyclical *Musicae sacrae disciplina*, nn. 31 and 34.

slowly but effectively into the consciences of the faithful. As they become accustomed to praying in common, to taking a mutual interest before God in the needs of every member of the parochial family, and to living together the most important acts of the life of piety, they feel themselves ever more joined in brotherhood and united by spiritual bonds, which they then express in works of charity and of authentic practical Christianity.

Pastors can never be too diligent in their efforts to instil into their parishioners an appreciation of the excellence of common prayer. Catechism for children and for adults, public and private instructions, the study groups of Catholic Action can be used profitably to instruct the various classes of people, according to the condition and the capacity of each one, on the meaning and the efficacy of liturgical prayer celebrated in common.

Most effective, however, is practice, personal experience. A beginning can be made with the children's Masses and the Masses for parish societies, usually attended by the more educated and better prepared members of the parish. When they have acquired a taste for collective prayer, they will readily desire the union of the individuals and the fusion of the various groups in the unity of the parish Mass. The spiritual and religious activity of the whole week should be centered entirely on the Sunday parish Mass.

On this point, let us insist on the need of preaching by example. The parochial clergy should never be absent from the official Mass of the parish, assisting at it around the altar and taking the active part in it that belongs to them. Instead, it frequently happens that ecclesiastics, accustomed to presiding over the liturgical assembly, do not know how to unite themselves with it when they are not the celebrants. It is not rare to see members of the clergy, even highly placed ones, who, when they have to assist at a liturgical service by reason of pastoral duty or out of devotion, let the faithful take their own part in the common prayer and action, while they take advantage of the time to recite their breviary. Then we have the paradox that the fulfilment of the canonical duty of praying officially in the name of the Church shuts them up, in practice, in an individualism which keeps them away from the public celebration of this same official prayer.

A community of offering should correspond to the community of prayer. The Mass is a sacrifice, an oblation. Jesus Christ, who offered Himself on the cross, wants to be offered now by means of us. In the unity of His Church, all of us Christians can unite ourselves to Him in the act of His offering, both to offer Him and to offer ourselves in union with our Head.

Among the first Christians it was the rule that each one present his own offering for the celebration of the Eucharist. This rite can be renewed, particularly in the solemn and parochial Masses. Pope Pius XII in *Mediator Dei* recalls favorably this practice according to which "sometimes—a more frequent occurrence in ancient times—the faithful offer to the ministers at the altar bread and wine to be changed into the Body and Blood of Christ."[29]

Special solemnity might be attached to the offering of the first fruits of the earth and the products of local industry on the occasion of the Ember Days. In one parish the parishioners offered the Lord part of a field and part of a vineyard, where they cultivated the grain and the vines that were to produce the wheat and the wine for the Mass celebrated during the year in the parish church. After the harvest and the vintage there took place respectively the solemn offering of the wheat and of the grapes at the offertory of a parish Mass.

The ecclesiastical community of the faithful is fulfilled in the Eucharistic communion. It is for this reason that there is so much insistence on the propriety of receiving in communion the hosts consecrated at that very Mass. Not that there is any intention of denying the value of communions received privately and outside of Mass; the idea is only to emphasize the fact that, if communion always gives that which it contains, the Body of the Lord, communion received during Mass realizes more fully that which it signifies, namely the unity of the Church.[30]

Hence the Pope says in recommending that the faithful communicate in this way if possible, so as to participate more closely in the sacrifice at which they have assisted, "Still though the Church with the kind heart of a mother strives to meet the spiritual needs of her children, they for their part should not readily neglect the directions of the liturgy and, as often as there is no reasonable difficulty, should aim that all their actions at the altar manifest more clearly the living unity of the mystical Body."[31]

The parish Mass as we have described it is the center, the most solid food and the surest guarantee of a strong Christian life within the parish. Hence it ought to be promoted with all the means at hand, beginning perhaps with a sensible arrangement of the schedule of Masses.

In very many parishes, the custom is to celebrate a Mass at eight o'clock in the morning with general communion as specified by the rules of certain parish societies. Later, around ten, there is usually a sung Mass with only a scattering of the faithful in attendance. The other Masses are distributed regularly, one every hour or every half hour, according to the number of priests in the place.

Would it not be better to combine the general communion Mass and the solemn Mass into a single act—the parish Mass—attended by the parochial community, clergy and people? All the societies—whose aim is not to divide but to unite—ought to consider it as their own, since it is properly the Mass of all the individuals and of all the collections of individuals in the parish. The celebration of the parish Mass, of course, would have to be set at a more convenient hour, to facilitate the communion of the faithful and

[29] *Mediator Dei*, n. 90.   73, 2 and 4; 79, 1; etc.
[30] St. Thomas, *Summa theol.*, III, 67, 2;   [31] *Mediator Dei*, n. 122.

their attendance in the greatest number possible. It should be *the* official Mass of the parish community, and thus it should take precedence over all other interests and considerations.

Singing or recitation on the part of the faithful, a short homily, some discreet clarifications of the liturgical texts, communion—these are elements that should not be lacking in the parish Mass. On the other hand, other readings and notices should be done away with, as they distract the attention of the faithful and often have a rather bureaucratic and even commercial character, or tend to excite the vanity or display the generosity of the individuals who have offered some alms or commissioned some Mass to be said.

The parish Mass demands the abandonment of the stingy notion of Masses lasting only half an hour. On Sunday, the day dedicated to the Lord, the parochial community cannot begrudge God the time necessary for a worthy celebration of the supreme act of public worship. On this point the clergy must be demanding with the people, so much the more as, with good organization, the parish Mass does not require too long a time.

It is true that those persons must be taken into account who really cannot spare this much time, by reason of their domestic obligations, the state of their health or other circumstances. It is well not to forget, either, that there are many persons not yet capable of understanding or appreciating the meaning of the parish Mass; and the fulfilment of their Sunday obligation must be facilitated. For these there are other Masses conveniently distributed; but the parish Mass must never yield its place to the needs or the convenience of these groups of the faithful, who, although they are perhaps a majority numerically, must be considered formally as an exception.

The pastoral zeal of the parish priest will succeed in bringing it about that the number of the "incapable" will decrease and that the parish Mass will take on increased importance and arouse increased interest. So also his zeal will find ways of arranging things so that the faithful will always be able to receive communion during Mass.

If we are to succeed in making the parish Mass an habitual practice and a spiritual need of the faithful, we shall have to have an intense labor of solid religious instruction, various trials and changes in a long-established parochial organization. But the faithful will welcome these innovations, especially if they are given to understand the reasons behind them. For, basically, these measures respond to a deep need of the Christian soul, which has as its center Jesus Christ and the sacramental penetration of His mystery as He has established it in His Church.

We need only look at the splendid results of the recent liturgical reforms in the places where they were celebrated with the spirit which they presuppose. The enthusiasm with which the faithful have received them, the interest and the pleasure with which they are discovering the spiritual riches contained in the liturgy, the eagerness and the sincere devotion with which they participate in the ceremonies of worship, show very clearly the fruit that can be expected from an intense liturgical life, brought about through the motherly solicitude of the Church and the intelligent, zealous pastoral action of her priests.

4. Roman Character of Our Liturgy

Constant contact with the mystery of Christ as offered by the liturgy gradually forms the perfect Christian. His mind, his heart, his spirit are nurtured on the superabundant grace contained in the sacramental rites, a grace which is life and light and warmth of charity. While he is being nourished on the supernatural content of the liturgical rites, the Christian is becoming accustomed to receiving these divine gifts through concrete media which also have their influence on him, communicating to him their own physiognomy. Liturgical spirituality begets a liturgical mentality. He who places himself in constant contact with the rites of the Church, who seeks to penetrate their meaning and submits gladly to their influence, will eventually be permeated by them, by their doctrine, by their procedures, by all that they suppose and signify, even in a purely human way.

The human element in the liturgical rites has been worked out by men who have necessarily imprinted upon it something of their style, their temperament, their formation, their personality. Every particular rite, every formula, every ceremony has had a concrete origin, at a definite time, and has received a personal imprint from its author.

Nevertheless, the more individualizing notes have disappeared when each new rite has come to form part of the Church's spiritual treasure. The combination of rites already in existence has assimilated the features of the new rite, the momentum of tradition and the passing of the centuries have rounded out its contours, its author has almost always succumbed to anonymity. Yet, all this notwithstanding, the new rite, absorbed by the principal nucleus of the liturgy, has brought to it something of its own personality. Thus over the course of the centuries the liturgy has acquired its own cast of features, in which are found fused and combined the elements that have entered successively into its composition.

The resultant character of the physiognomy of our liturgy has a name: *Romanity*. Our present liturgy is the Roman liturgy, not only because Rome is the see of its hierarchical head, but also because it was the particular liturgy of the Roman See before it became universal. Born at Rome, developed at Rome, propagated with the spread of the Roman empire and civilization, our liturgy is clearly Roman. The indigenous elements of other churches which for various reasons have been added to it have not succeeded in changing its original character.

The outward forms which clothe the mystery of Christ and bring it within reach have been molded by the Roman character. Roman laws, traditions, institutions, temperament and history are reflected in the liturgical forms.

Our calendar is fundamentally the Roman calendar: our Proper of the Time cannot be well understood if it is not related continually to the customs of the Roman Church; our Proper of the Saints has as its central nucleus the group of saints honored by the Church of Rome from the earliest days. Many martyrs whose history is unknown to us and whose very names are almost unknown to us are still venerated today in our liturgy because they are Roman martyrs, whose tombs were venerated by the Christians of Rome.

The greater solemnity with which the liturgy marks the feasts of some saints finds its explanation in the special relation they had with the Church or the city of Rome, as its holy patrons and protectors, its most famous bishops, etc.

Many Mass texts of our present repertory reveal their full meaning only when they are related to a particular Roman basilica for which they were composed. That is why our missals still carry the indication of the Roman basilica where the solemn liturgical station was held that day.

Whoever is formed in the school of the liturgy cannot escape the powerful influence of its Roman character. Whoever loves the liturgy loves Rome as his country, as his mother and mistress, as the norm of his Christian thinking and of his spiritual life. Every year on the principal solemnities and throughout Lent the liturgy makes us visit Rome's basilicas and shrines. The tombs of its martyrs frequently attract our attention, and the majority of their names are familiar to us, especially those that enter into the canon of the Mass as our special intercessors.

Roman institutions gradually shape our spirit, forming it for Christ, through our present rites; and the collects of the liturgical books bring down to us the profundity of Roman thought, the sobriety of Roman expression and the classical elegance characteristic of Rome.

Inherited from Rome and transmitted by the liturgy, by canon law and by the writings of the Roman pontiffs, three great virtues give character to our Christian life: love of law, love of justice and love of liberty.

We are pleased to make our own the sentiments of Dom Beauduin: "Thanks to the liturgy understood and daily lived, Rome ought to occupy in the love and the worship of Catholics the place that Jerusalem occupied in the love and worship of Israel: 'Our feet were standing in your courts, O Jerusalem!' "[32]

Rome for us is the pope, bishop of Rome, with his priesthood, his teaching, his directives. It is the church of the Lateran, as synthesis of all the Roman churches and as "head and mother of all churches." It is the Holy See, with its departments, its laws and its rules. It is the Eternal City, with its basilicas and catacombs, its streets, its monuments and its history. It is Roman civilization, with its culture, its character and its institutions. All this is reflected in

---

[32] Dom Lambert Beauduin, *La piété liturgique* (Louvain, 1922), p. 33.

our liturgy. And because we live by the liturgy we feel ourselves to be profoundly Roman. He who does not feel himself to be Roman will find it hard to assimilate the whole spirit of the liturgy.

Romanity is the safeguard of the purity of the liturgical spirit. Deviations in the matter of liturgy, as in so many other fields of thought and practice in the Christian life, usually have as their basis a lack of Romanity. An excessive and exclusive patriotism looks on love of Rome as a rivalry, considers Roman regulations as lacking in understanding and Roman laws as despotic impositions. Romanity is the basis of our Catholicism.

The Roman liturgy does not exclude an adaptation to the characteristics of any place: it admits of particular calendars, accepts local privileges and preserves local traditions. But it is imperative that these peculiarities of each nation do not smother or disfigure the characteristic physiognomy of the Roman liturgy. In particular and concrete matters it is permissible to take into account that which is national; in everything that refers to the mind of the Church and the principles of the Christian life, that which is Roman must always prevail and impose its standard of judgment.[33]

In the liturgy, as in the hierarchical and pastoral organization of the Church, differences of a civil and political basis count for little. In the liturgical and ecclesiastical reality, the Christian has only three intermediaries for reaching Christ and receiving divine life from Him: his pastor, his bishop and the pope, bishop of Rome; the parish, the diocese, the Roman See.

Let us close these pages on liturgical spirituality by turning to Rome and welcoming with love and devotion the desire which Pope Pius XII expressed as the epilogue of his great encyclical on the liturgy: that all Christians "may more fully understand and appreciate the most precious treasures which are contained in the sacred liturgy: namely, the Eucharistic

---

[33] Although the trait in question is an accidental one, we want to point out a desire of the Holy See that involves this sense of Romanity. On July 31, 1919, four years after the first national liturgical congress had been celebrated at Montserrat, Cardinal Gasparri wrote to P. D. Antonio M. Marcet, then coadjutor abbot of Montserrat, asking him in the name of His Holiness Pope Benedict XV that he see to "the introduction of the Roman pronuncation of Latin," as he had personally indicated to him in an audience the preceding year. And he added, "Having now decided to insist on this point both for Spain and for other regions, His Holiness would be pleased to hear from you what reception this wise reform has met with. The Holy Father, who has not forgotten that at one time he spoke Spanish, has often reflected on the fact that the Roman pronunciation of Latin is necessary for Spain . . . . Aside from this, here is a point to think about: just as he who wants to speak the *Castilian* language well must pronounce it as it is pronounced in *Castile,* so he who wants to speak *Latin* well must pronounce it as it is pronounced in the capital of *Latium.*" In another letter dated September 13 the same year, the same Cardinal Secretary of State wrote, "The very reverend Father, in response to my letter dated July 31, informs me of the reception accorded the introduction of the Roman pronunciation of Latin in this monastery . . . . His Holiness, who is very well pleased, has instructed me to extend his compliments . . . and while he is giving thanks, through me, for this fine testimony of respect, he expresses the wish that the praiseworthy example of the Abbey of Montserrat will find numerous imitators everywhere and will give rise in the whole of Catholic Spain to a holy emulation in seconding this timely reform according to his desires."

sacrifice, representing and renewing the sacrifice of the cross, the sacraments, which are the streams of divine grace and of divine life, and the hymn of praise, which heaven and earth daily offer to God."[34]

[34] *Mediator Dei,* n. 205.